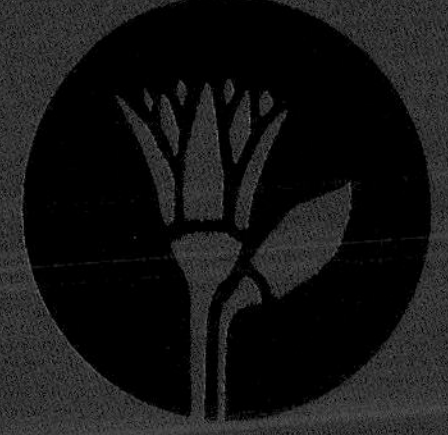

British Library Cataloguing-in-Publication Data
A catalogue record of this book is available from the British Library

ISBN 0 86356 080 6
EAN 9-780863-560804

© Chant Avedissian, 2006

All texts by Rose Issa unless otherwise indicated
Copyright for individual texts rests with the authors

Cover Illustration by Chant Avedissian; 'The Best Lady of them All'

All rights reserved. No part of this book may be reproduced or transmitted in any form or by any means, electronic or mechanical, including photocopying, recording or by any information storage and retrieval system, without permission in writing from the Publisher.

Editing   Katia Hadidian & Saeb Eigner
Design   TANK Publishing & Petra Kottmair
Photographs   Heini Schneebeli
Printing   Chemaly & Chemaly
Paper   Euro Art Silk 150 g.

Produced with the kind support of Dr Anwar M. Gargash, Dubai, UAE

This edition first published 2006

SAQI
26 Westbourne Grove
London W2 5RH
www.saqibooks.com

Chant Avedissian

Cairo Stencils

Edited by
Rose Issa

SAQI

I dedicate these images to the editors, writers, photographers and designers of the Egyptian newspapers and magazines whose portrayals of the Nasser era (1952–70) inspired much of this work.

Also, to the women and men whose high hopes for their recently independent country and belief in their progressive future created a buzz and momentum that was shared in most of the developing world.

Chant Avedissian, 2004

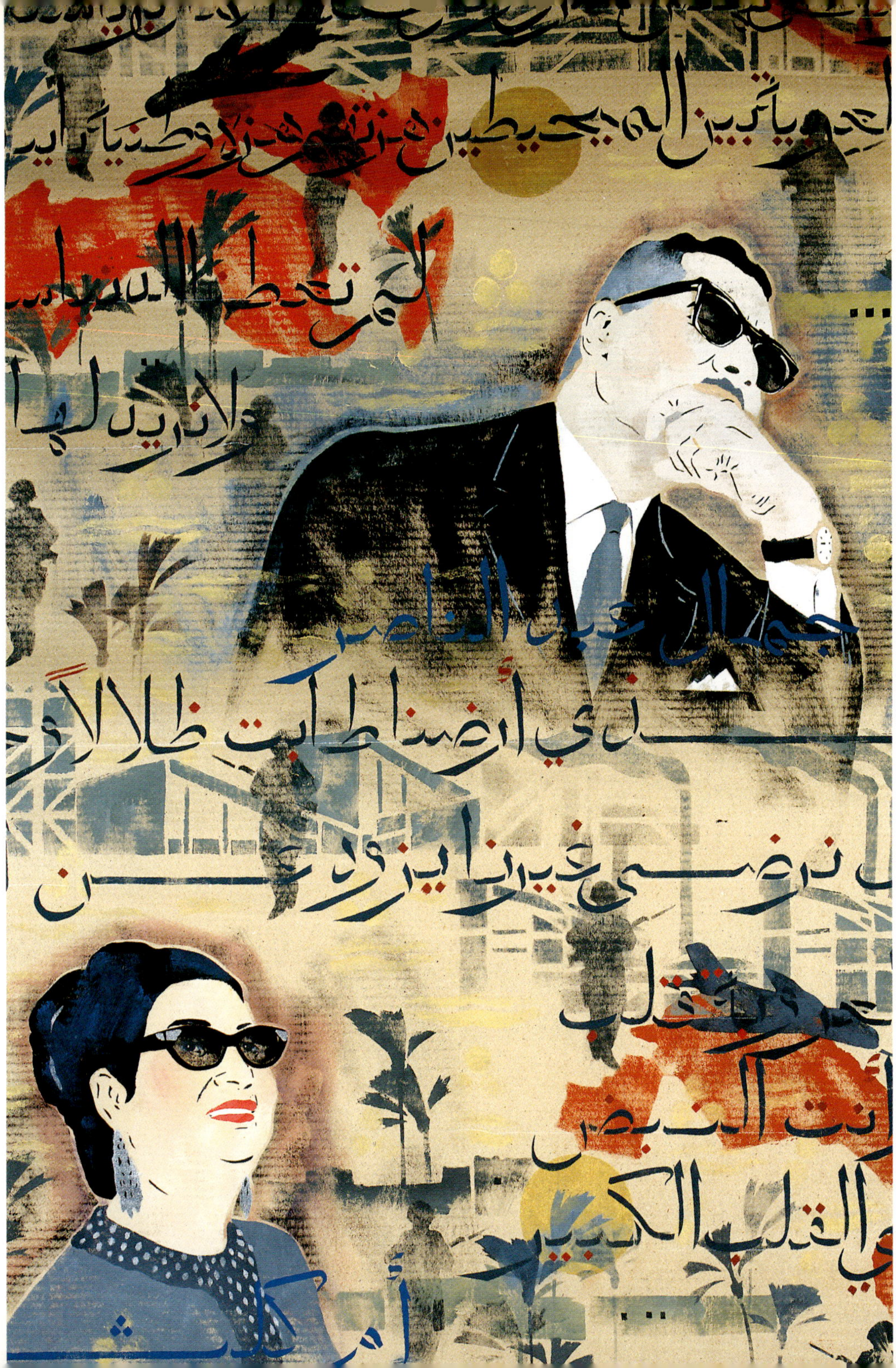

6

An Iconography of Egypt

Chant Avedissian's stencils are the result of more than twenty years of peripatetic research during which he integrated his formal studies in Canada and France with the iconographic heritage of unknown pharaonic artists; the geometric and abstract concepts of Arab architecture; the baroque and floral motifs of Ottoman textiles; and glamorous twentieth-century images of well-known figures in the Arab world. The series started in 1991, in Luxor, Upper Egypt, during the Gulf War, and was a turning point in Avedissian's career – his earlier work was based mostly on photography and hand-dyed and hand-sewn textiles – art objects for the 'architecture of the body'.

While studying in the West, first fine arts in Montreal, then printmaking and silkscreen at the Ecole Supérieure des Arts Décoratifs in Paris, Avedissian soon realised that Western modern academism and its cultural mechanism was part of a system in which he would become an exotic outsider if he lived outside its centre. Yet he made the decision to return to his birthplace in Cairo. Here he fused the techniques he had acquired in the West with the heritage of his complex Armenian-Egyptian background. Egypt – his grandparents' adopted homeland after their flight from the massacres in Armenia – became essential to his art.

Back in Cairo, Avedissian's work and vision were soon influenced by the Gandhi-like approach of the late Egyptian architect Hassan Fathy (1900–89), with whom he worked for some ten years, archiving and cataloguing his drawings and writings and photographing his projects for the Aga Khan Foundation. His fascination with Fathy's sustained focus on primal Egyptian art led to his search 'for the essence of an Egyptian way of doing and seeing'.

Avedissian is not in awe of the West. He encourages his audience to look to the East for inspiration, knowledge and craftsmanship. He even painstakingly learnt Chinese in Egypt and travelled to China, Japan and Korea to find alternative connections through architecture, calligraphy, folding screens, costume and even food. Equally, he never resorts to self-protective inwardness, or to proclaiming a culturally exclusive 'Egyptianness'. On the contrary, he has a fascination for cultural differences, affinities and similarities, as well as an ability to translate pharaonic, Nubian, Arab, Eastern and Western sources into new visions. He does this in brave, unconventional ways.

The main themes of his monotypes are the bygone eras of romance and glamour, musicals and melodramas, revolutions and ideals, beloved childhood heroes – stars, divas and leaders, the famous and anonymous people of the Egyptian socialist propaganda machine, and urban and rural daily scenes. These depict an era, the Egypt of the 1950s, when the country was at the height of its cosmopolitanism and Middle Eastern intellectuals mingled. The era also represents the height of Egyptian popular culture: when Egyptian cinema – 'Hollywood on the Nile' – dominated most of the Arab world. Booming publishing houses made Cairo a meeting place to discuss anti-colonial ideas.

Avedissian's first stencil of the singer Om Kulthoum, the most iconic figure of the Arab world, was followed by a series of more than 200 different monotypes in small format, which were later combined and superimposed on large panels in different permutations of background and colour.

Om Kulthoum (1904–75), 'The Star of the Orient', diva *par excellence*, who almost thirty years after her death is still number one in the charts, is given special prominence in his work. Her short-lived rival, the Druze princess and singer Asmahan, and Asmahan's brother, the composer Farid al- Atrash, a heart-throb who had to compete with the 'Dark Nightingale' Abdel Halim Hafez, are among the many stars to whom he pays homage. Other well-known screen goddesses include Samia Gamal and Tahiya Carioca, the greatest Arab dancers of all time, and Yolanda, a dark-haired beauty queen who became internationally famous when she re-invented herself as the blonde disco queen Dalida. The melodramatic lives of these superstars, who incarnated, each in their own style, an idealised character, were well-documented, and their iconic status was kept alive with postcards sold near cinemas and popular fairs (*mouled*).

The glamorous era that preceded and continued during the reign of King Farouk (1937–52) transformed Cairo into one of the most sophisticated cities in the world. During Farouk's time, Cairo was a party capital, where the court was mostly French-speaking and government finances were under British control. When King Farouk, the last king of Egypt – whose life story is just as tragic and melodramatic as that of any star – was dethroned in 1952, the glamour was gradually replaced by socialist concerns, with the dawn of a new era led by the leader of the Free Officers Group, Colonel Nasser. Today, King Farouk's family's contribution to many cultural institutions and charities, which was demonised and suppressed for decades, is gradually being reassessed.

Egyptian president Gamal Abdel Nasser (1918–70), the father of Arab nationalism and pan-Arabism, is a key figure among these icons. Nasser's charisma, his endorsement of Arab values and culture and his anti-colonial stand, which crushed British-French ambition with the nationalisation of the Suez Canal in 1956, made him the most popular Arab leader of the twentieth century. Here was a president who was of the people, who spoke their language, preferred Om Kulthoum and Abdel Halim Hafez to Verdi's *Aida*, and aspired to progressive values. Although he was not popular with most Arab and Western regimes, he remained, despite several military defeats that clouded his career, an enigmatic leader to his Arab public.

The only non-contemporary figure among Avedissian's icons is the nineteenth-century anti-colonial activist and philosopher Jamal al-Din al-Afghani. Al-Afghani's unusual life and charisma are the source of much mythmaking: he travelled widely and was expelled from Egypt and several other countries for his anti-British and anti-colonial writings. His speeches, stressing the pragmatic aspects of internal reform and self-improvement, reflected ideas that remained increasingly popular, including nationalism and pan-Islamism – which was then voiced in more progressive, anti-imperialist forms.

Egypt, under Soviet influence, was keen to promote the image of an idealised working class, of war heroes and builders of a new progressive nation. When women were given the right to vote, an entire propaganda machine was put in place to encourage female parliamentarians, freedom fighters and sportswomen, in order to reflect a secular egalitarian regime. The Aswan High Dam, Egypt's new pyramid, gave momentum to rural society.

Avedissian's own rediscovery of Egypt and its rural life was greatly due to his mentor, Hassan Fathy. Photographing his work helped him reorient his gaze to local aesthetics. For Fathy, the distinction between high art and folk art did not exist. He encouraged looking for traditional local specifications, for what was particular to a nation, to a culture – its history, atmosphere, aesthetics – and what constituted an identity. Talismanic objects and words, such as 'Kol Hal Yazoul' ('Nothing is Permanent'), reflect Avedissian's belief in the ephemeral. This is supported by the materials he uses – recycled cardboard and corrugated paper that convey the idea of 'dust to dust'.

Depicting subjects who are mostly dead is not an innocent choice. Avedissian commemorates subjects who have been ignored by the Egyptian media. In his portfolio are more than 200 portraits and images taken mostly from the covers of Egyptian photo magazines of past decades, such as *al-Musawar, Akhar Saa, al-Gil, Bena al-Watan* and *al-Kawakeb*, which he carefully archives and sources. He creates images of images and explores the way historical documents and symbols shift. His acute sense of observation and humour, his play on words, semantics and phonetics, add a final touch to these unashamedly great decorative artworks. He mixes amusing words in Latin or Arabic with his own photographs of monuments under environmental threat (Luxor, Aswan, the Valley of the Kings, famous streets of Cairo); everyday objects that he and many Egyptians still use (cooking utensils, fly whisks), animals (parrots, donkeys, stray dogs) and landscapes and people. No amount of personal angst intrudes on the humour and wit of these paintings.

Overlapping motifs are intertwined with historical characters and names, landscapes, objects and symbols, stencilled in seemingly random directions and painted with local pigment mixed with gum arabic and bordered by hand-coloured textiles, to become the vehicles for his memories. How histories and societies overlap in real life as in art is layered in past and present. This is his way of paying homage to his host country, Egypt. Even the technique of stencilling, a process that demands the reduction of lines and colour, is for simplification. By repeating the images, already reduced to simple lines, not unlike ancient hieroglyphics, he perpetuates a process in use for thousands of years. This is the magic of Egypt: the permanent and the transient.

Today, when not travelling, Avedissian divides his time between Yerevan, in Armenia, and Cairo. His fondness for popular art, Sufi poetry, Chinese and Japanese Zen concepts and aesthetics, have resulted in Avedissian's own version of a Wabi Sabi lifestyle.

Rose Issa, London 2004

CHANT AVEDISSIAN

Cairo Stencils

Diva

Diva

Om Kulthoum was the most charismatic and famous Middle Eastern singer of the twentieth century.

She was born in 1904 in a small village in the Egyptian Delta and arrived in Cairo in the 1920s. She immediately attracted the best poets, composers and musicians of her time, and by the 1930s began to appear in films.

Every Thursday night, for more than ten years, her concerts were broadcast on the radio, and millions of people throughout the Arab world would gather in cafés, restaurants or their homes to hear her sing.

She recorded some 300 songs. During Egypt's turbulent period (1946–54), she sang lyrics with nationalist and political overtones, which came to embody the hopes and aspirations of the Arabs. A great supporter of Nasser, after the 1967 war she gave concerts to raise funds for numerous Egyptian charities. Her funeral in 1975 was the largest ever attended in Egypt.

Saeb Eigner, London 2004

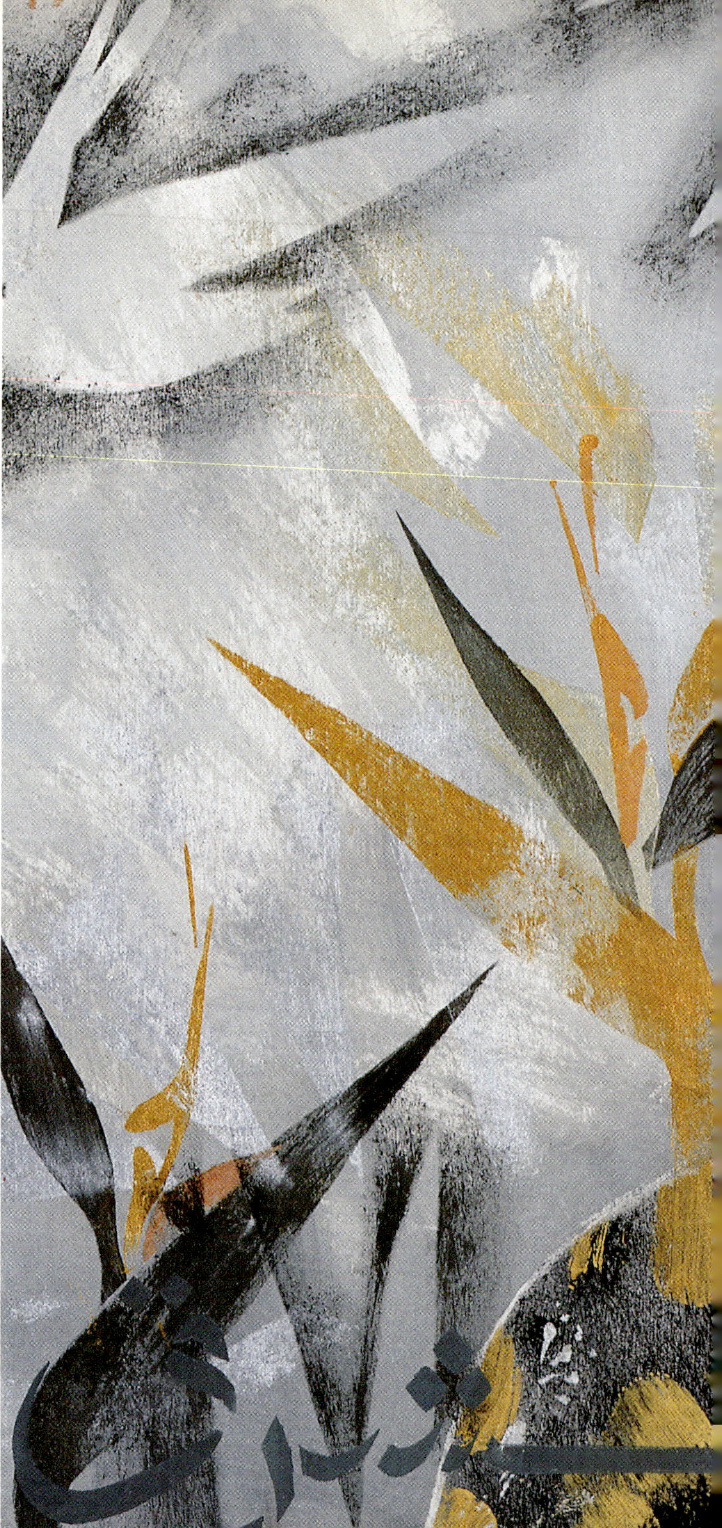

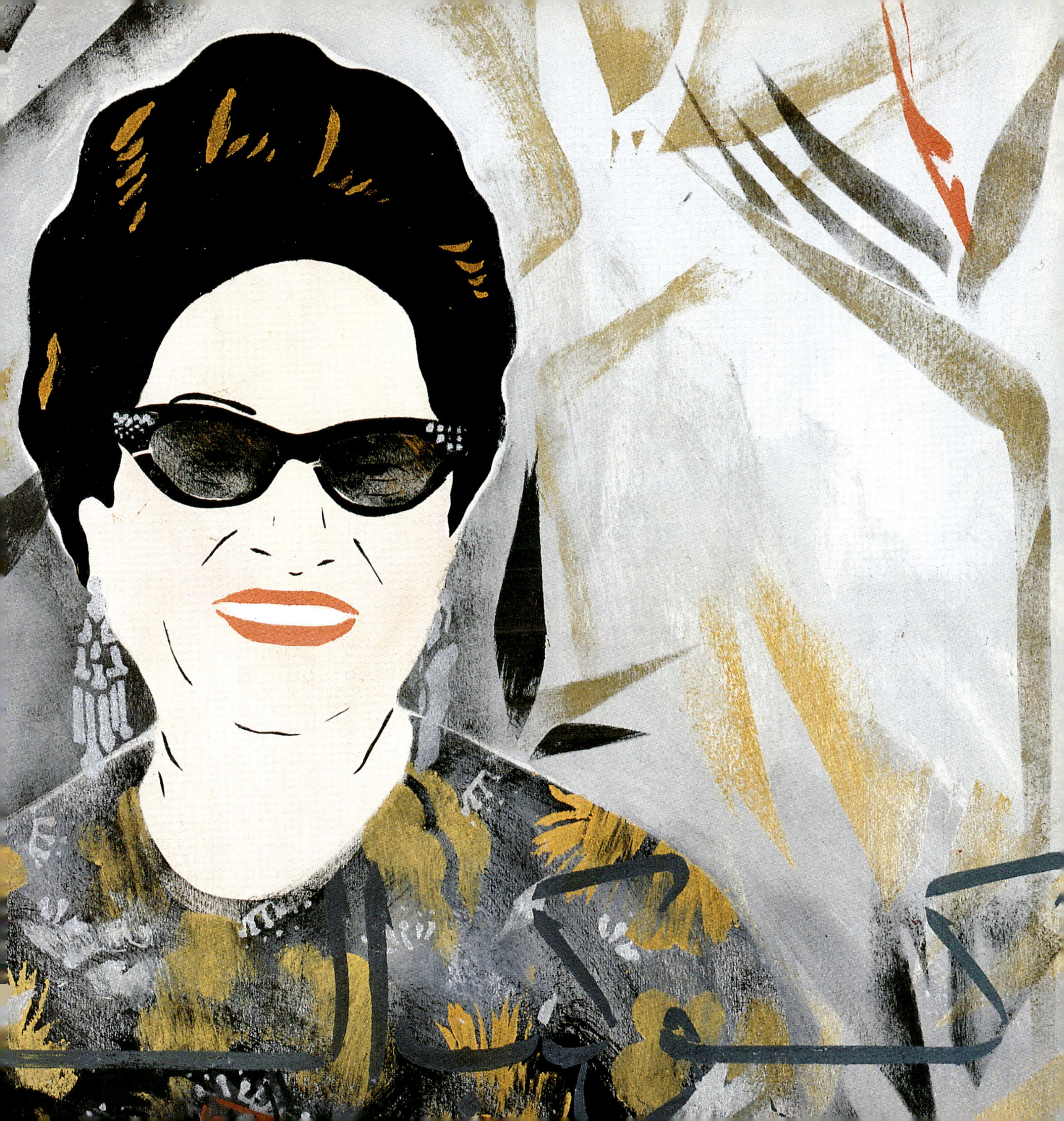

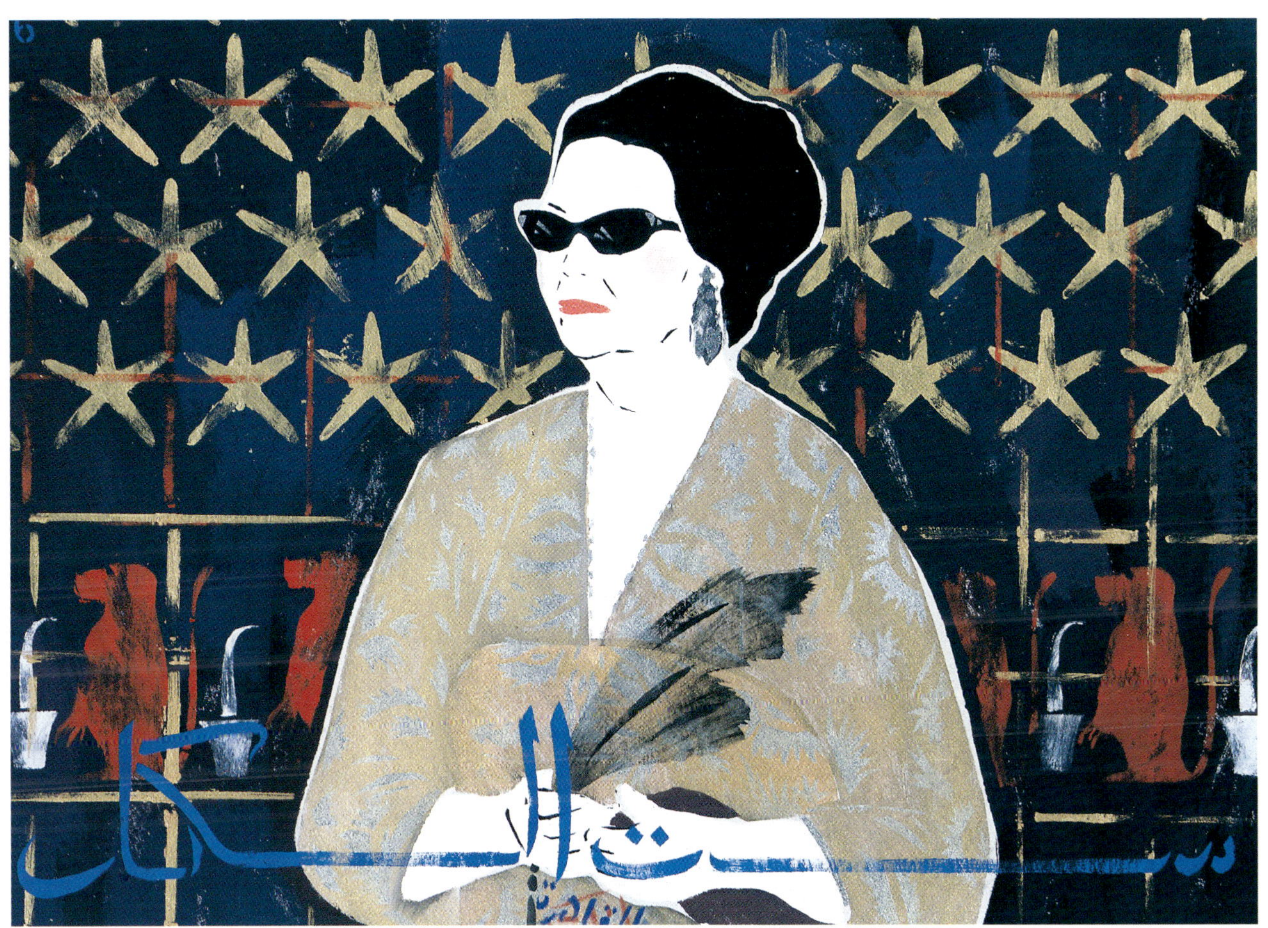

The Best Lady of Them All

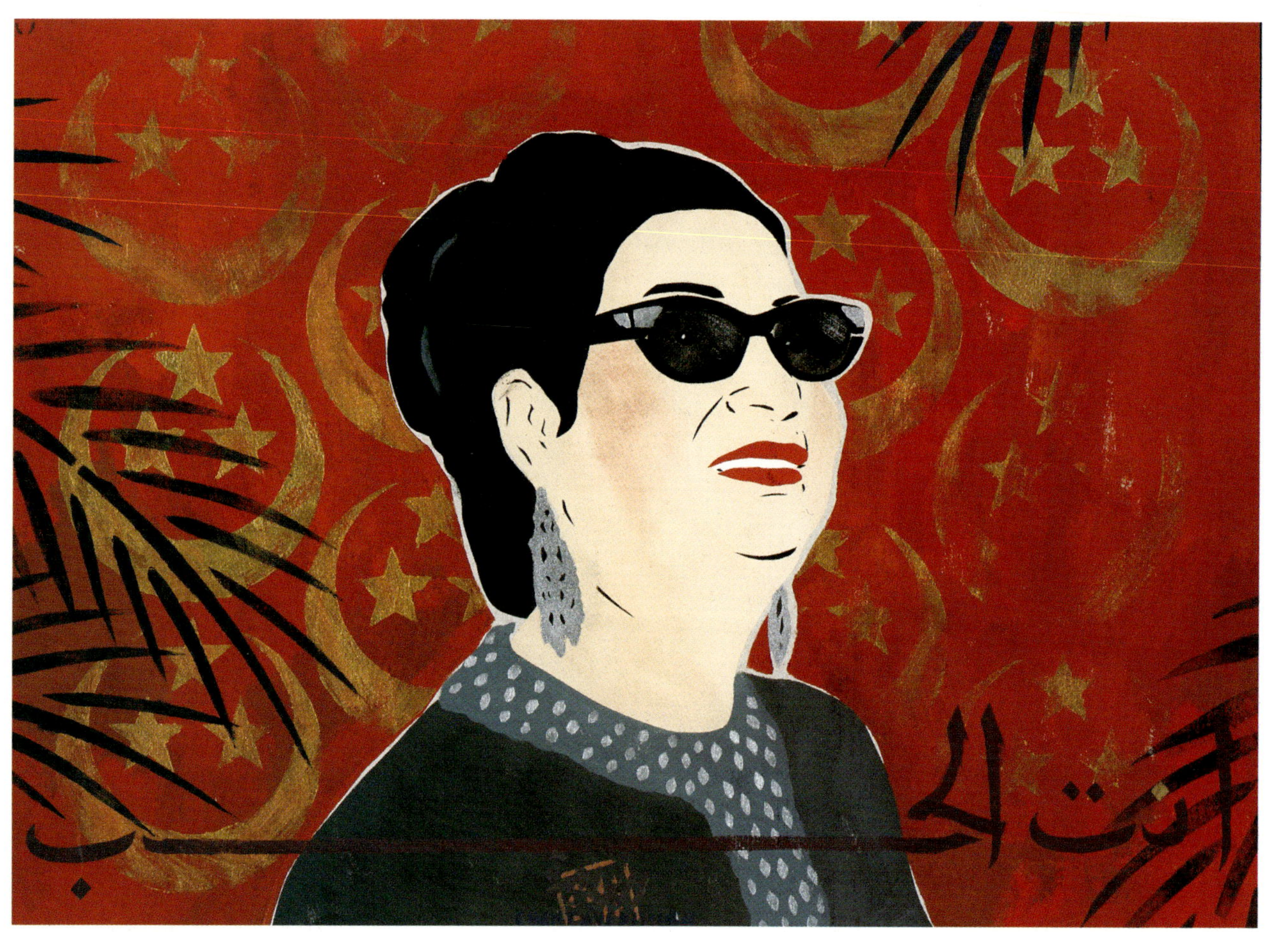

You Are Love

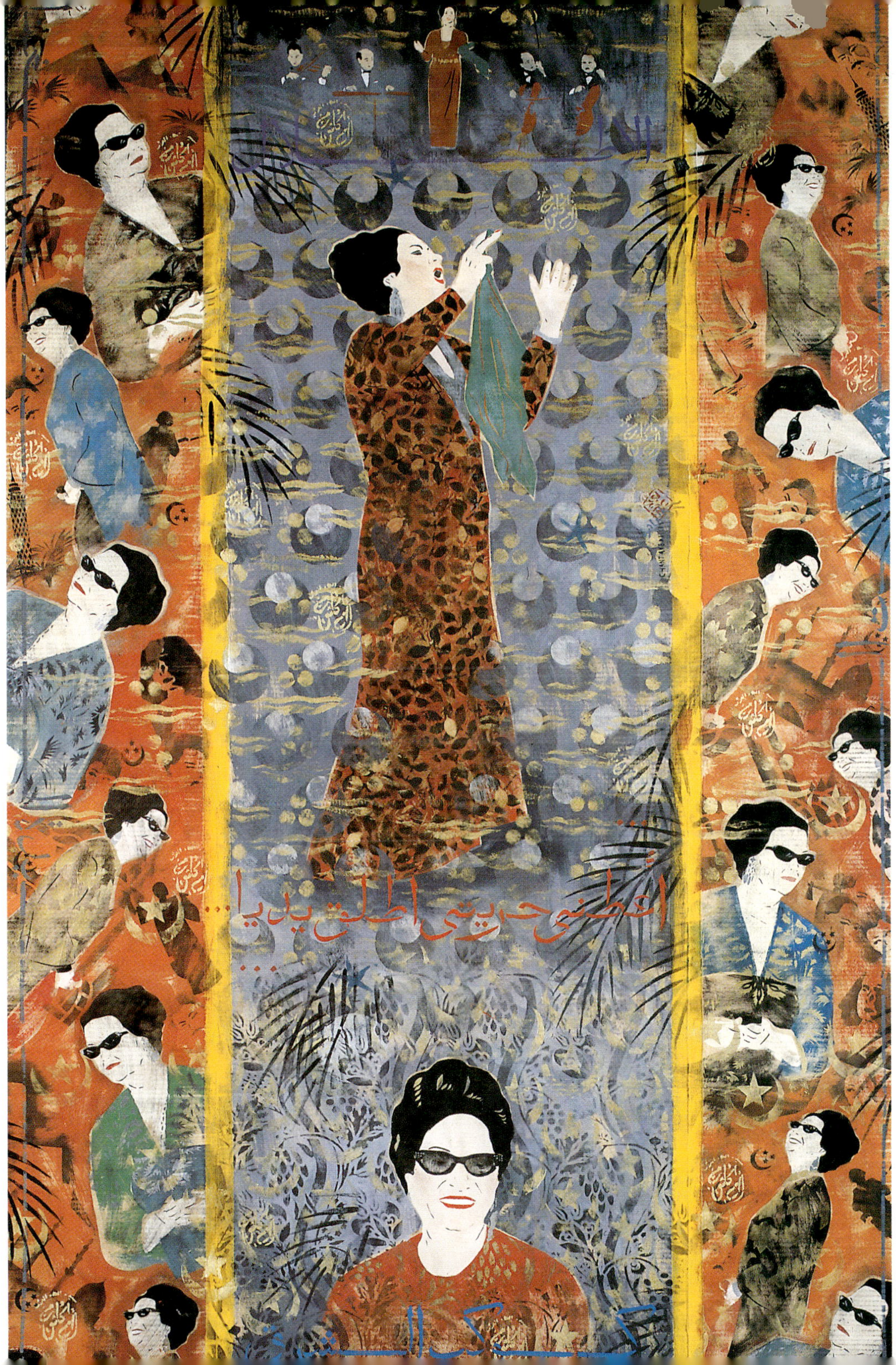

Icons of the Nile

Icons of the Nile

During the Golden Age of Egyptian cinema, from the late 1930s to the early 1960s, the dream-makers of the Nile created an industry that would dominate the Arab world for decades.

This era of glamour was dominated by greatly talented singers, like the legendary Om Kulthoum, the Arab diva *par excellence*; Asmahan, a stunning Druze princess with a thrilling voice whose mysterious death at the age of twenty-six is still the subject of endless speculation; her heart-throb brother Farid al-Atrash, a composer who accompanied many stars with his romantic songs, including the alluring great dancers Tahiya Carioca and Samia Gamal; his rival, Abdel Halim Hafez, the 'Dark Nightingale', the romantic idol of the 1950s and 1960s generation, whose death in 1977 was followed by a wave of suicides; the sex symbol Hind Rostom; the classic 'bad guy' Zaki Rostom; the director-actor Anwar Wagdi; Shadia, the 'Coquette of the Screen'; Kouka 'the Bedouin'; and the fragile-looking Faten Hamama, the 'Lady of the Screen', who acted in more than 100 melodramas.

Most of these artists, still hugely popular decades after their deaths, incarnated each in their own style an ideal character, and remain to this day matinée idols throughout the Arab world.

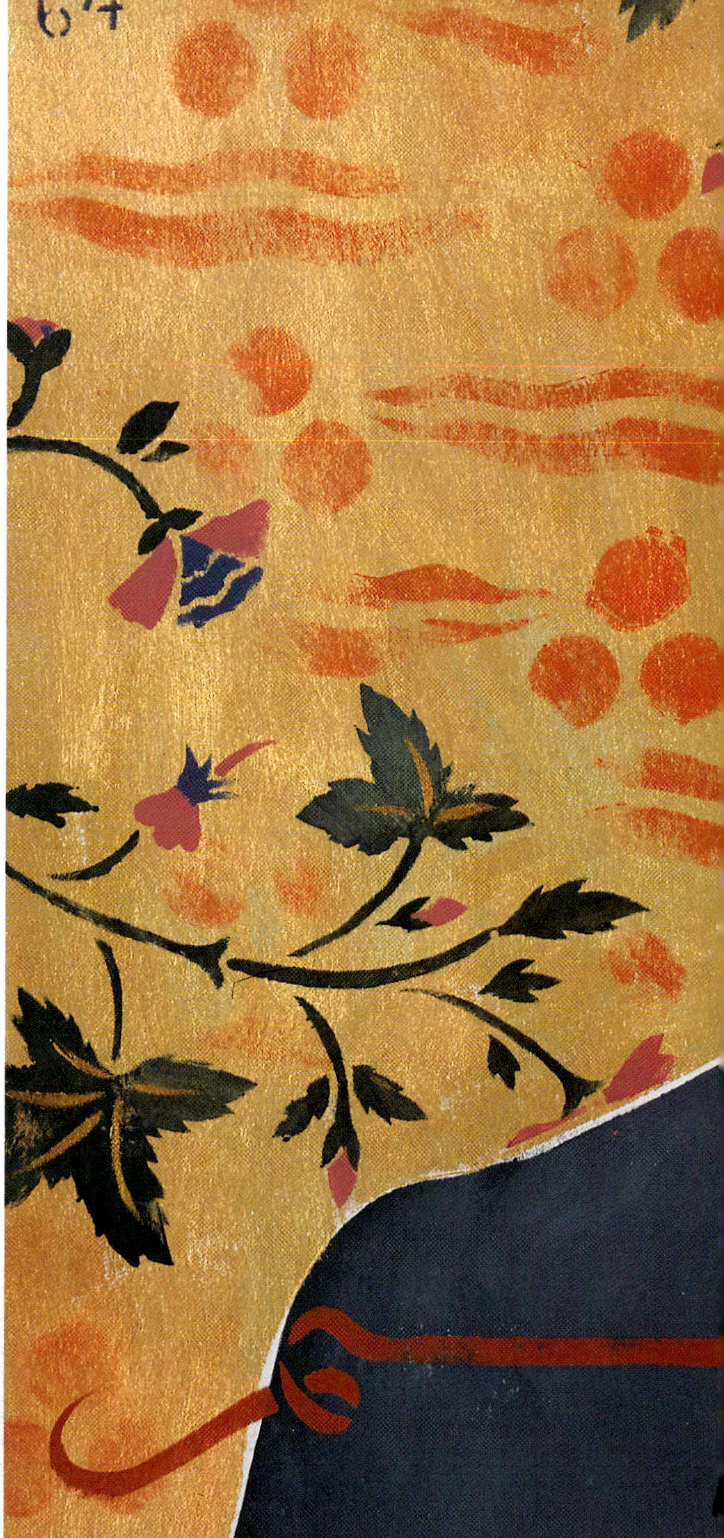

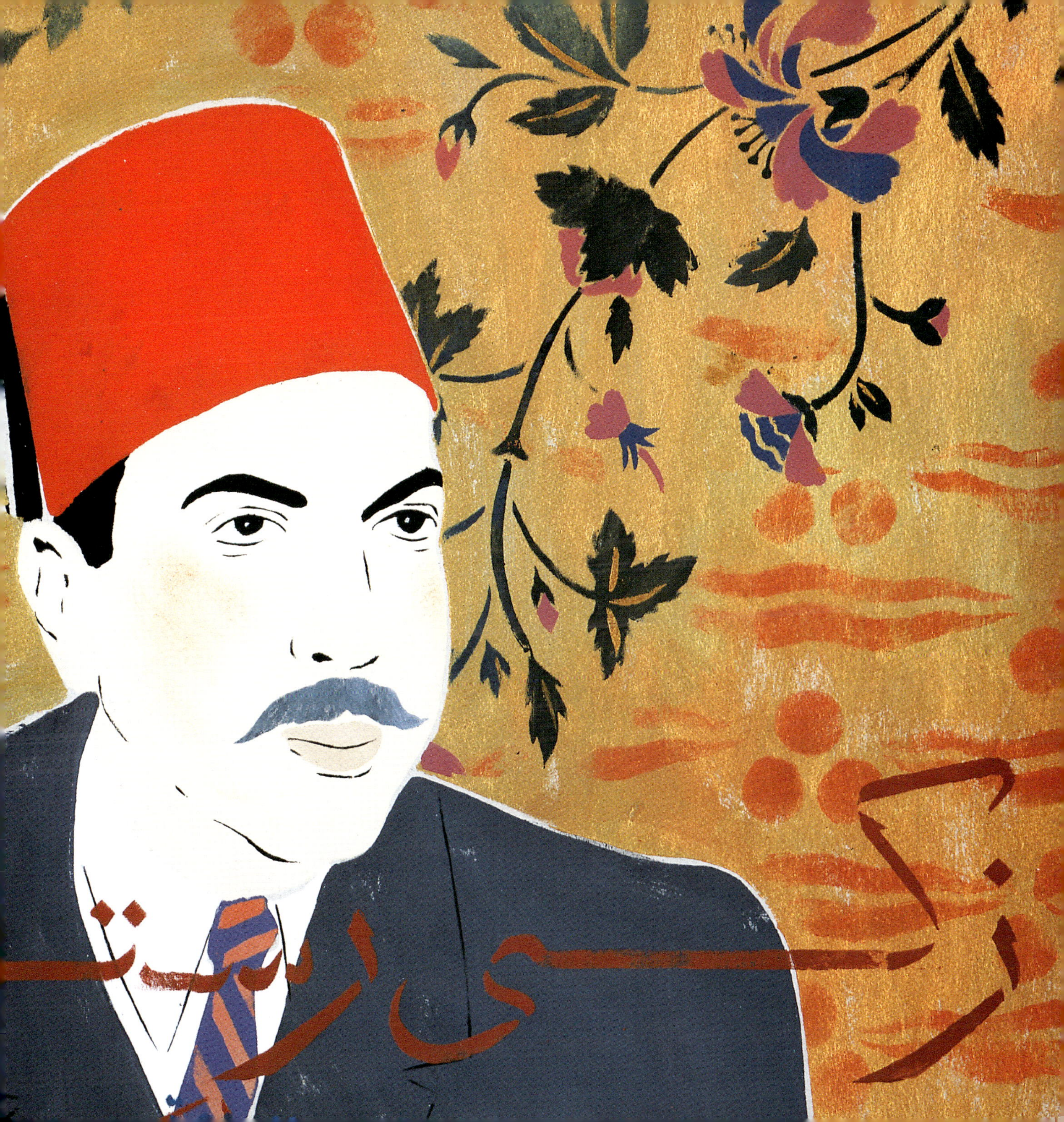

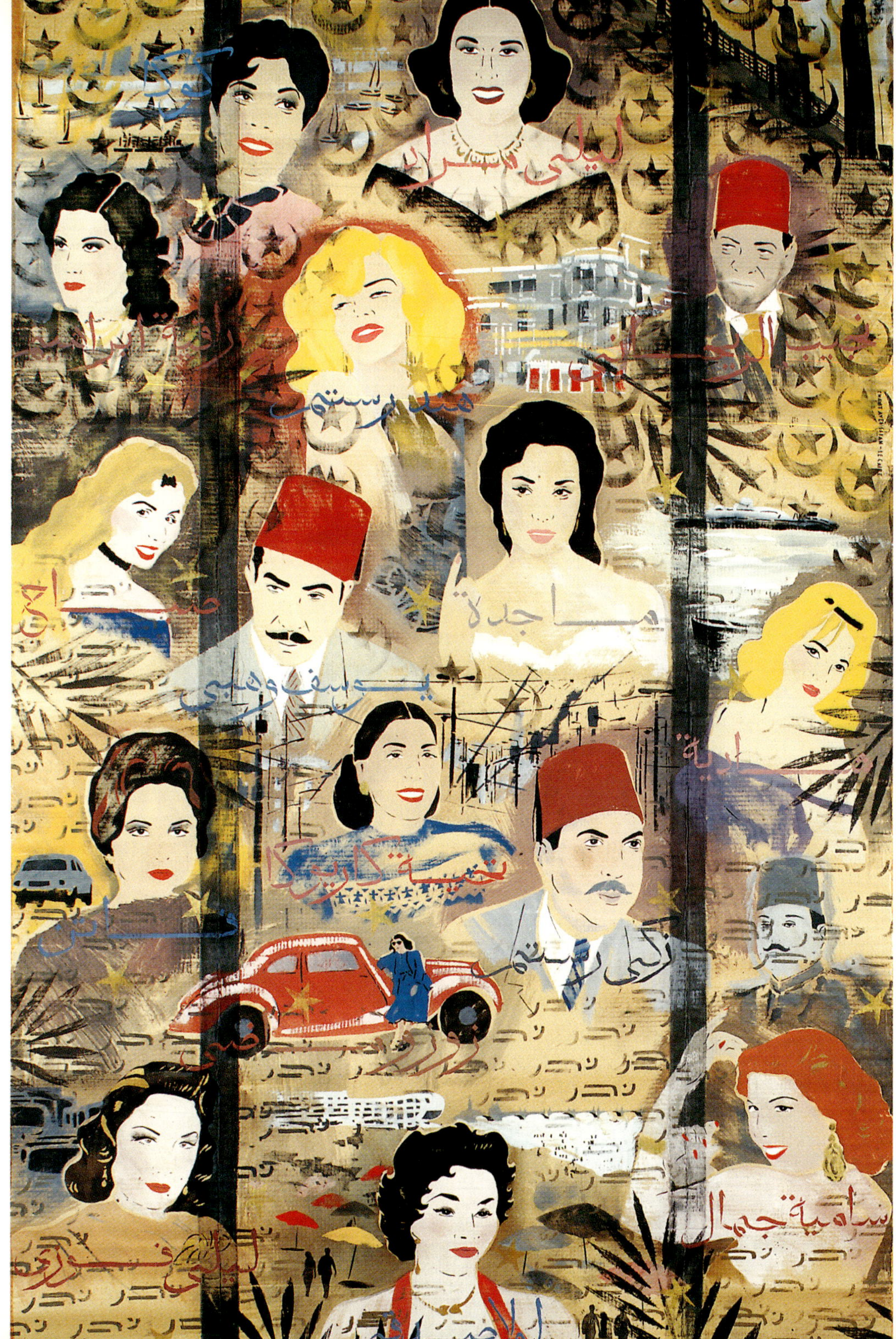

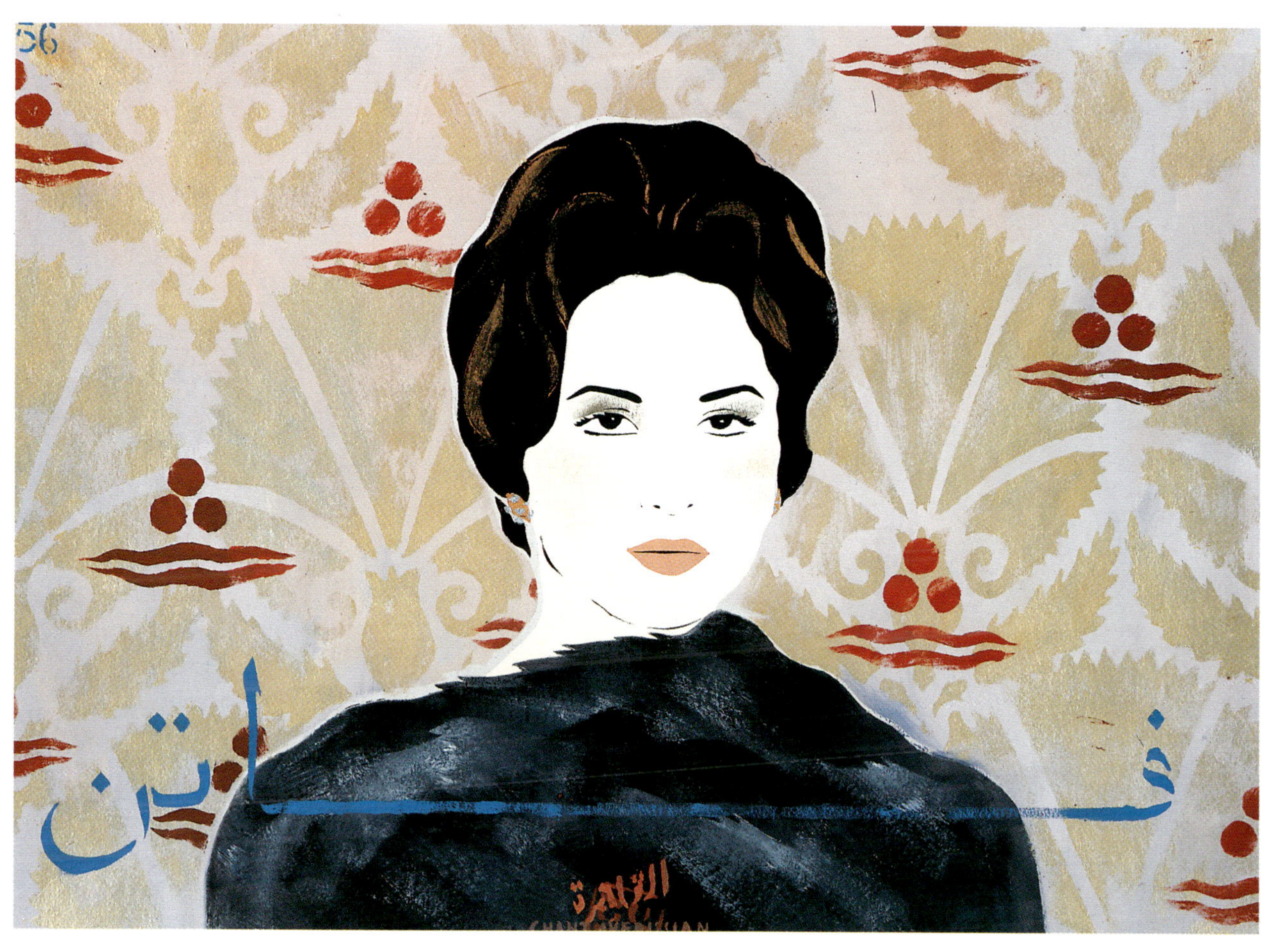

Faten Hamama

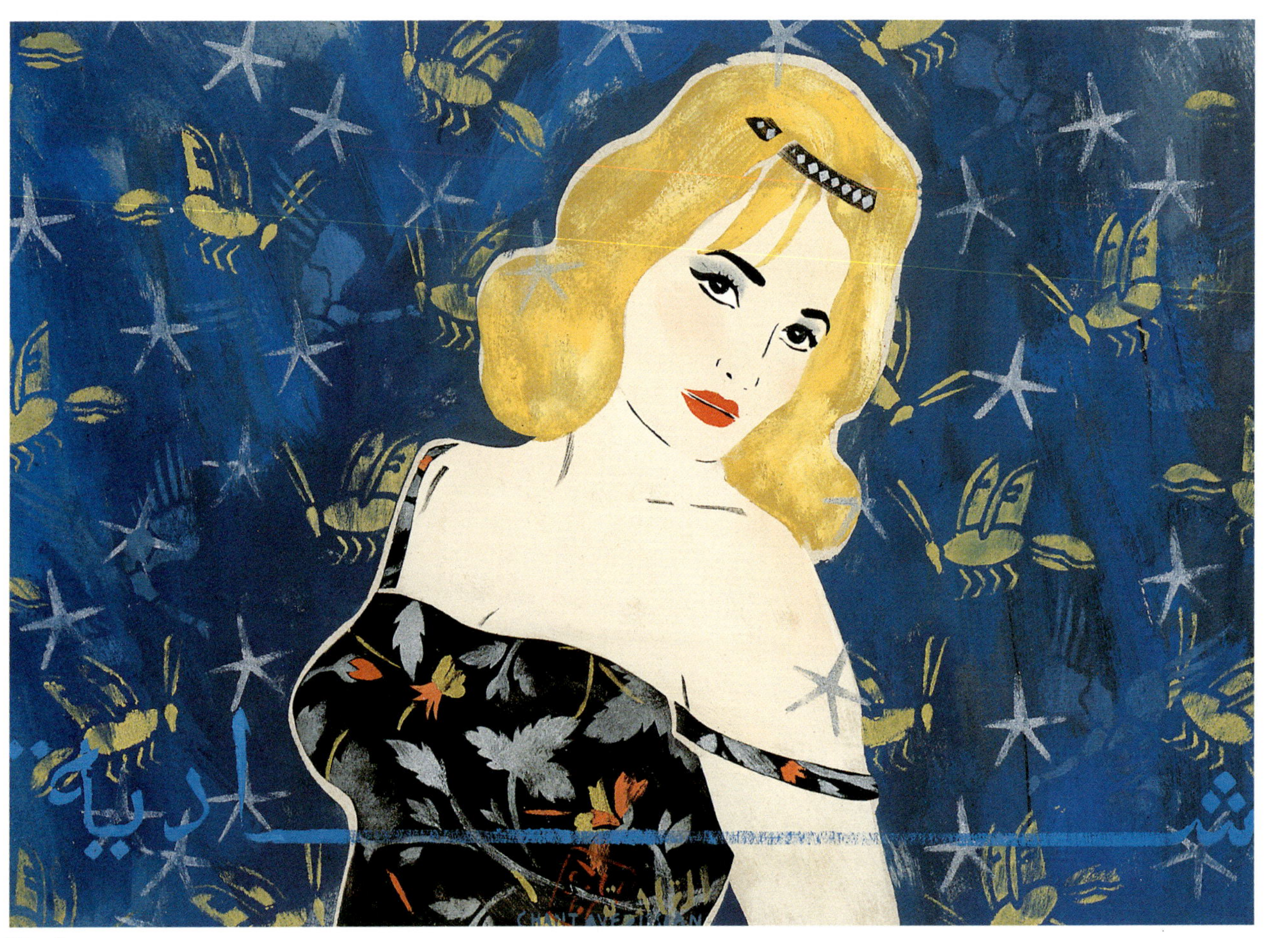

Shadia

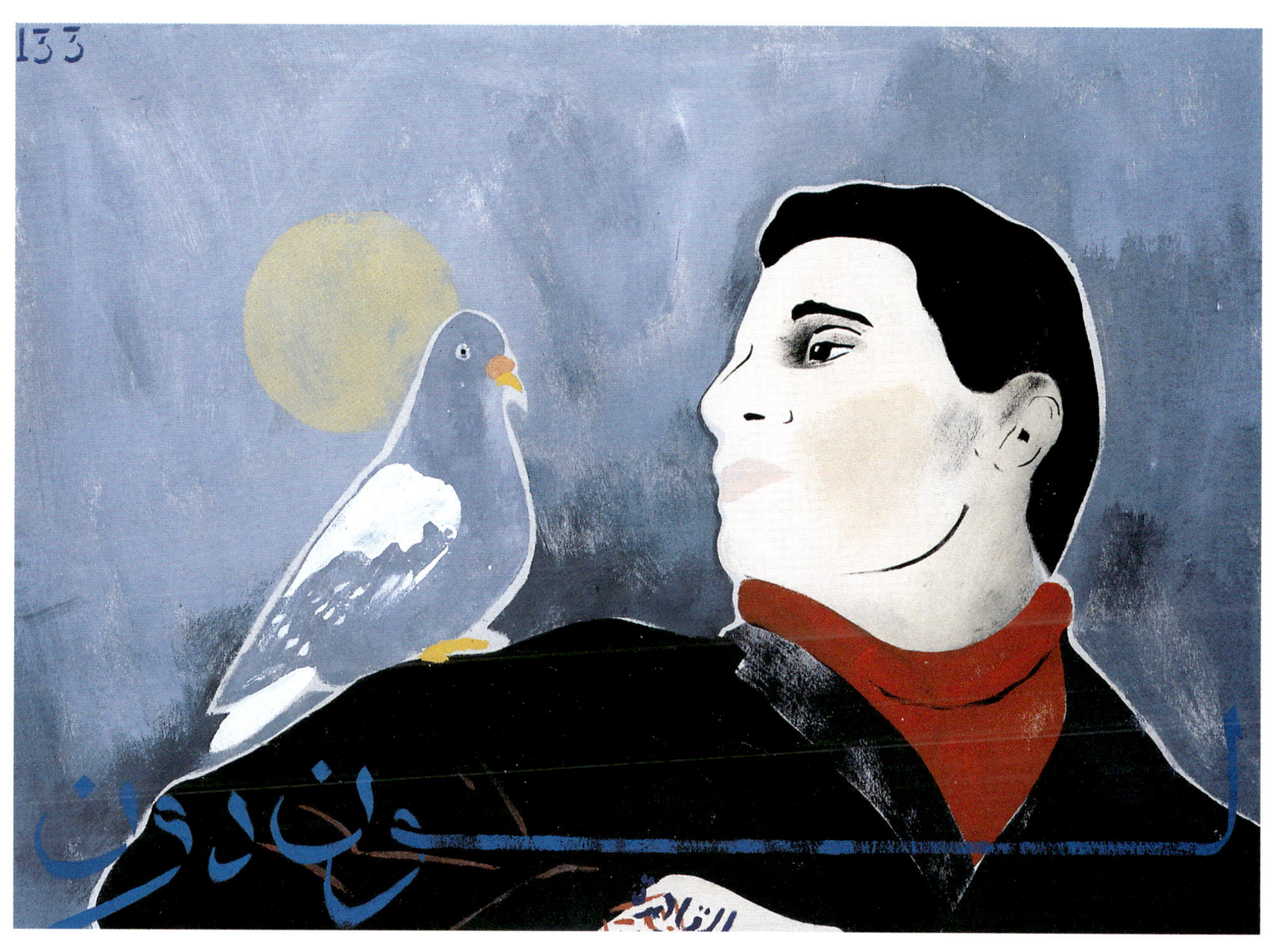

Abdel Halim Hafiz, in London

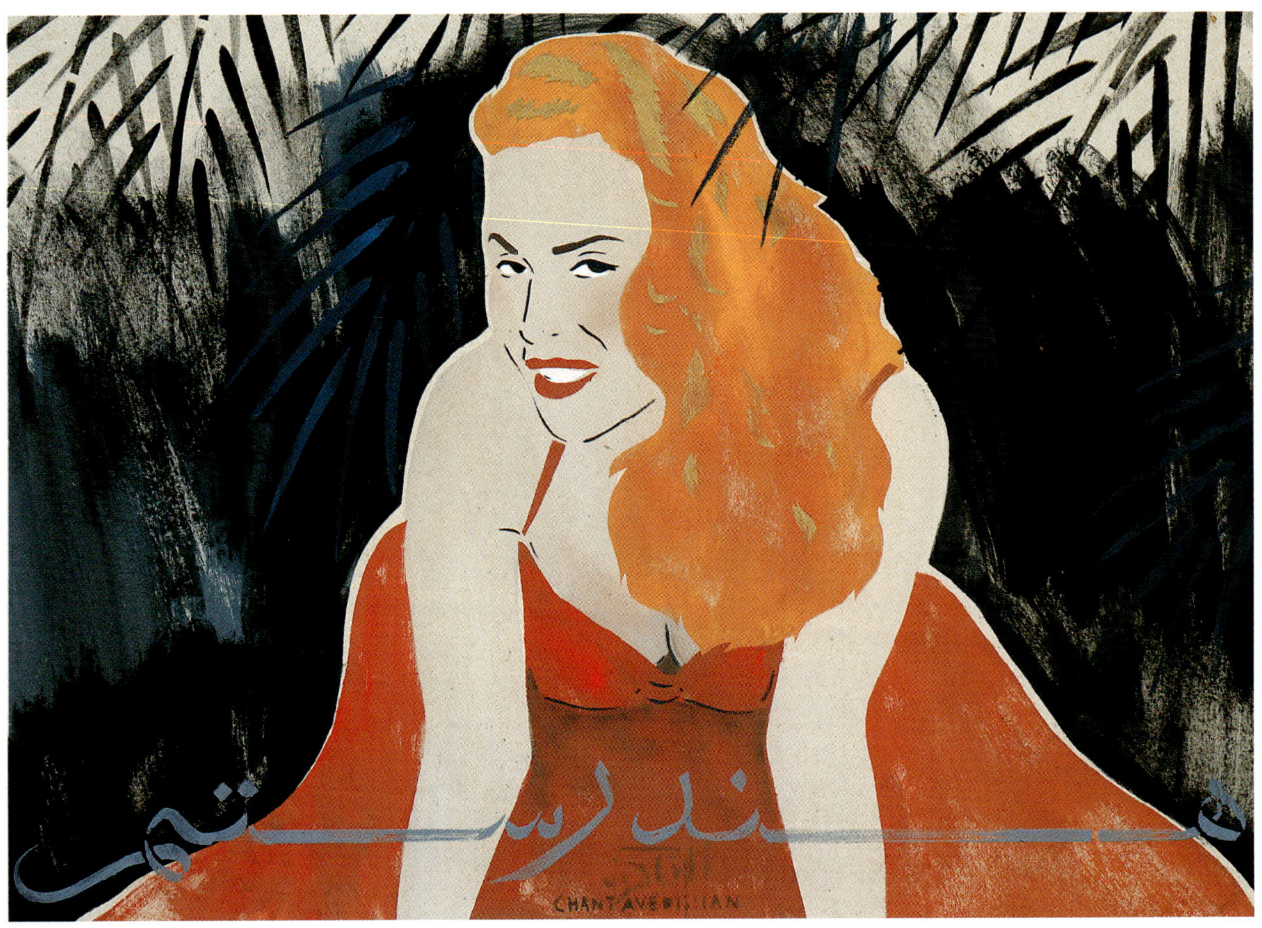

Hind Rostom

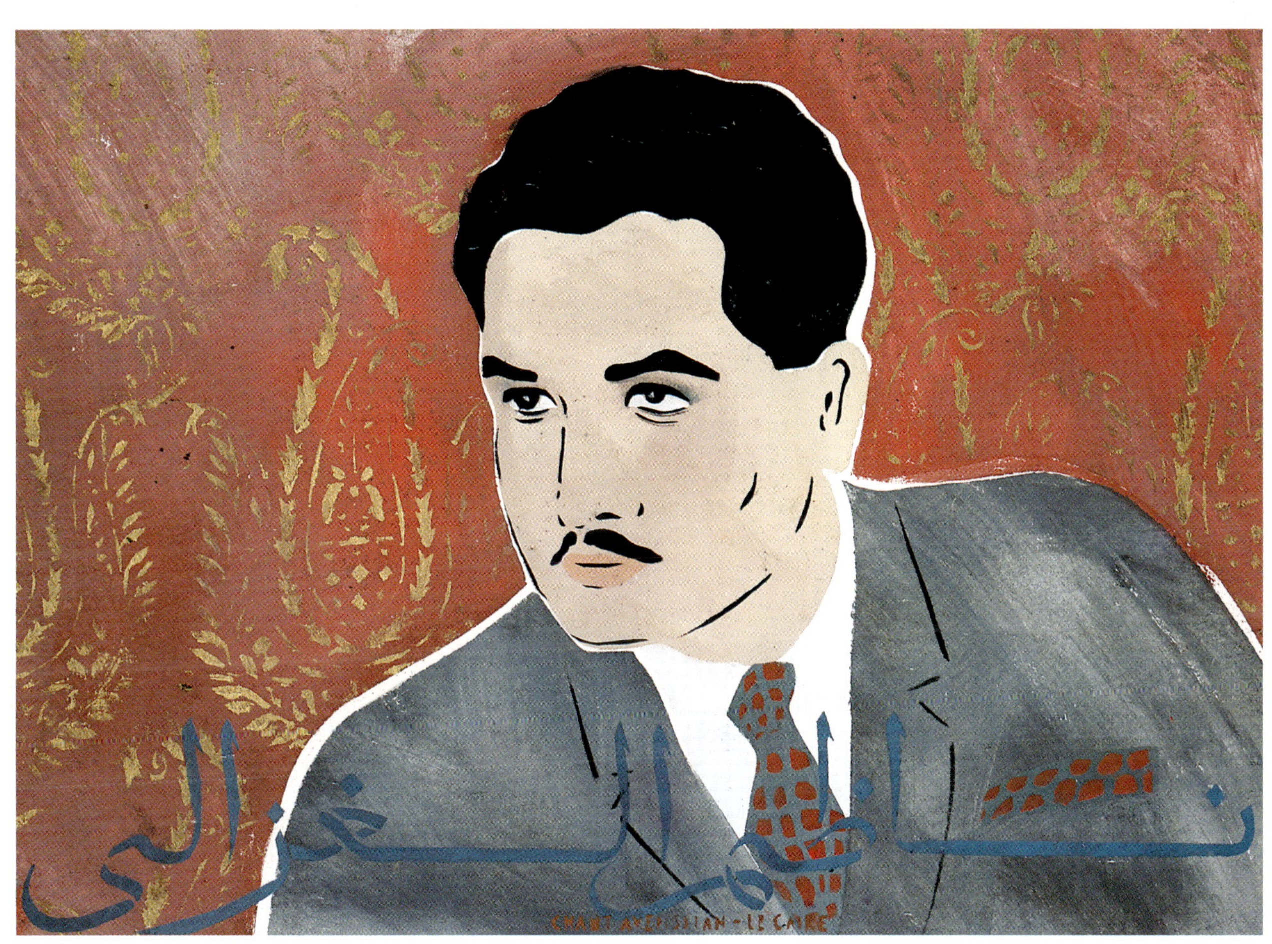

Nazem al-Ghazali

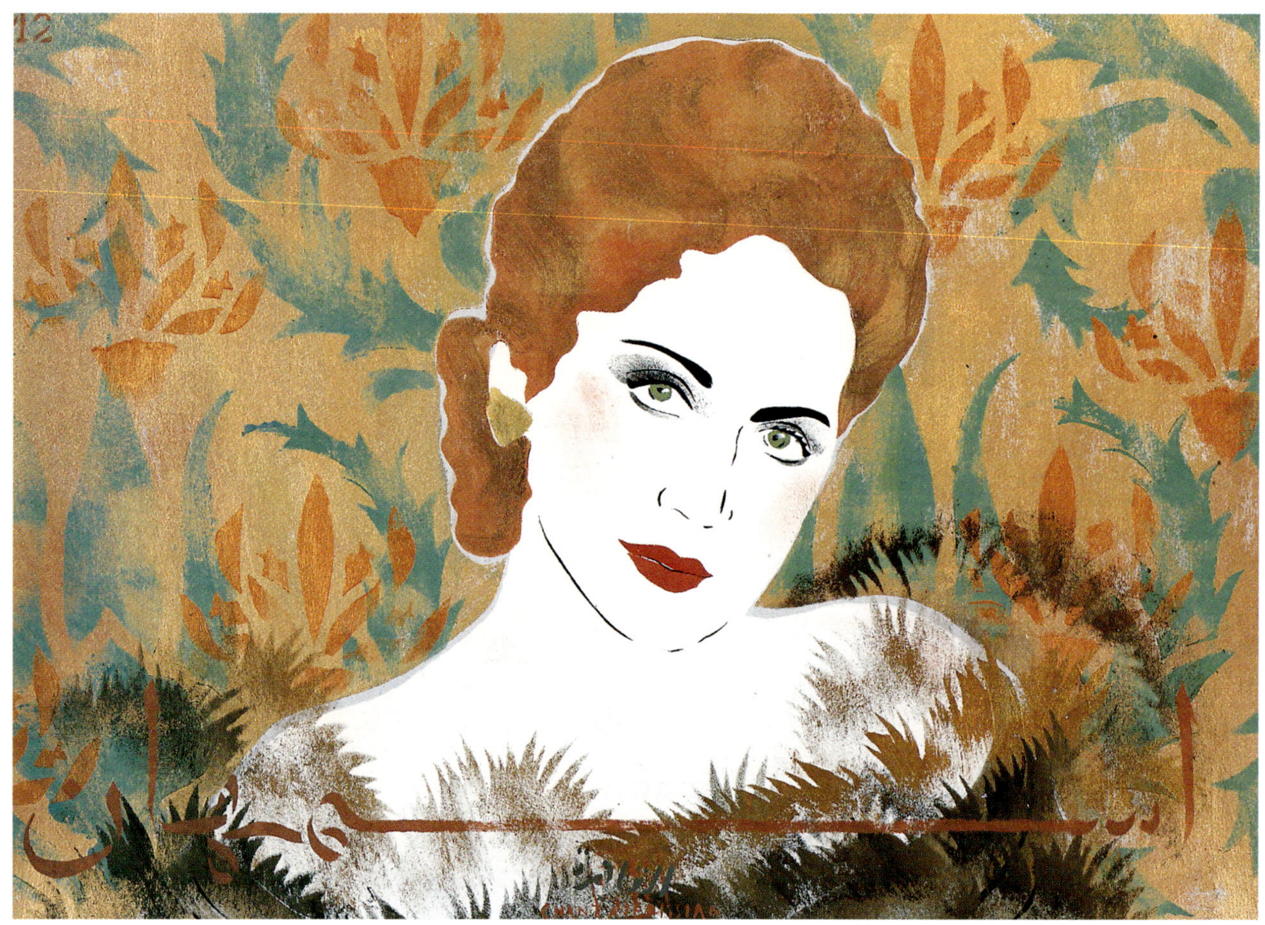

Asmahan

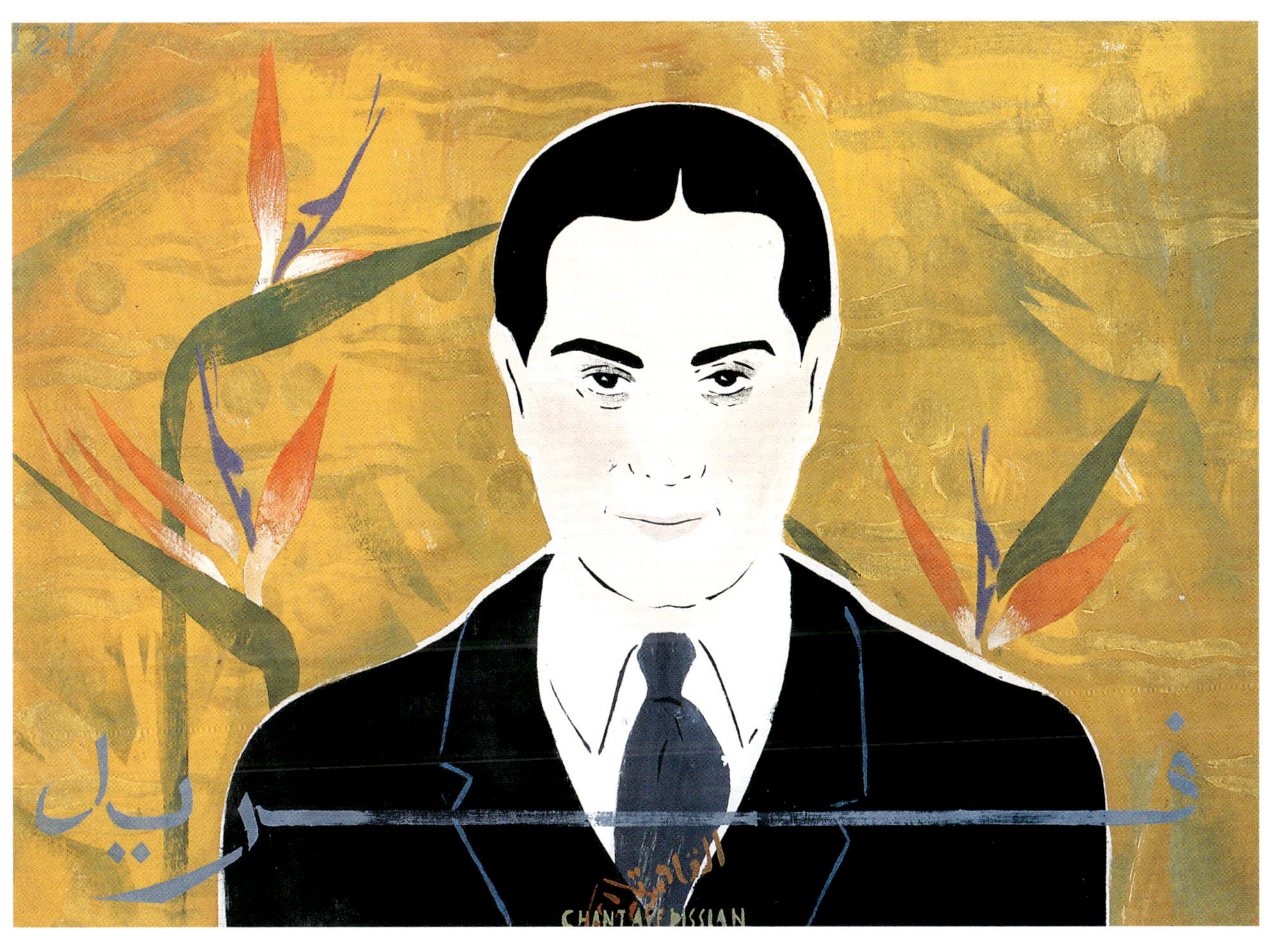

Farid al-Atrash

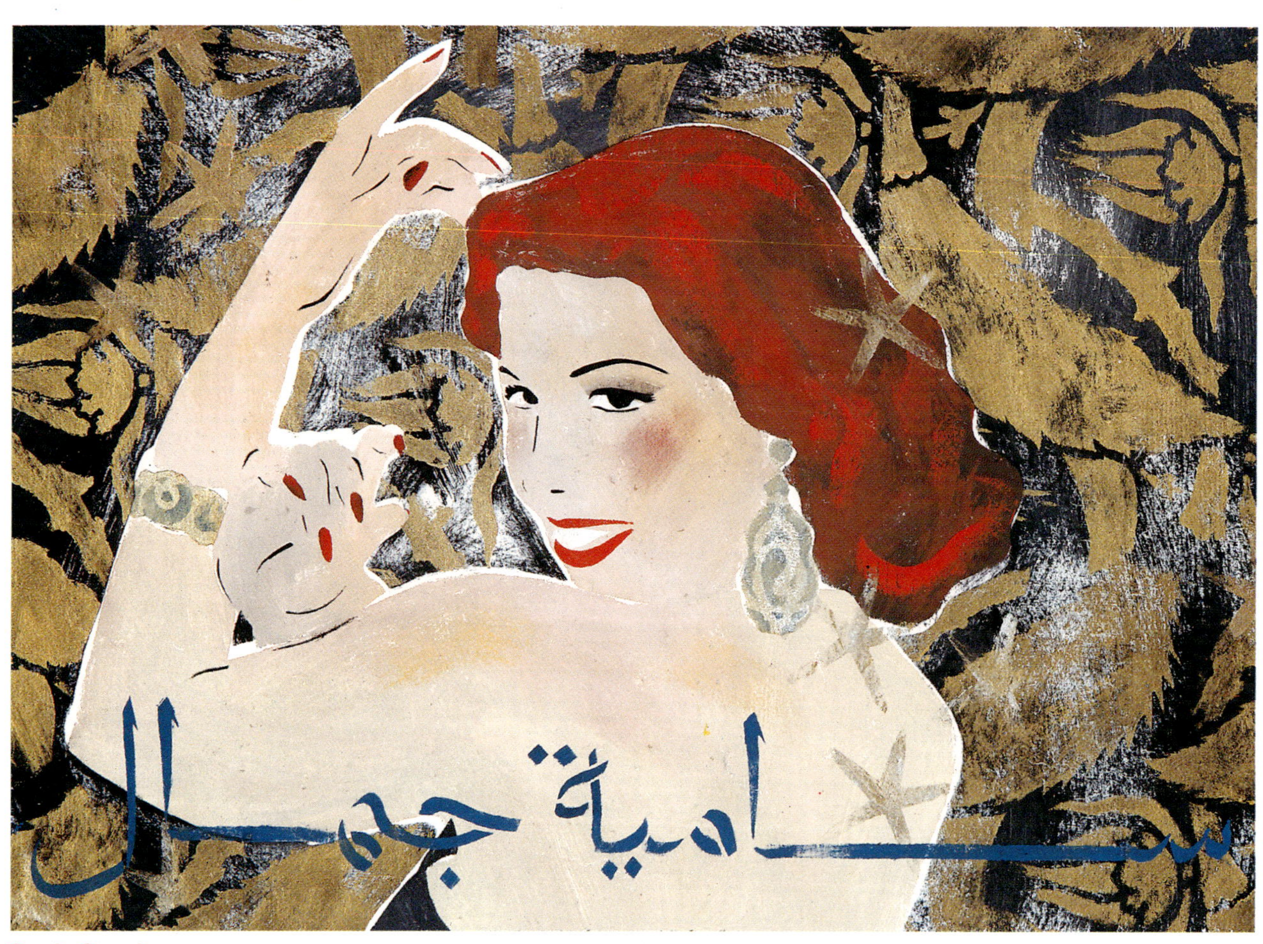

Samia Gamal

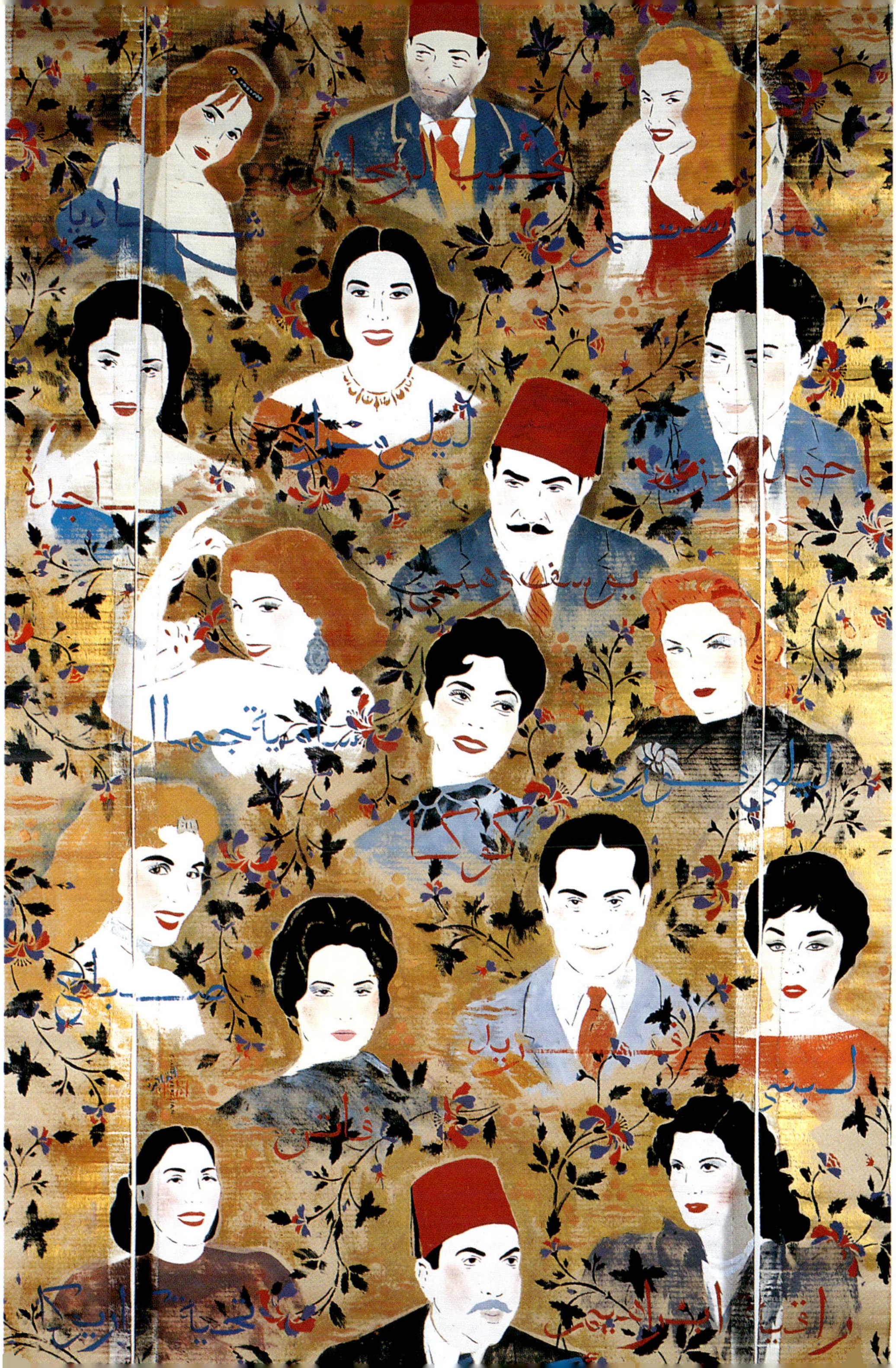

شادية
حبيب الوطن
ماري منيب
ليلى مراد
يوسف وهبي
ليلى فوزي
ماجدة
كوكا
ليلى
لبنى
فاتن
تحية كاريوكا
فريد الأطرش

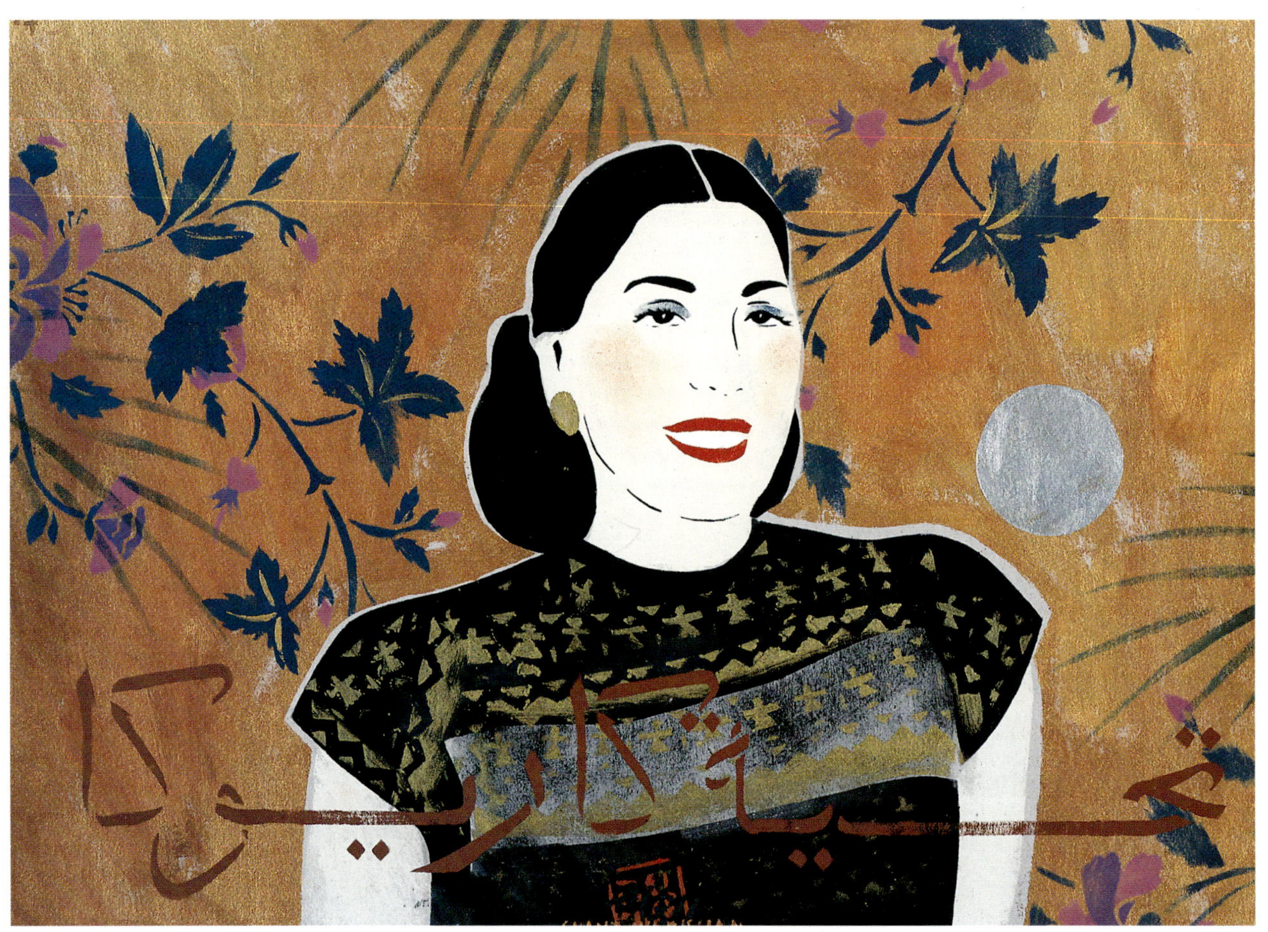

Tahiya Carioca

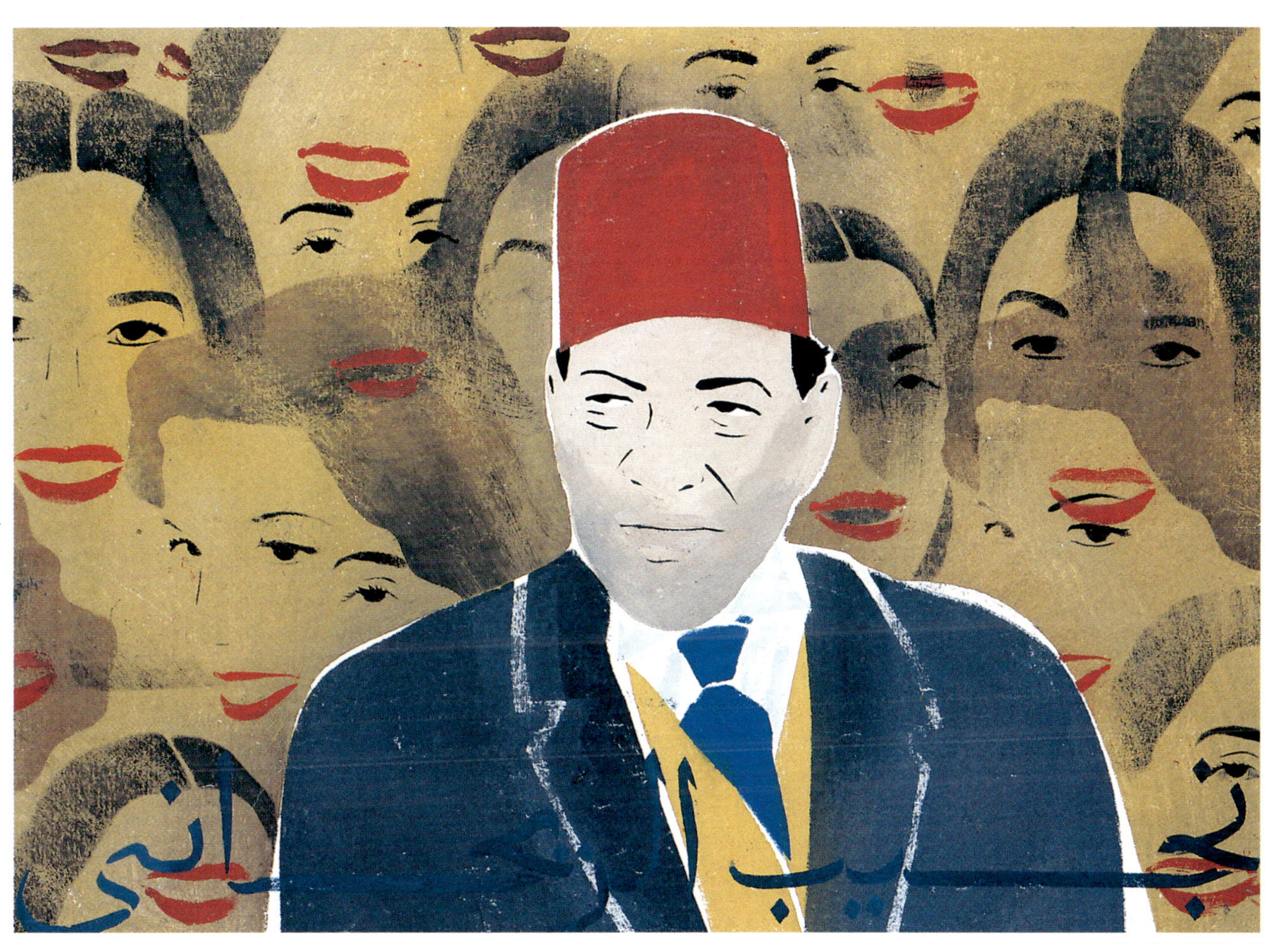

Nagib al-Rihani

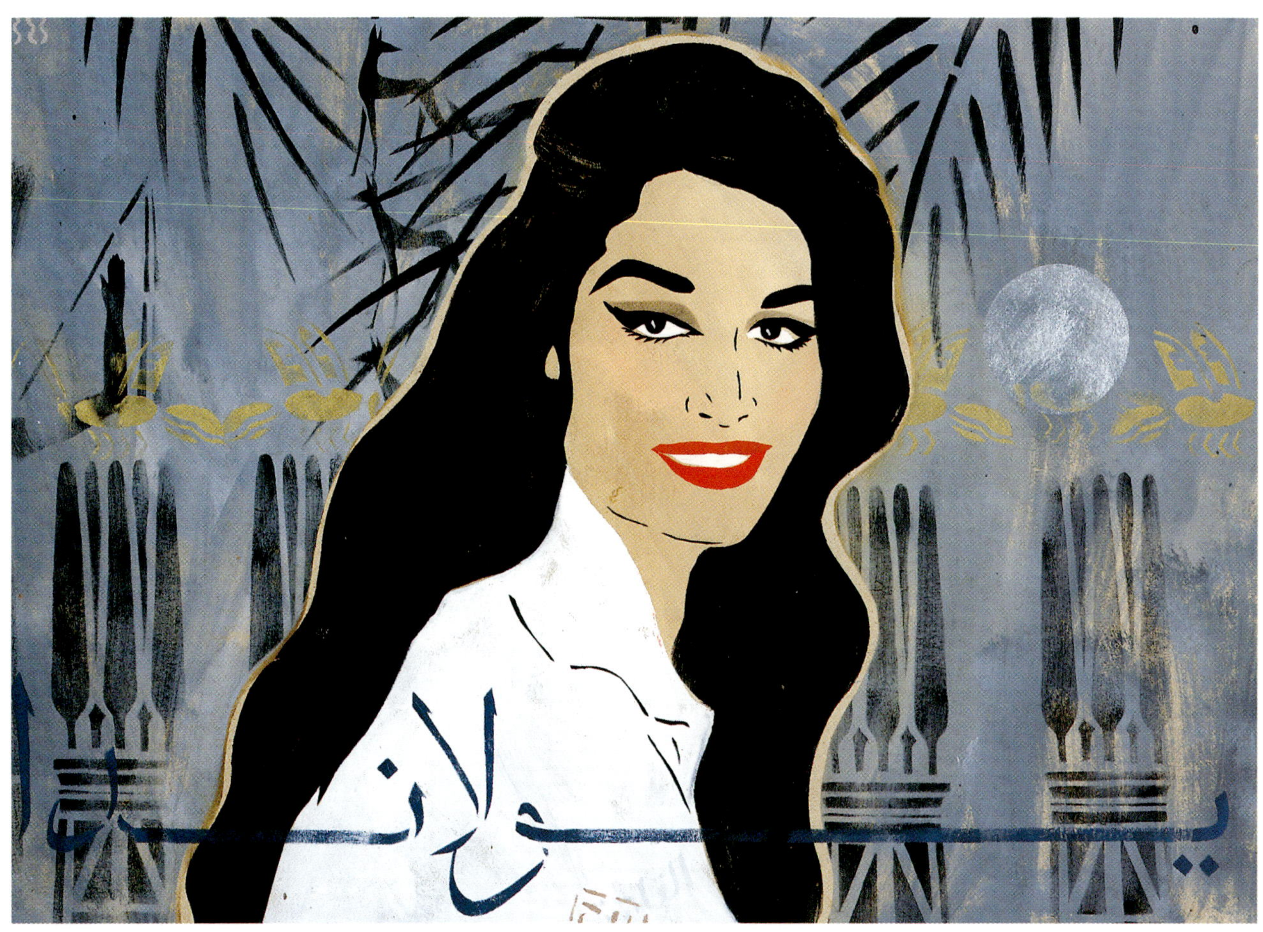

Yolanda

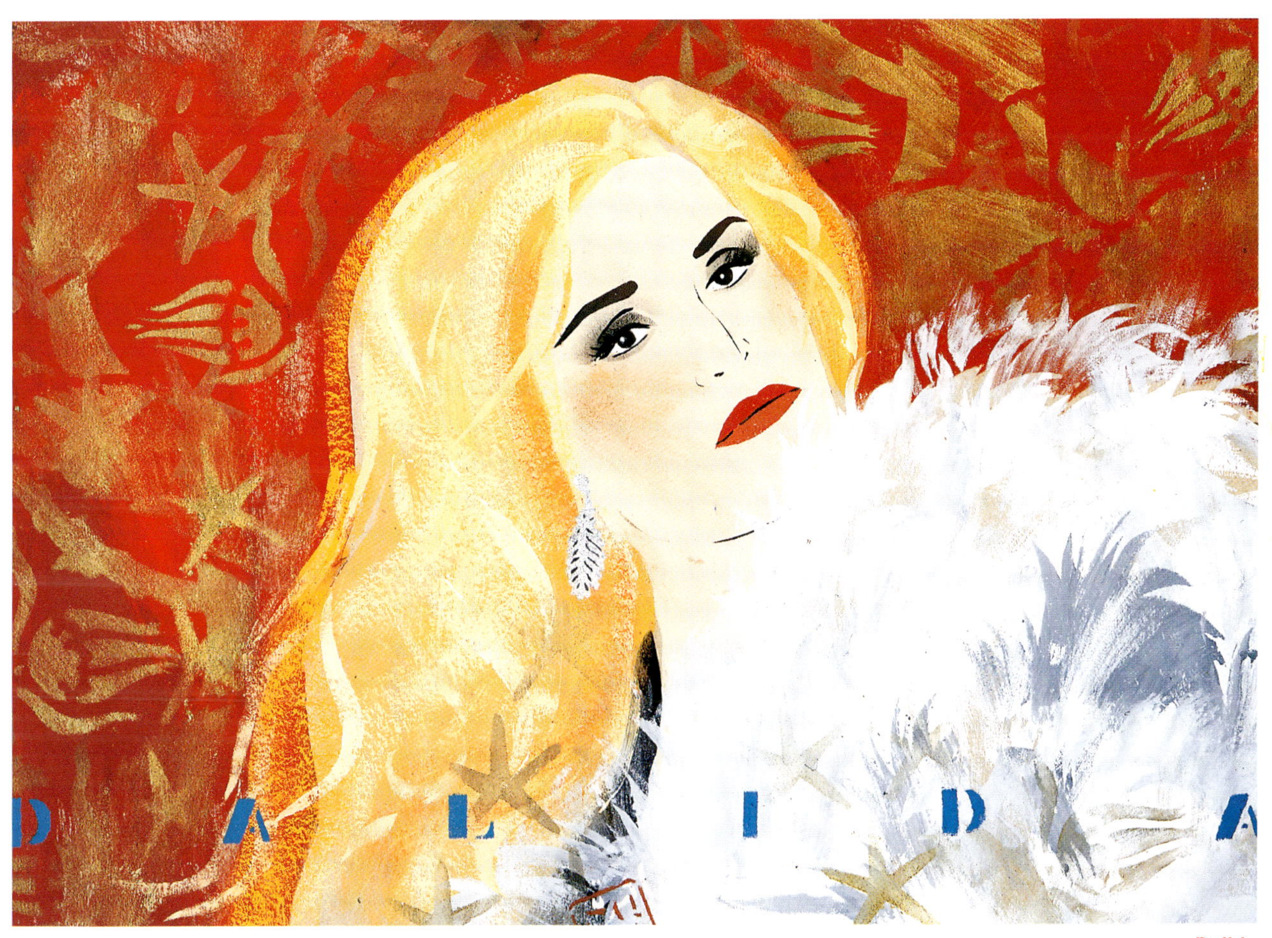

Dalida

Kings & Pharaohs

Kings & Pharaohs

Farouk became King in 1936, aged sixteen, and soon afterwards Cairo became one of the most cosmopolitan and sophisticated cities in the world – so much so, his legendarily beautiful sister Fawziya, married to the Shah of Iran, left Tehran to return home.

Farouk's personal life was almost a soap opera. The British humiliated him by invading his palace in 1942; a year later he was immobilised for many months by a serious car accident; and in 1950 his adored mother, Queen Nazli, was expelled from the royal court with her daughter Fathia, who had married a Christian. Fathia was later murdered by her ex-husband; Nazli died in exile. Farouk married twice, first to Queen Farida, with whom he had three daughters, and then to Queen Nariman, in the hope of having a son.

Under King Farouk, Cairo became the headquarters of the Arab League (1945), and it was on his initiative that Egypt fought the first Arab-Israeli war (1948). He loved his people and was the first Egyptian king to mix directly with the populace, but, surrounded by manipulative courtiers and a pawn of the British government, he increasingly took refuge in pleasure. On losing his throne in 1952, Farouk lived a life of lonely idleness in Italy, where he died aged forty-four. He epitomised the problems of a Middle Eastern monarch, torn between East and West, modernity and tradition.

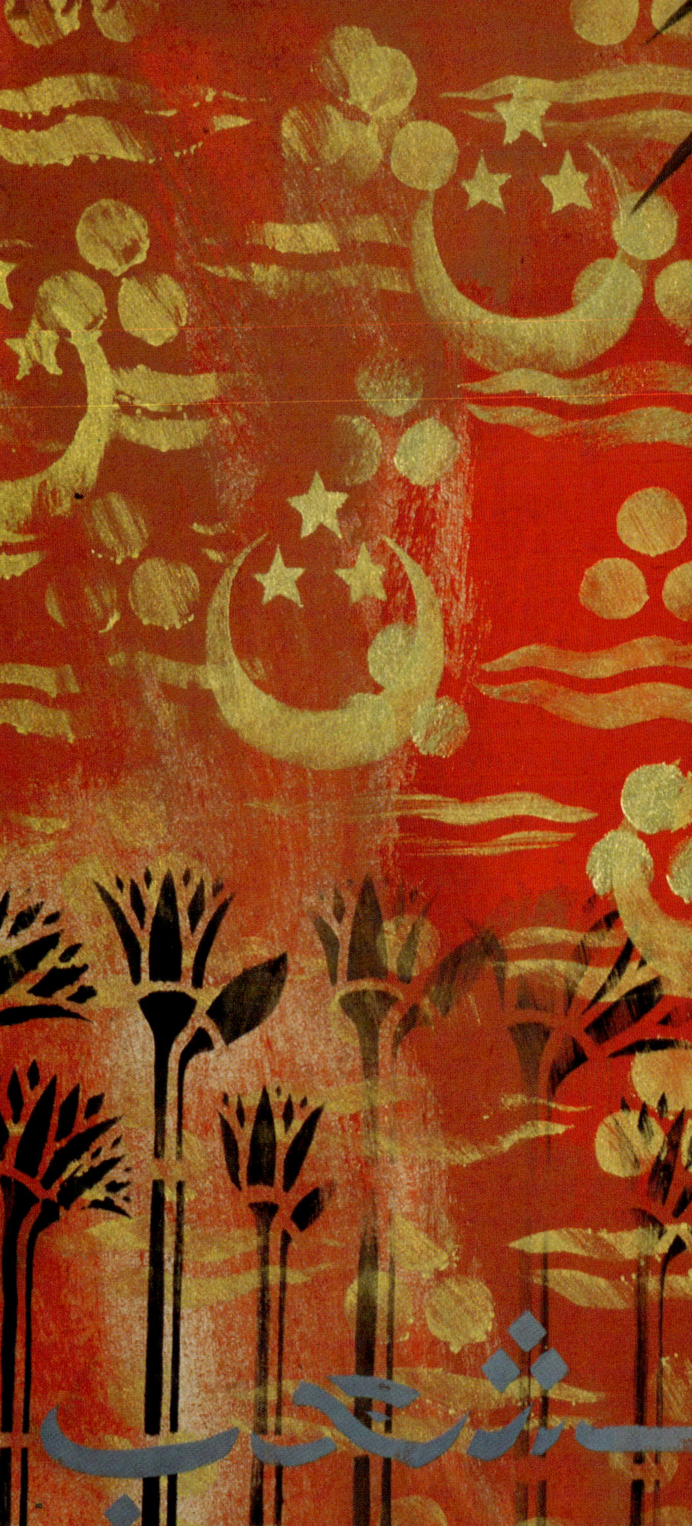

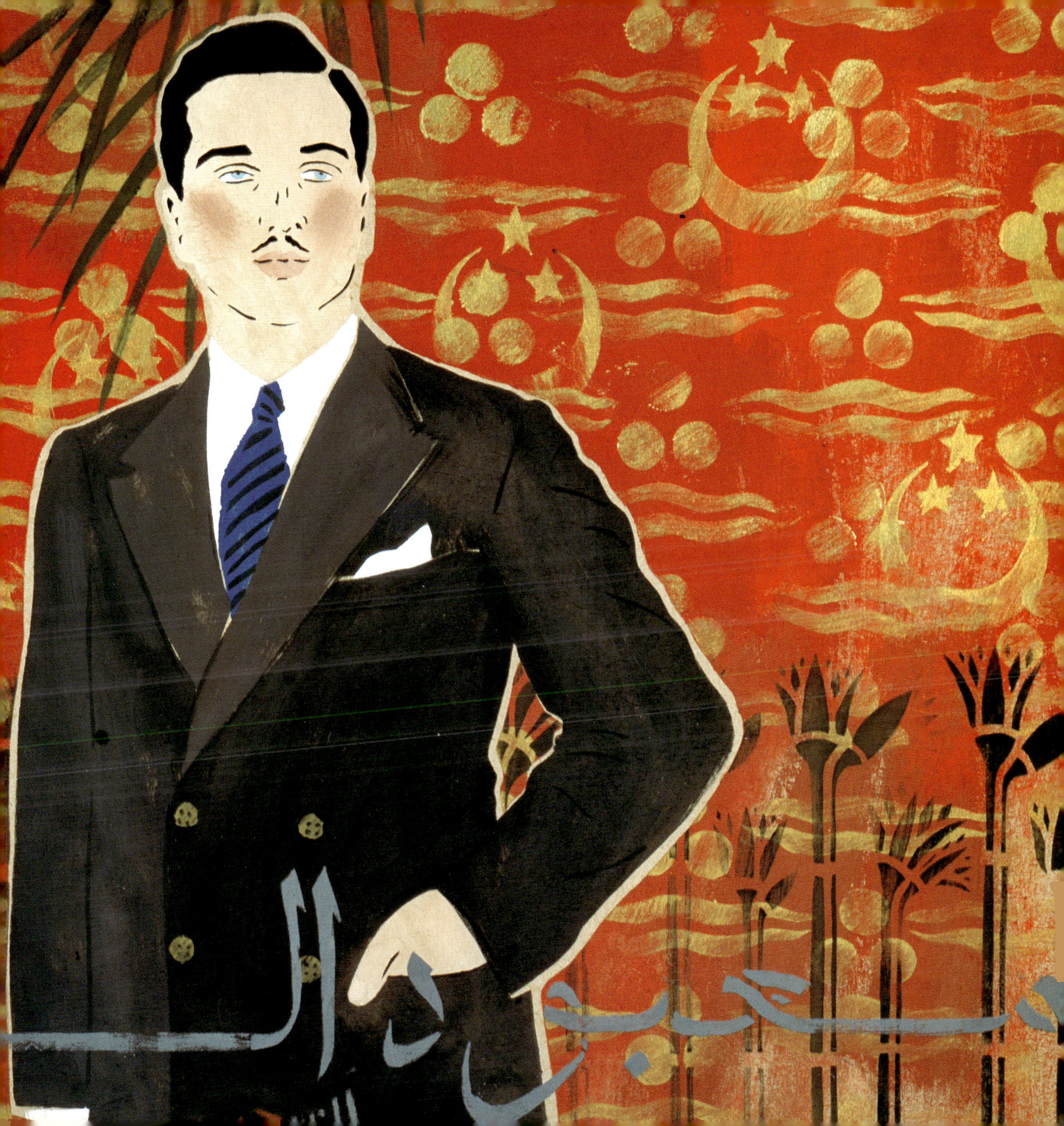

بـحـبـوبـة دلال

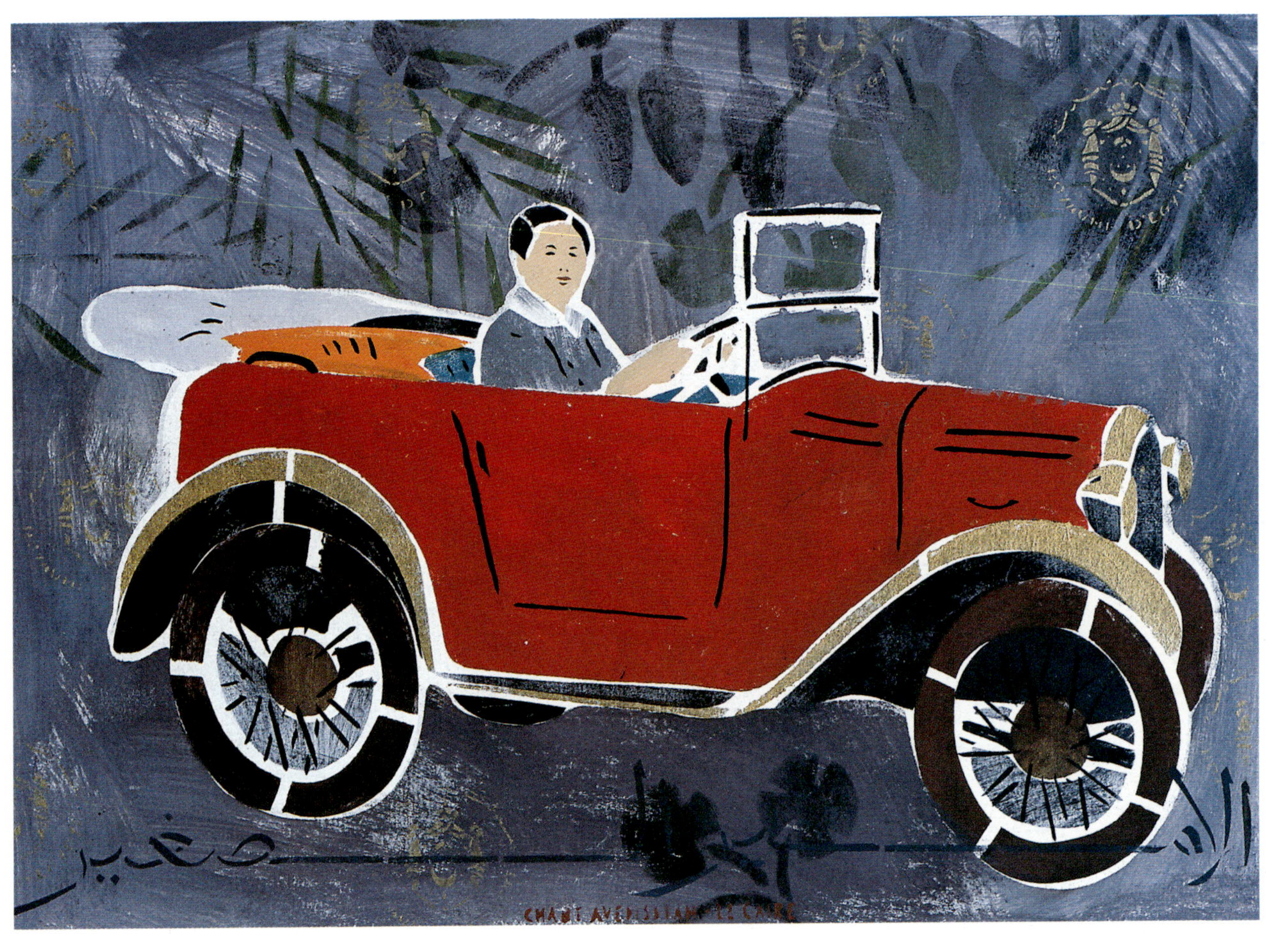

The Young Prince

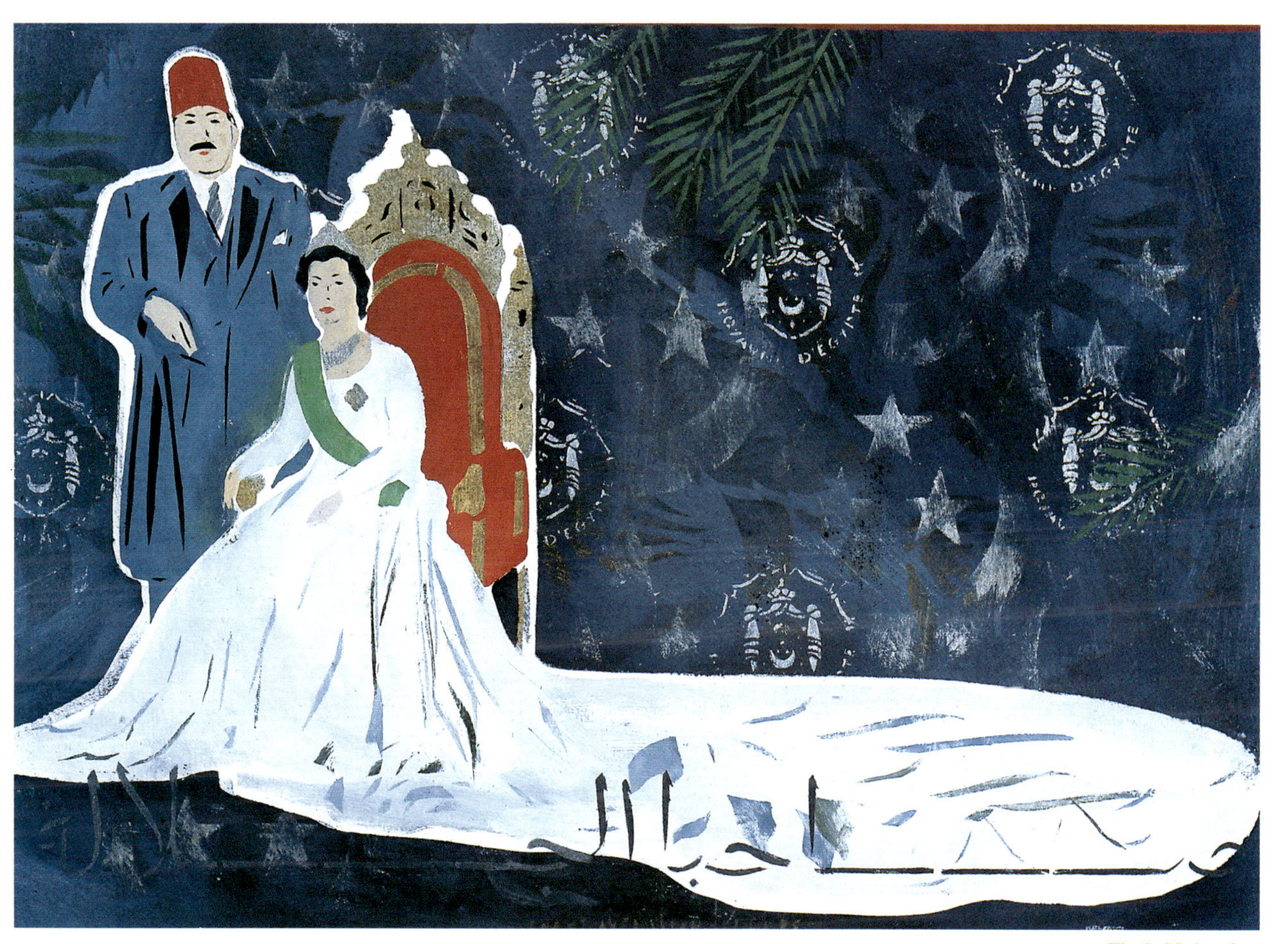

Their Majesties

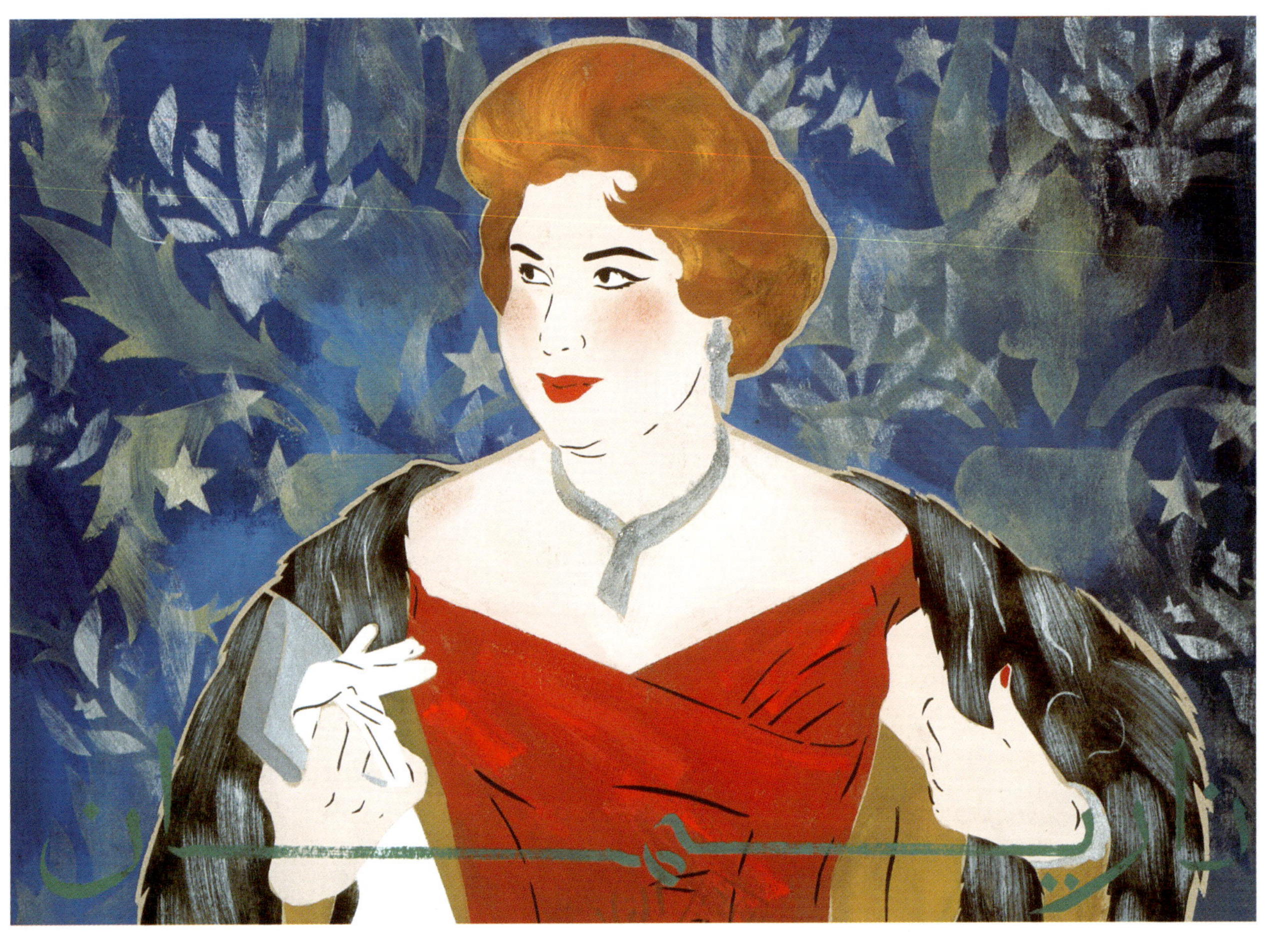

Queen Nariman

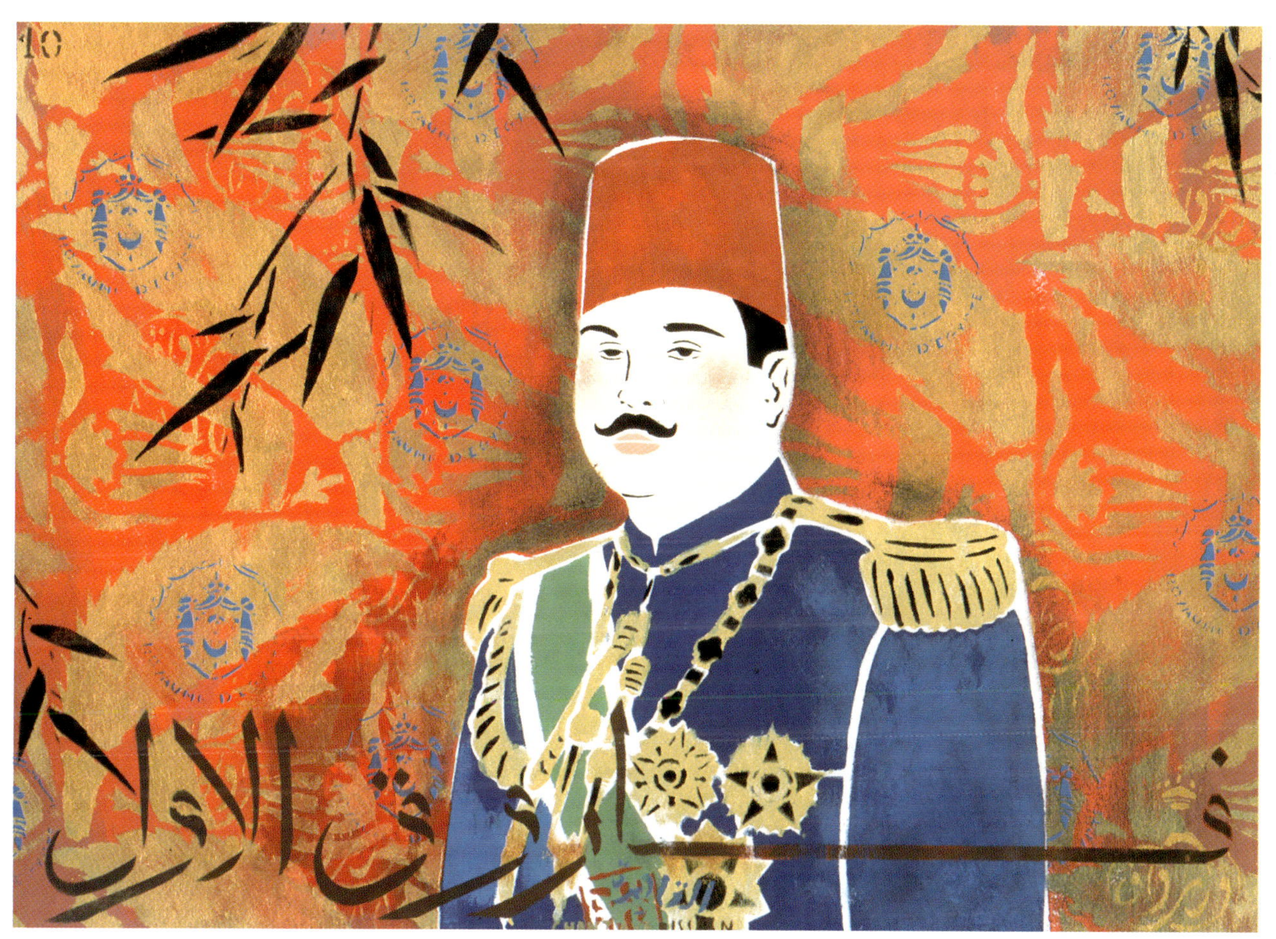

King Farouk the First

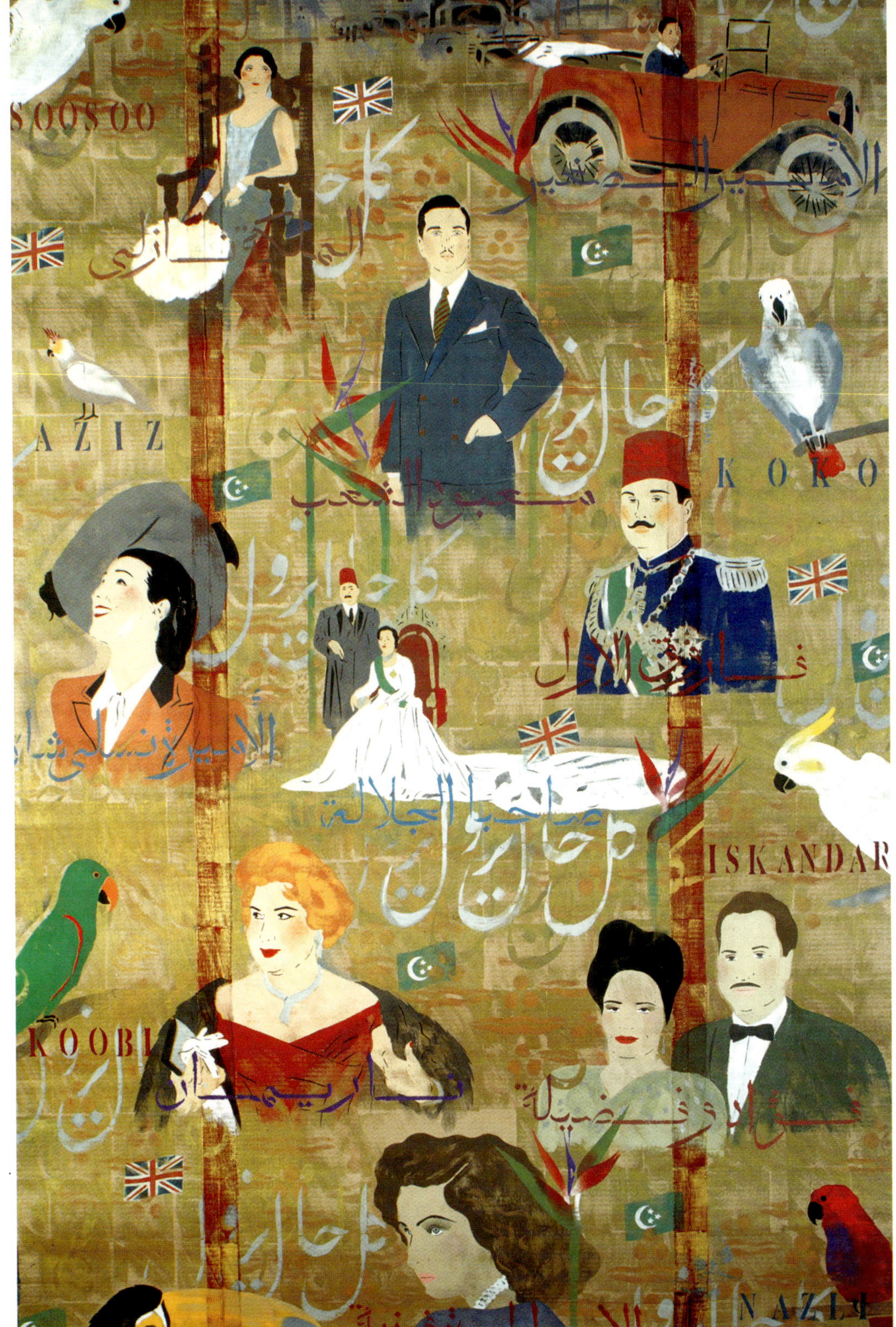
SOOSOO
AZIZ
KORO
ISKANDAR
KOOBI
NAZLI

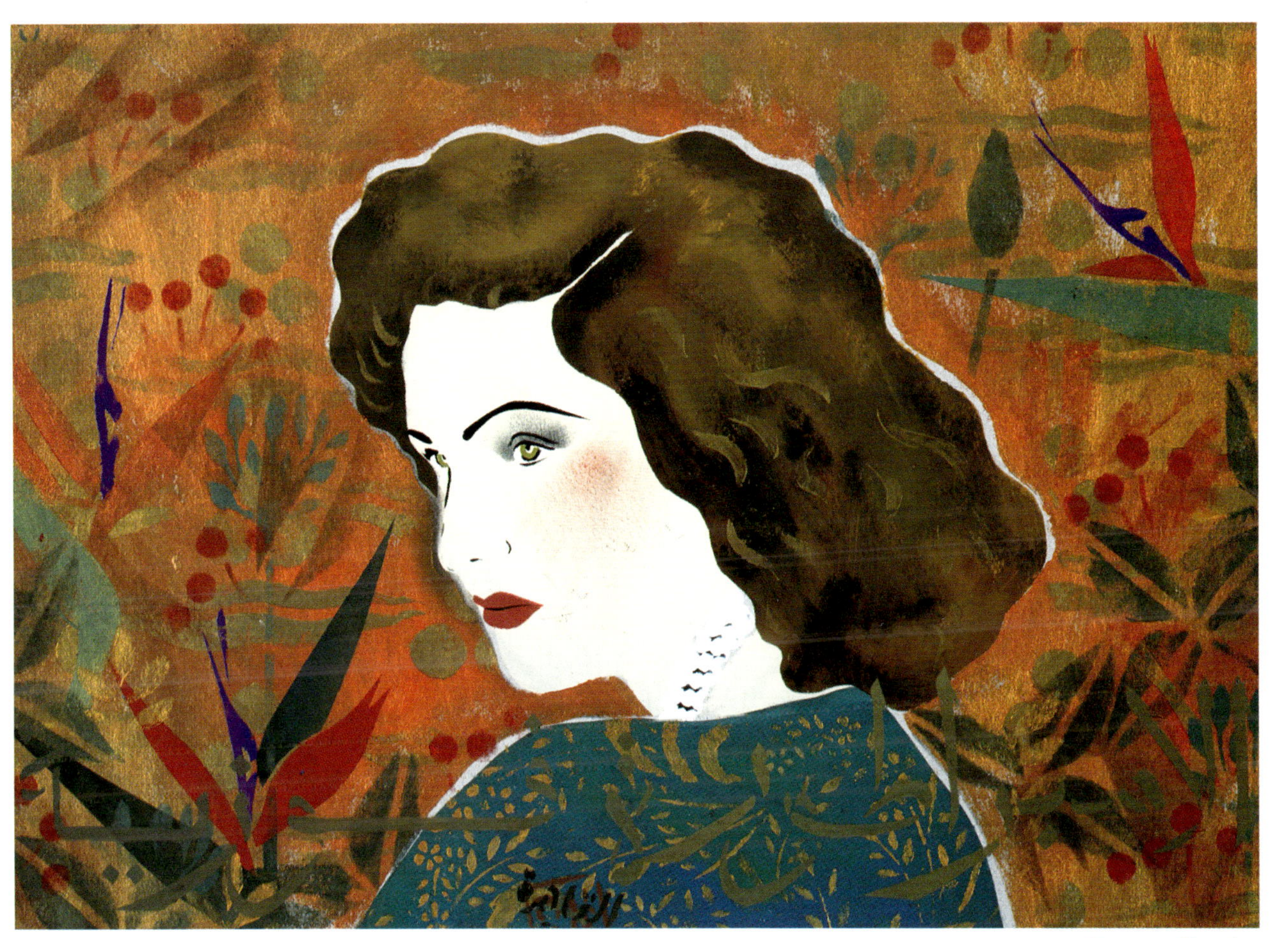

Empress Fawziya

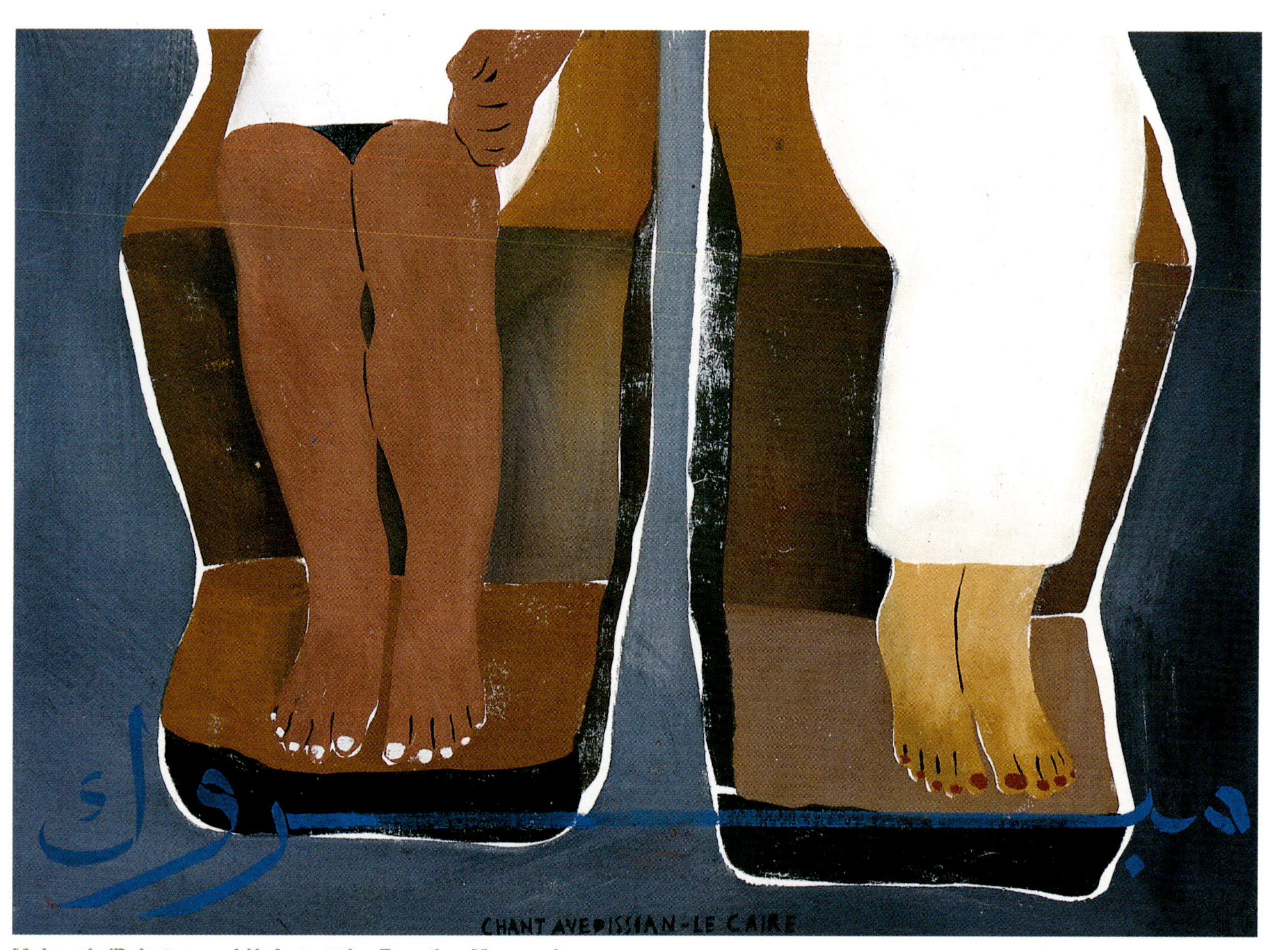

Mabrook (Rahotep and Nofret at the Egyptian Museum)

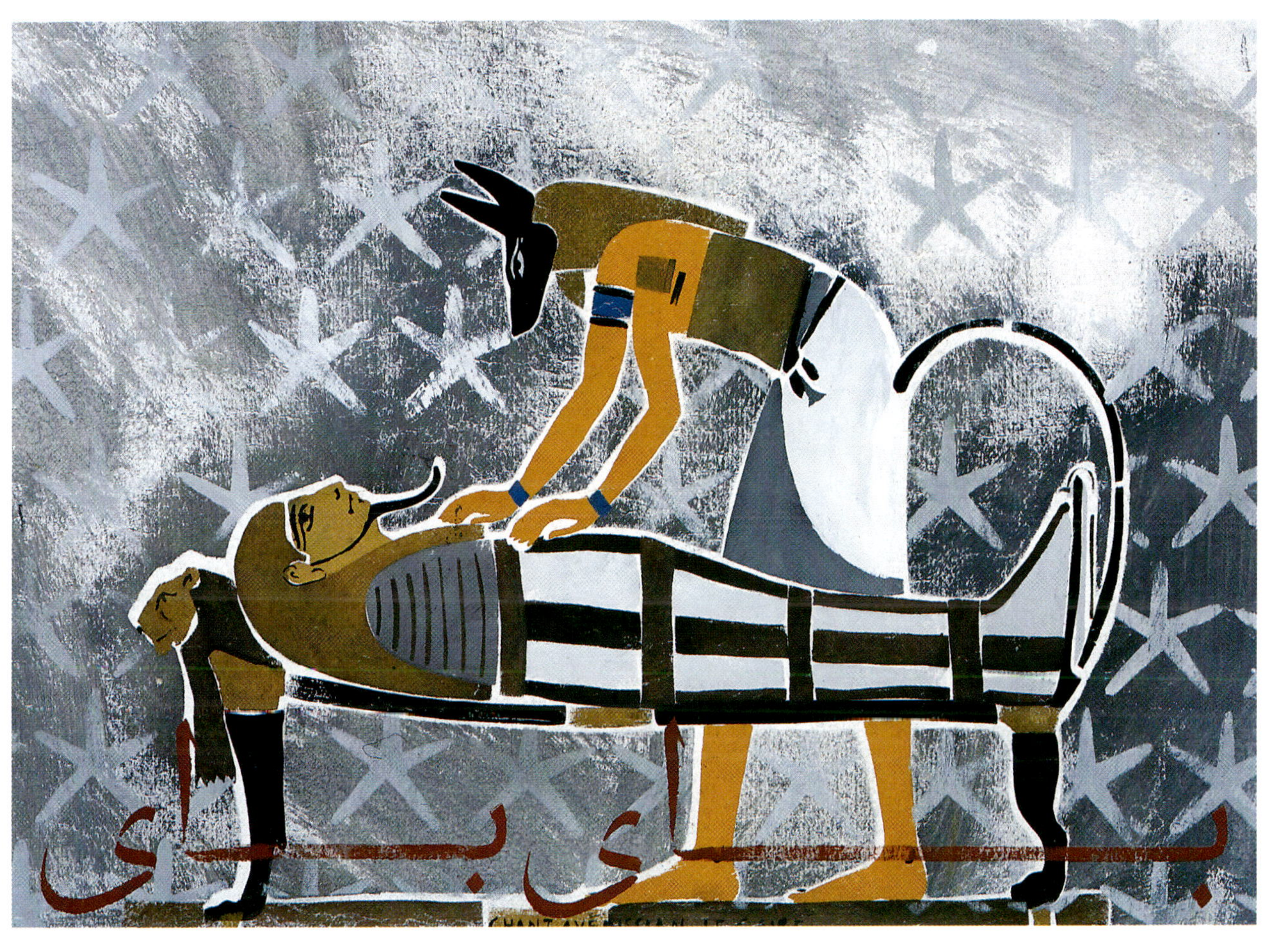

Bye-Bye

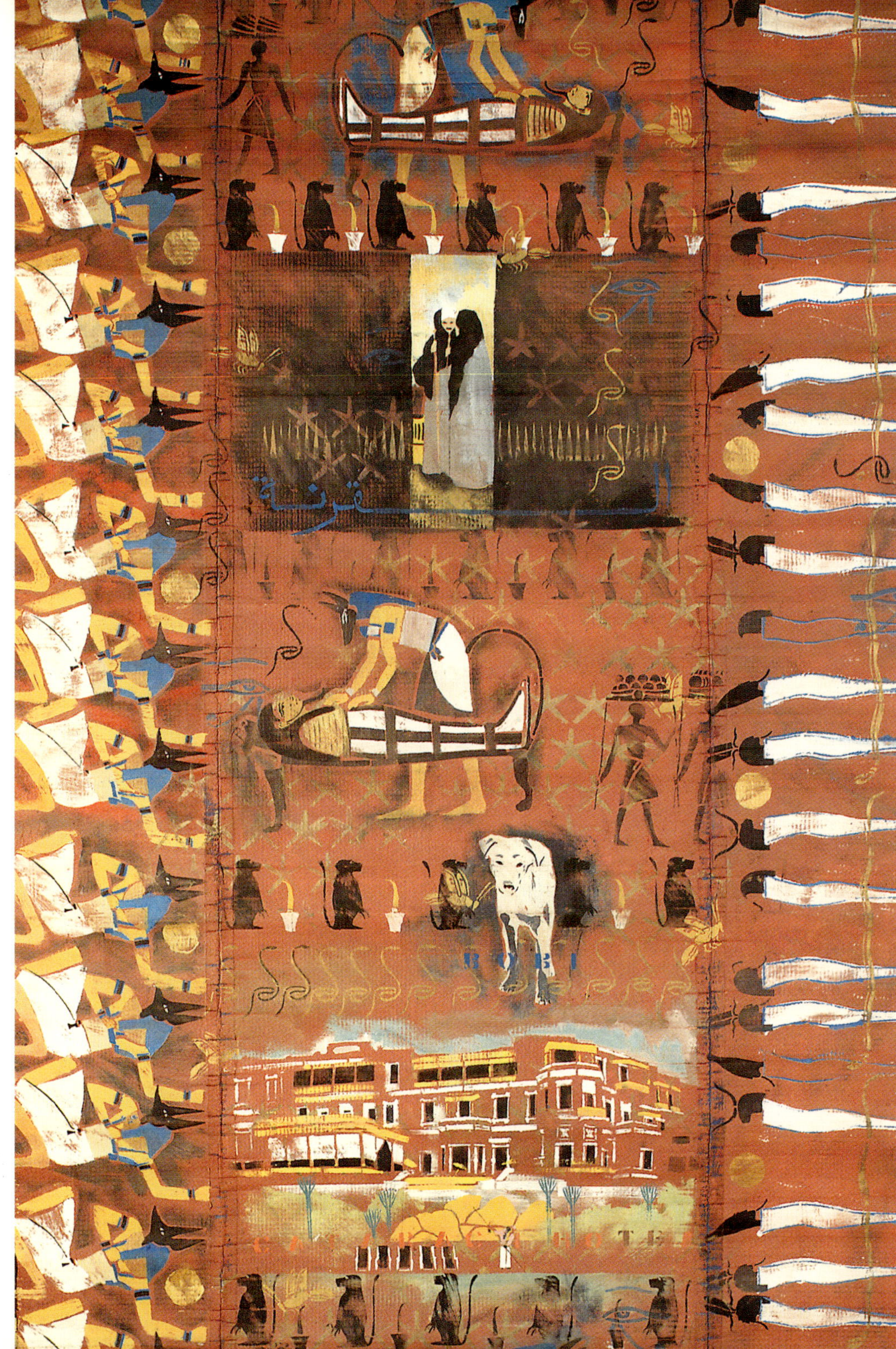

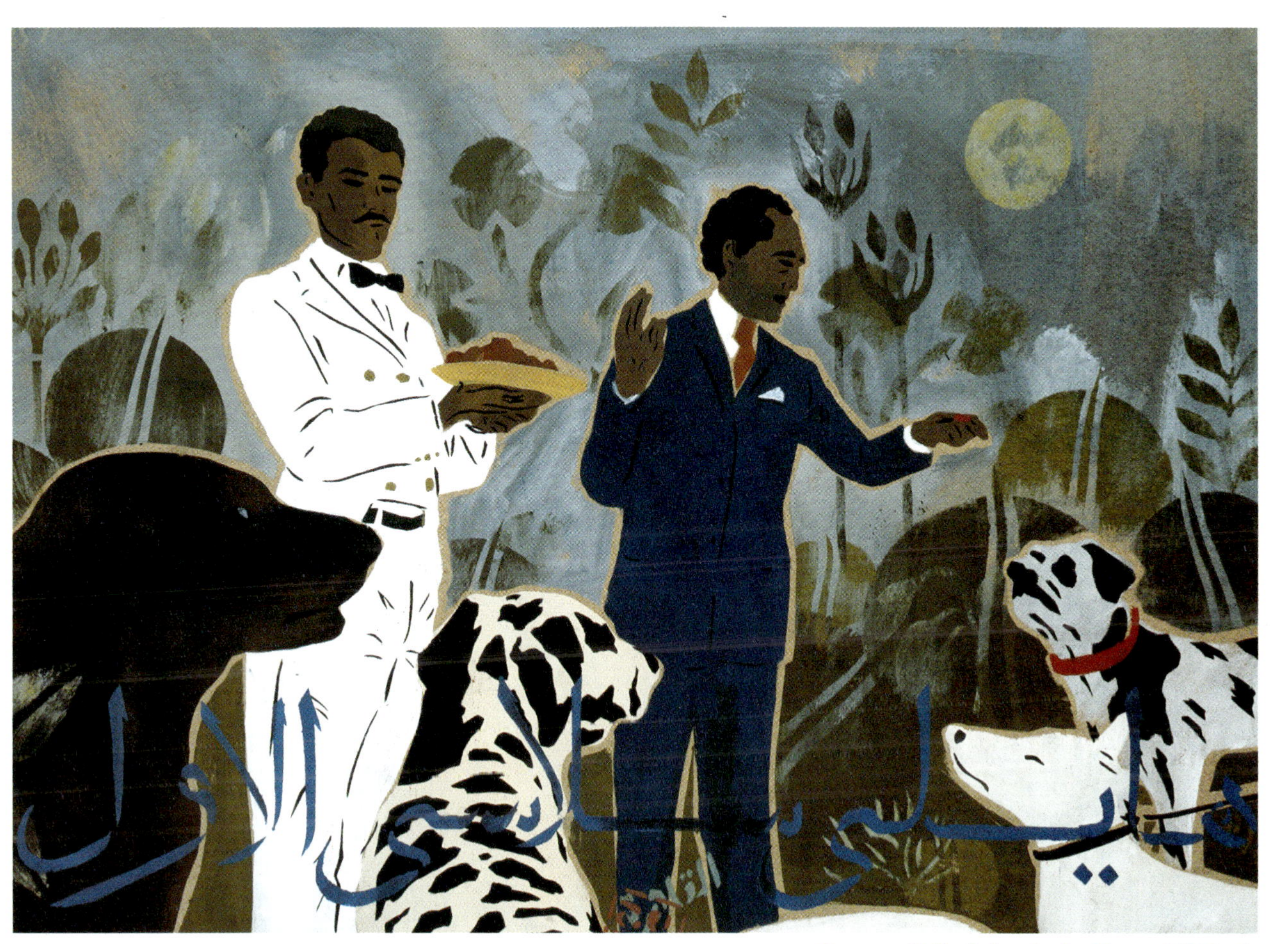

Emperor Haile Selassie the First, of Ethiopia

Nasser

Nasser

Born in 1918 to a postal clerk, Gamal Abdel Nasser came to dominate Egyptian and Arab politics throughout the 1950s and 1960s until his premature death in September 1970. As Egypt's revolutionary leader, Nasser championed Arab nationalism and dreamt of Arab unity, with Cairo at the centre of this vision. An ardent anti-colonialist and anti-imperialist, Nasser's legend grew as a popular Third World leader, especially after the Suez crisis of 1956. He tried to modernise and transform Egyptian society with a programme of agrarian reform, women's emancipation and nationalisation. The Aswan Dam stands as a symbol of these efforts. However, after 1956, his adventures led to various military defeats – most notably his entanglement in Yemen and the Arab-Israeli debacle of June 1967. Furthermore, his dependence on the security services and internal repression established the mould for various other Arab military regimes.

Anwar Gargash, Dubai 2004

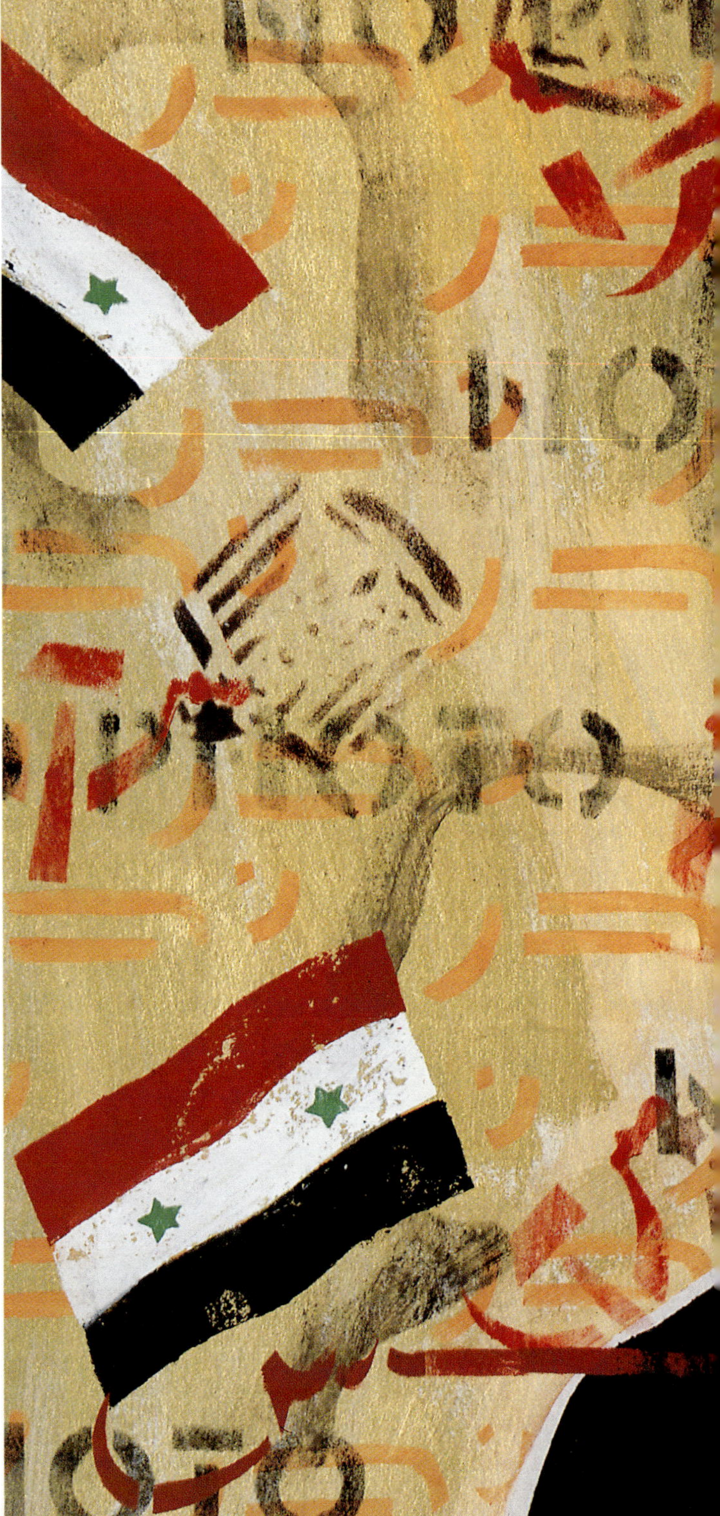

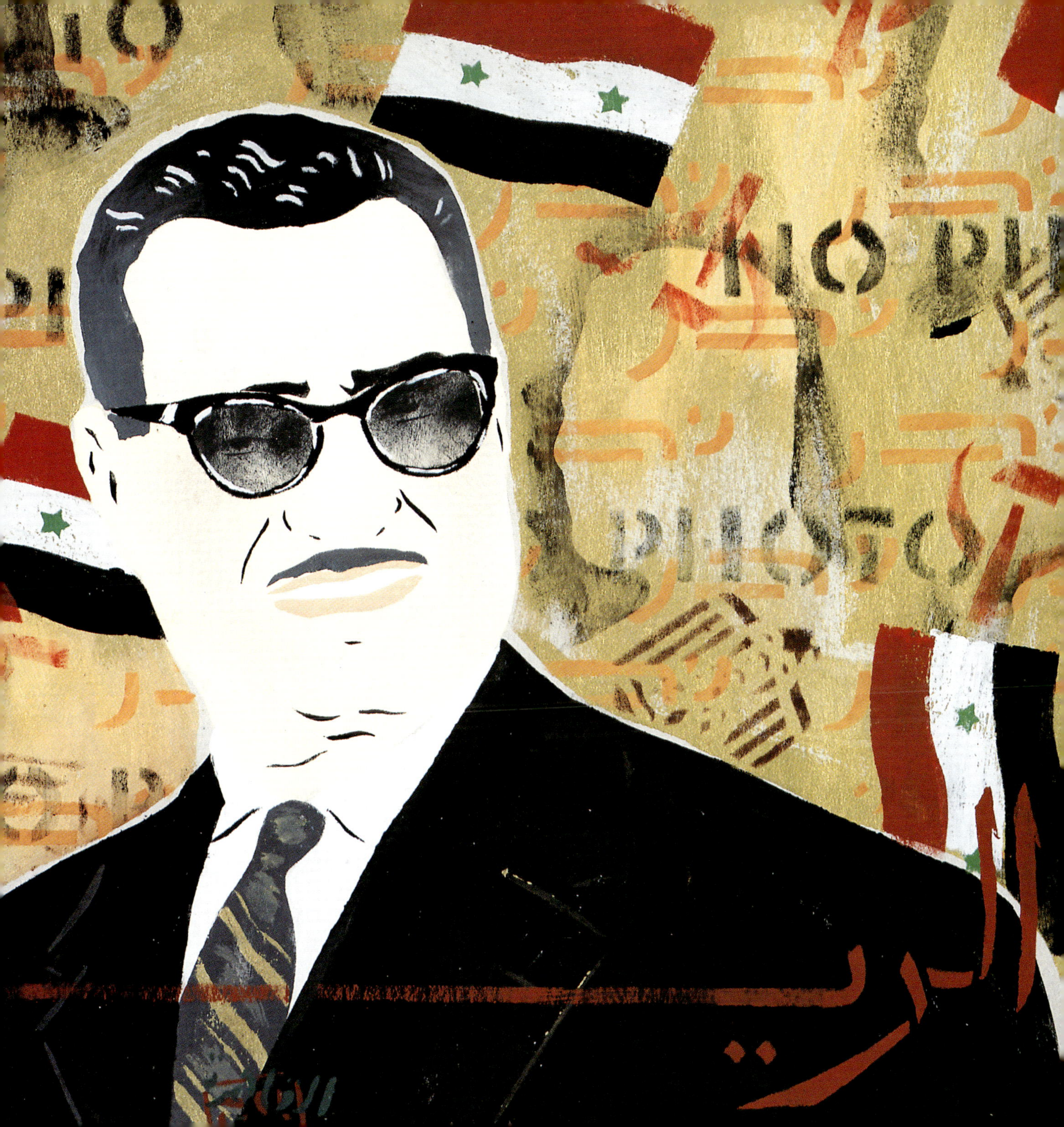

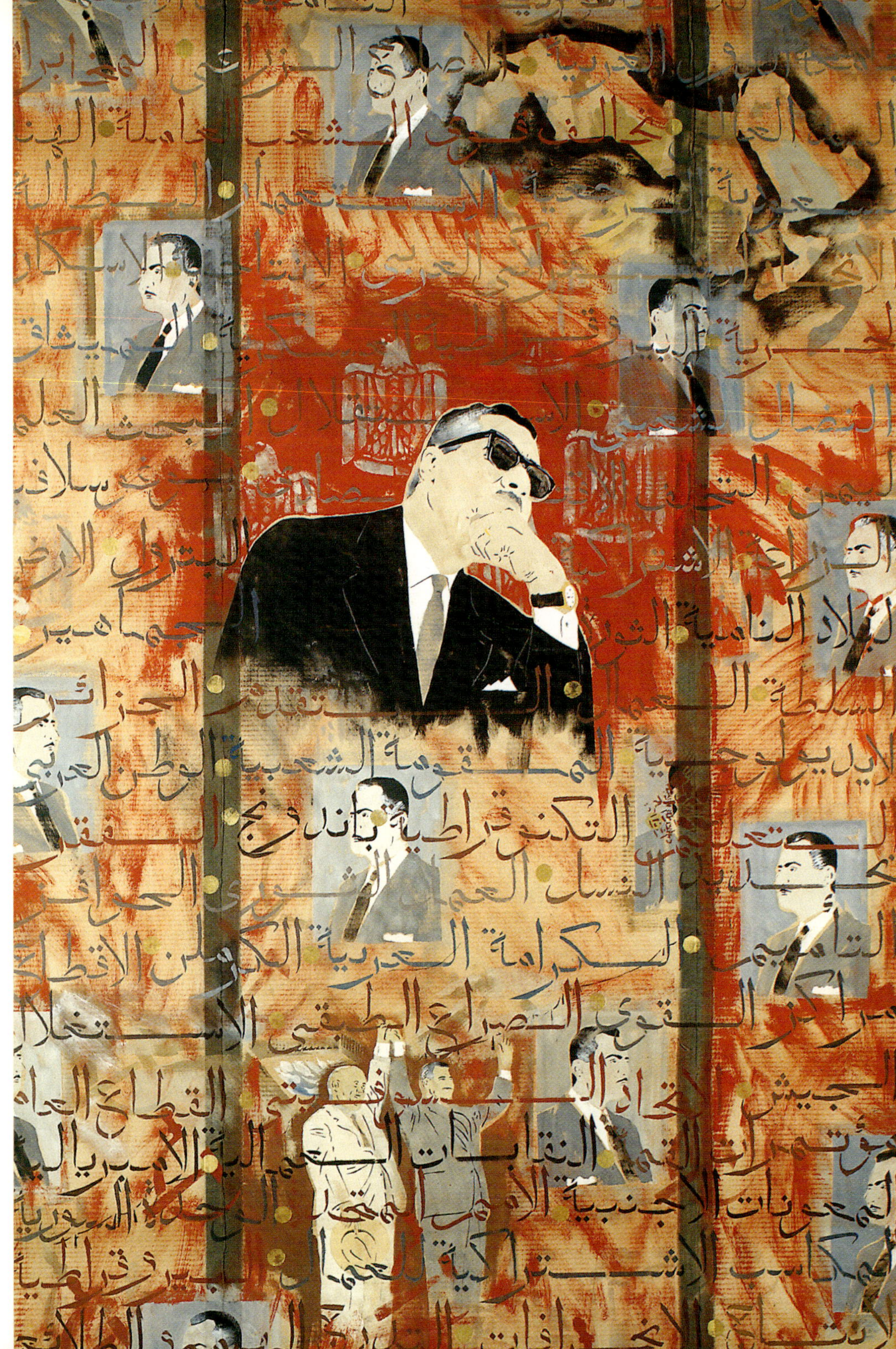

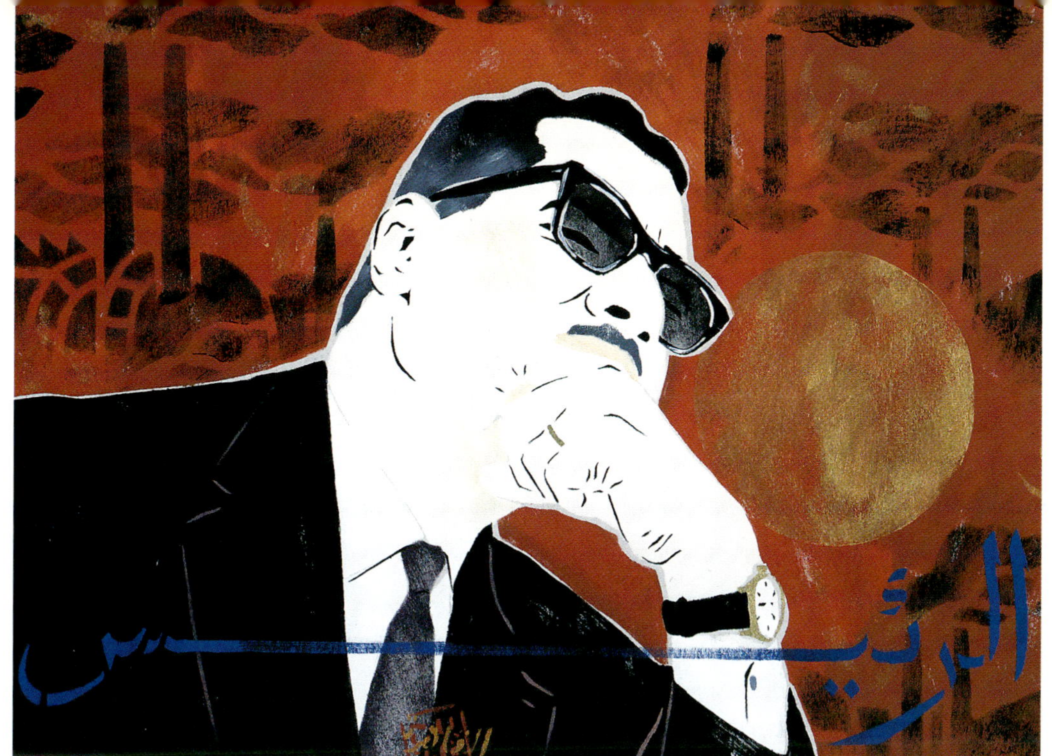

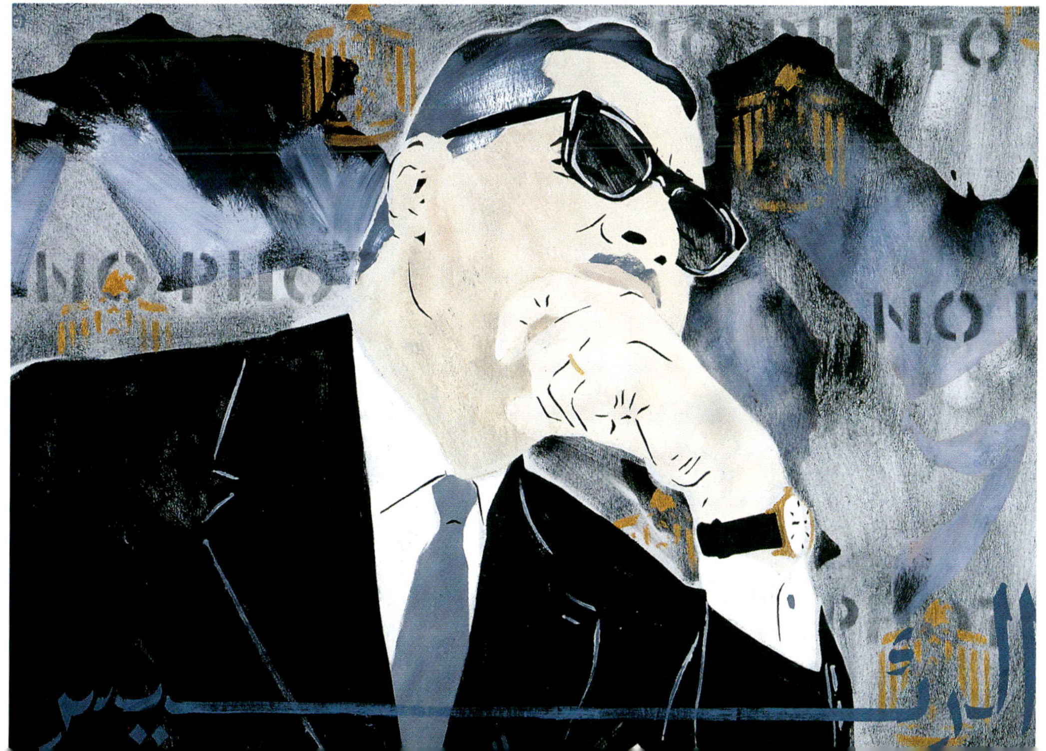

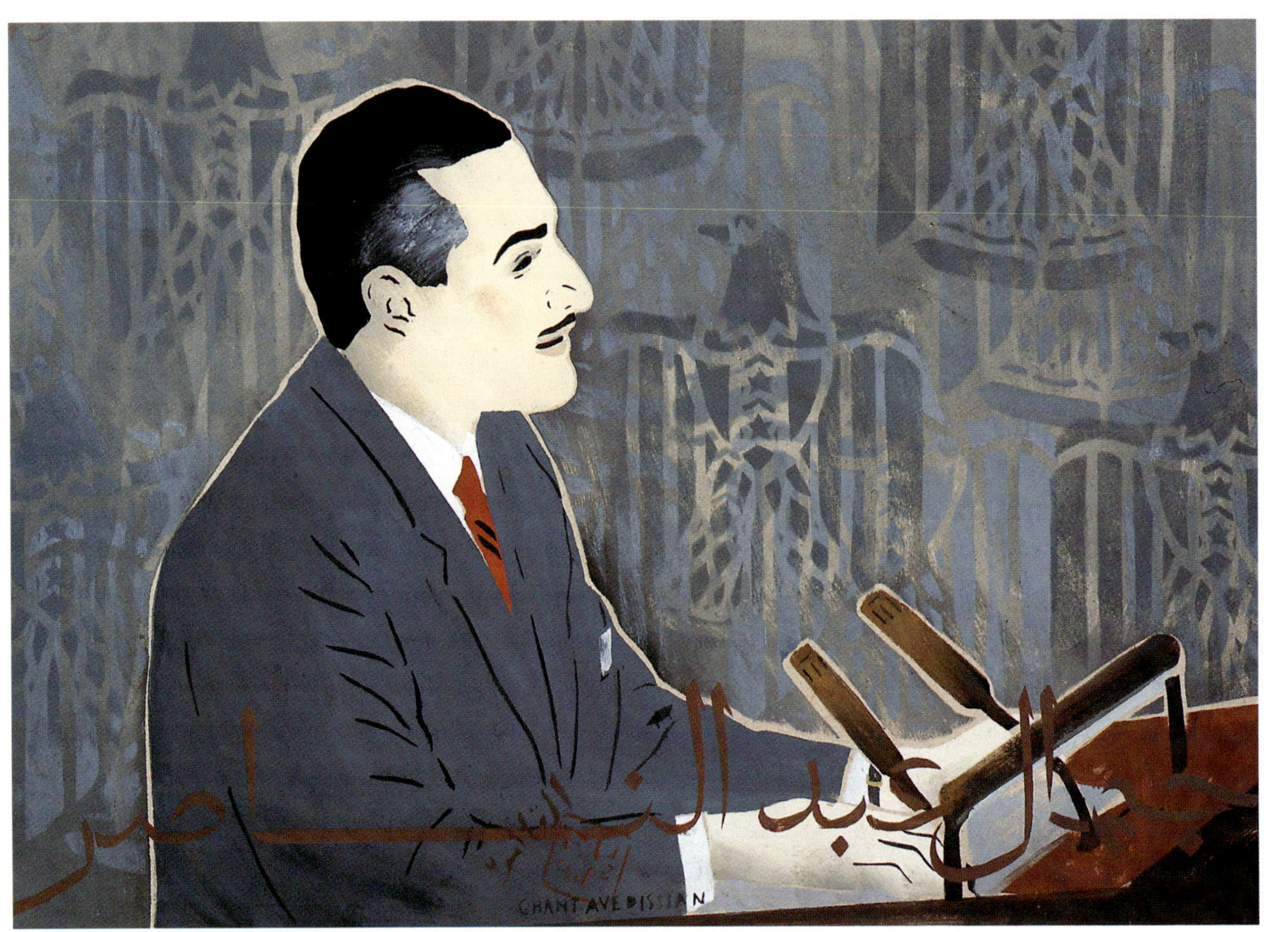

Gamal Abdel Nasser

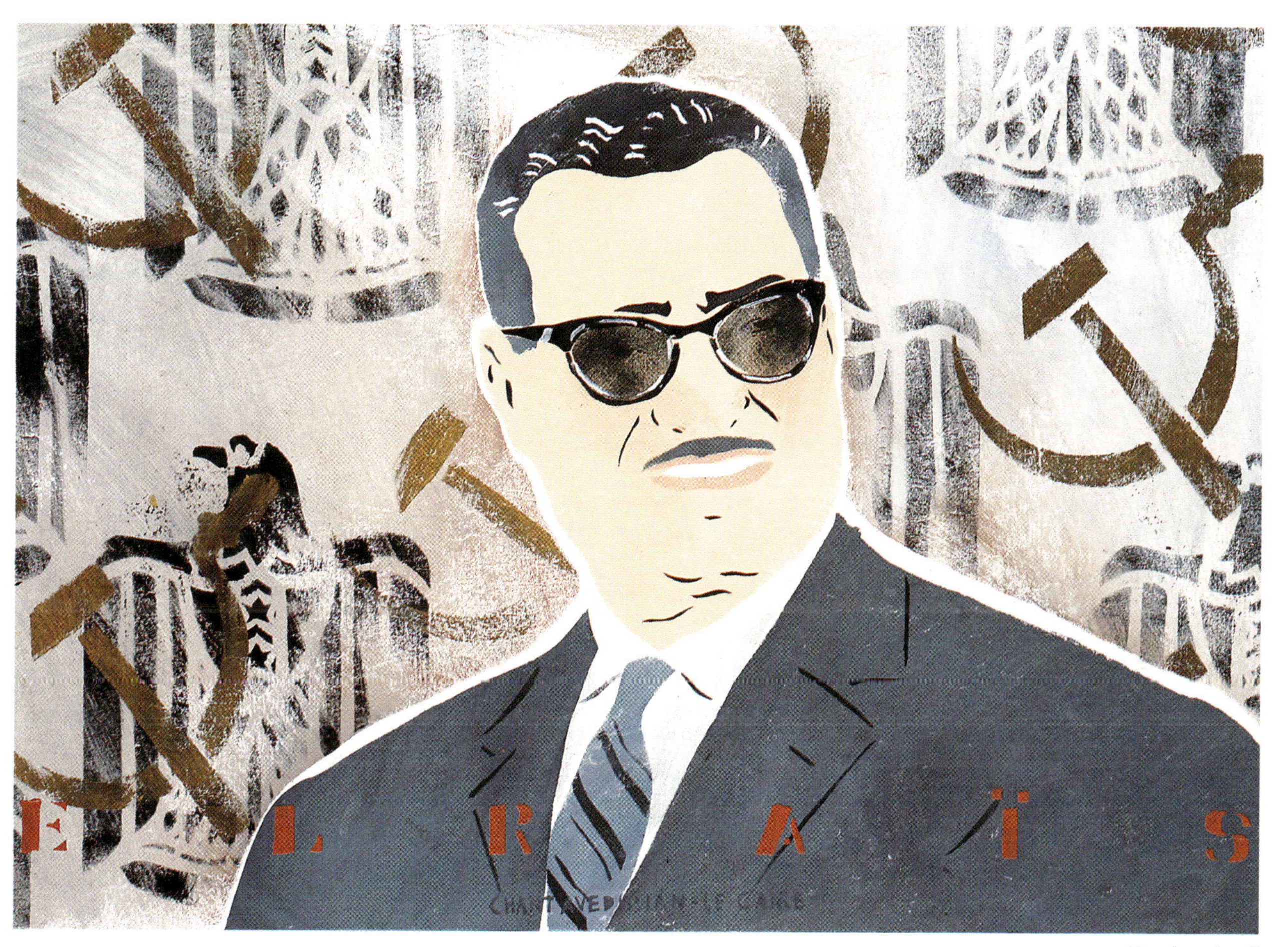

The Leader II

Socialism & Nationalism

Socialism & Nationalism

These words symbolised a colourful and eventful era in the Middle East and the Third World.

Nasser's era was a period of breaking the shackles of colonialism and imperialism. Nationalist fervour and planned socialist economies would lead the way for progress and emancipation. Years of Western domination and backwardness would come to an end. The Arab world, with Egypt at its centre, would control its destiny and seek the political kingdom. Hope was in the air, expectations were rising. The cynicism of later years was millions of miles away. Revolutionary regimes replaced monarchies and the traditional ruling classes. Socialism and nationalism mobilised millions of the previously disenfranchised, but the emphasis was on the collective, not the individual.

This was not a democratic era, but an era of conformity and little tolerance.

Anwar Gargash, Dubai 2004

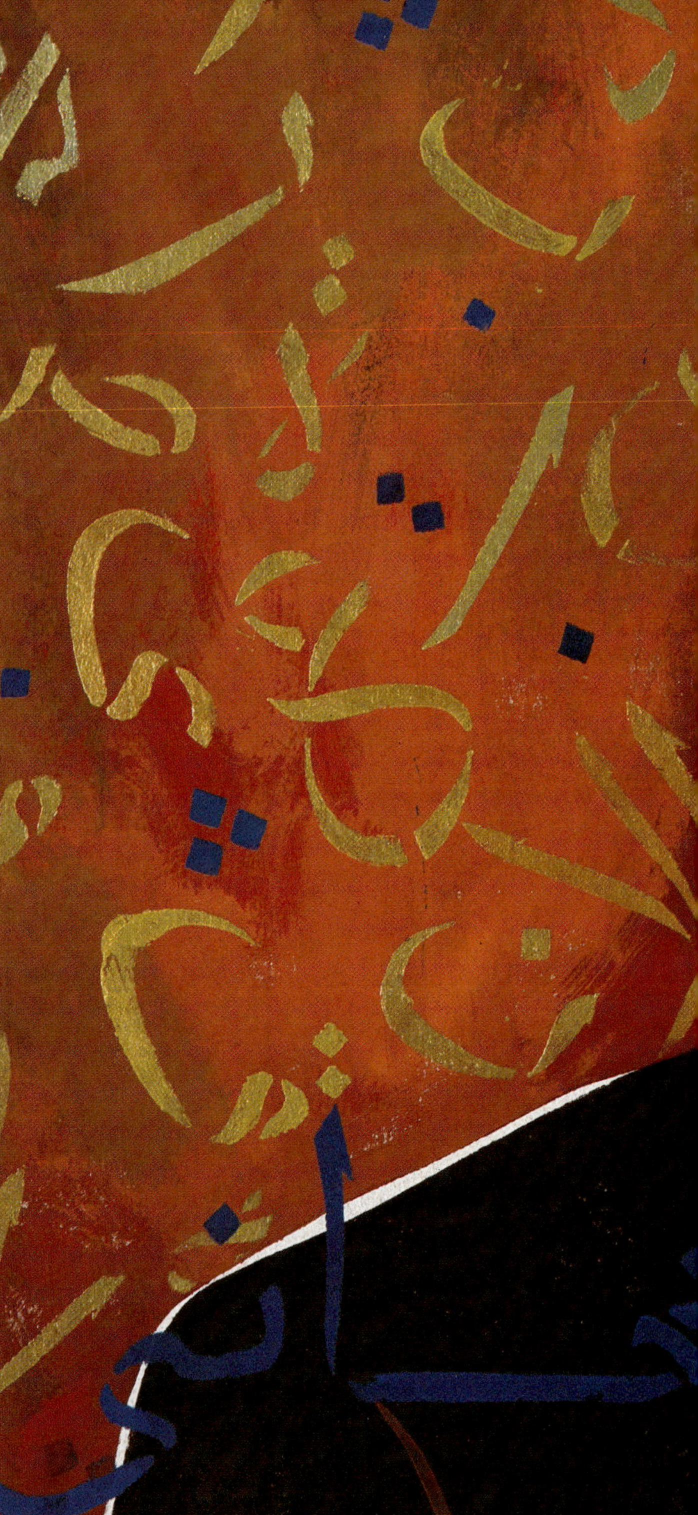

Jamal al-Din al-Afghani

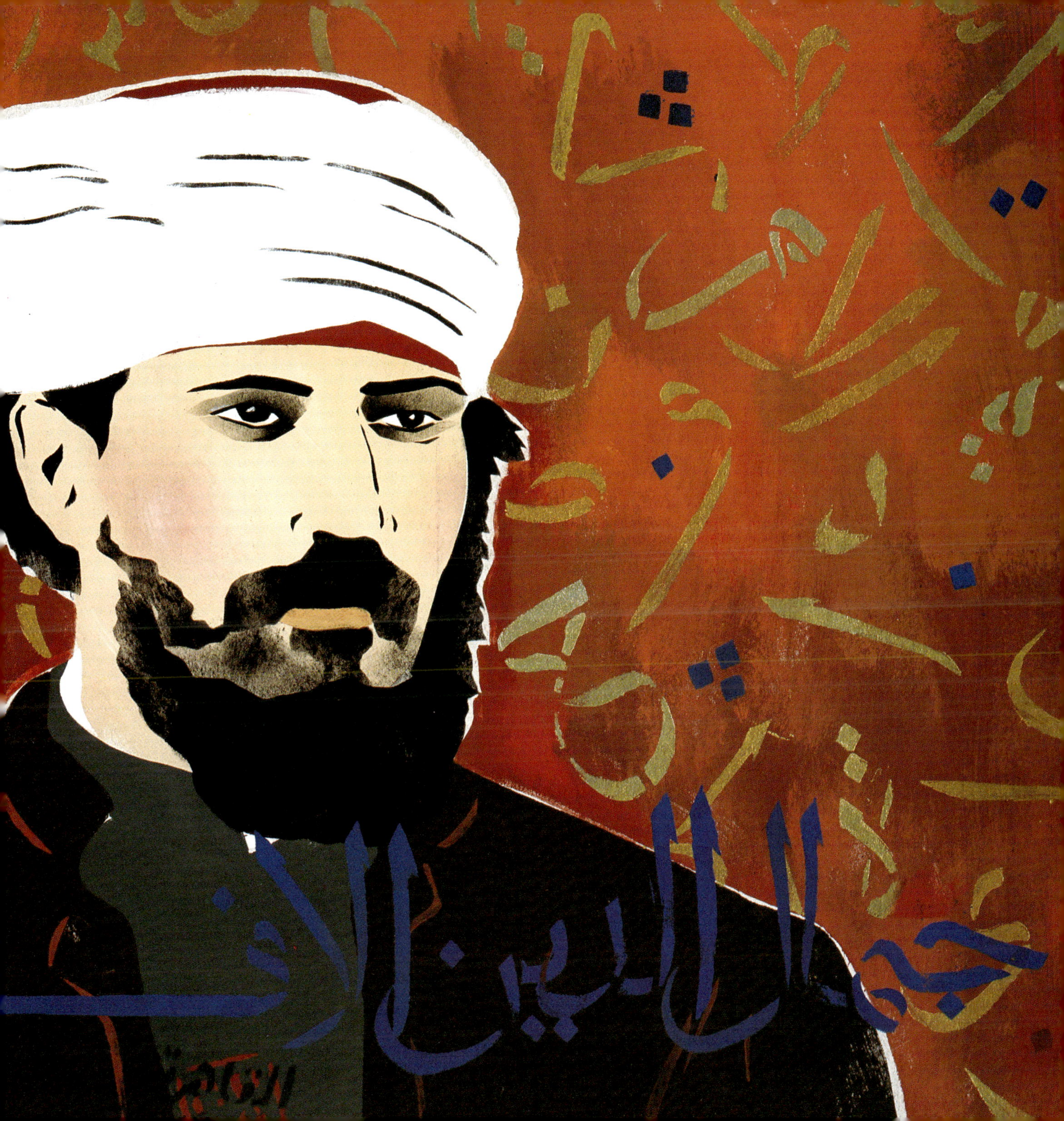

جبران خليل جبران

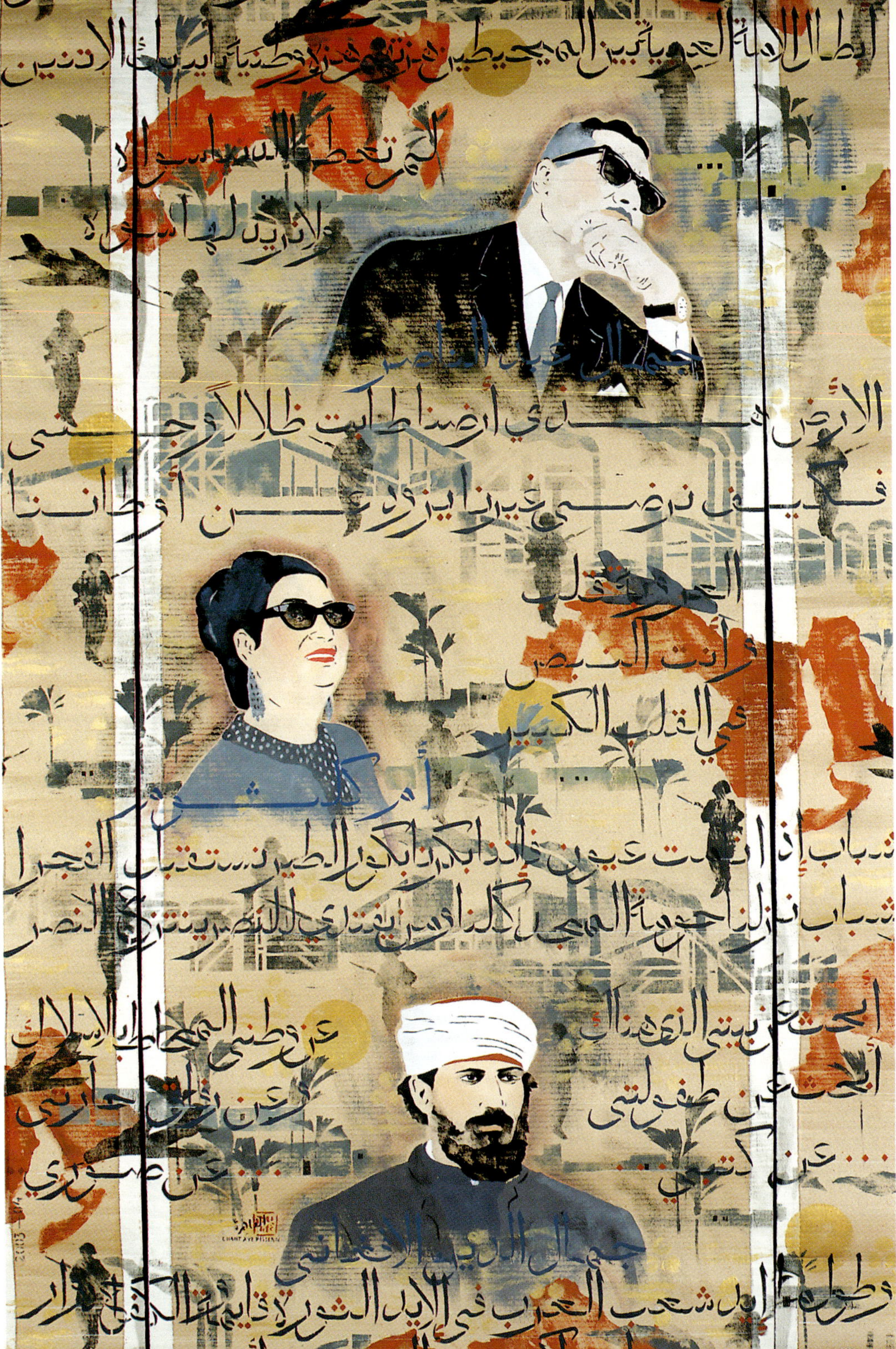

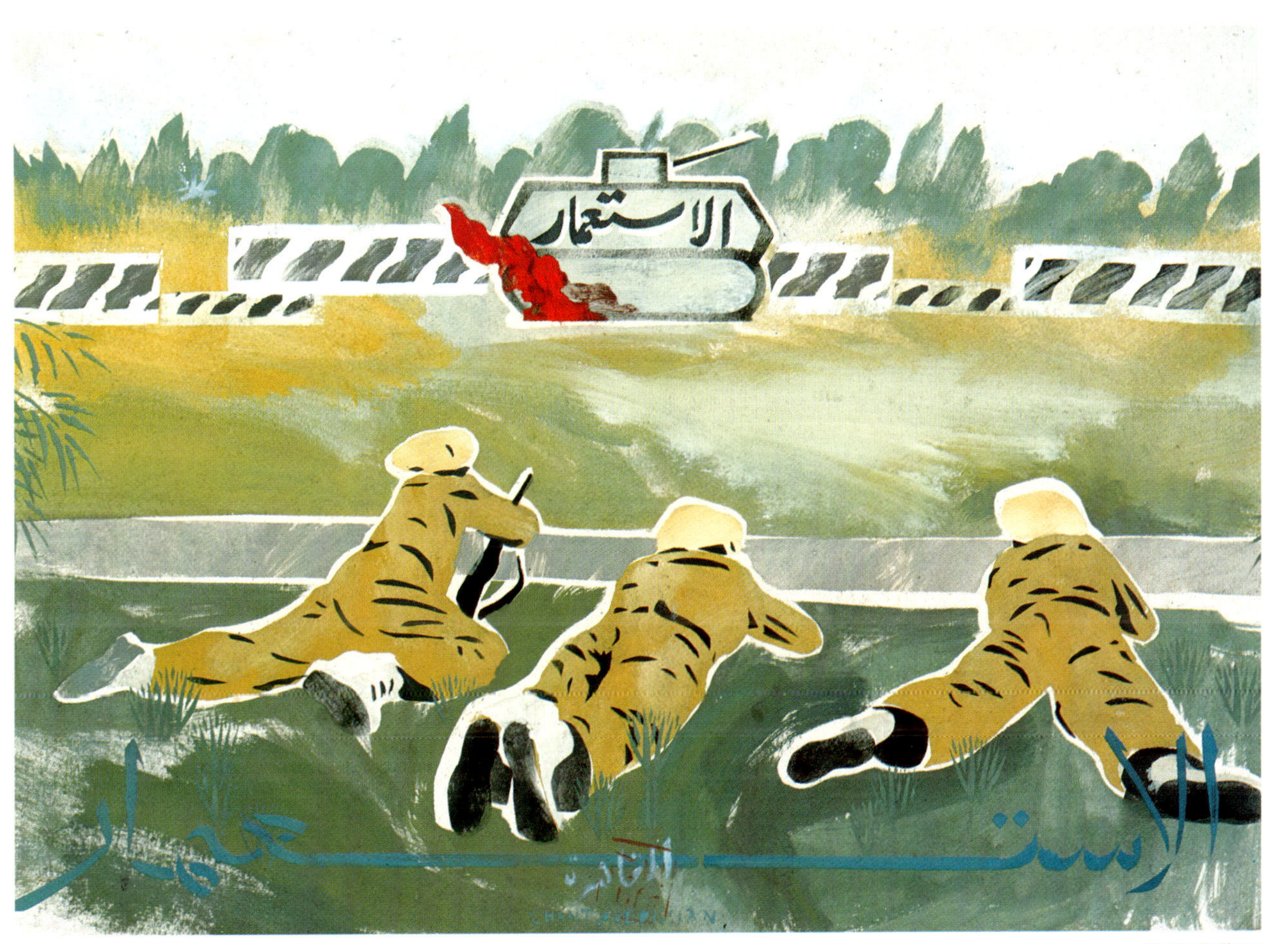

Colonialism

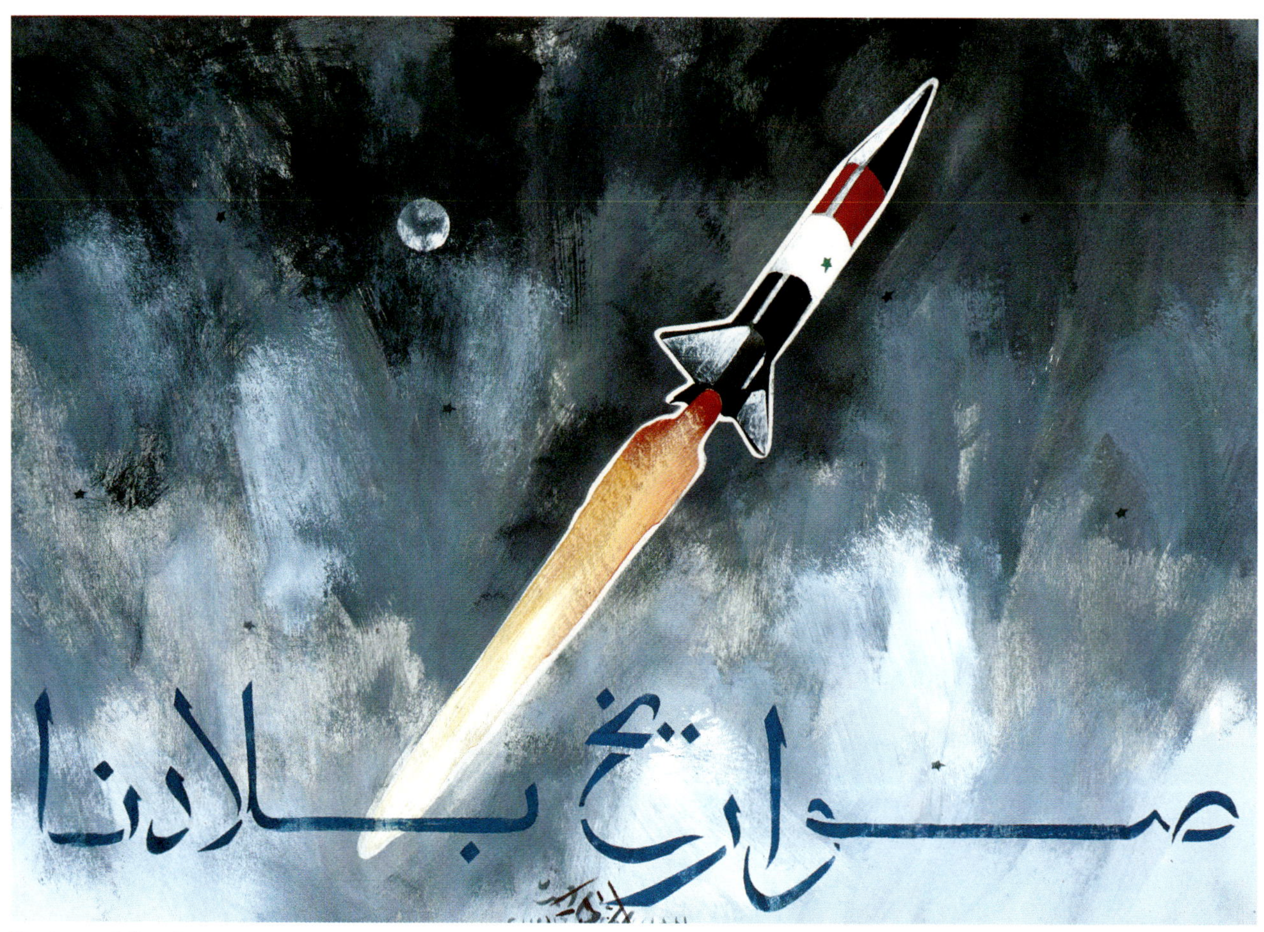

Rockets of Our Country

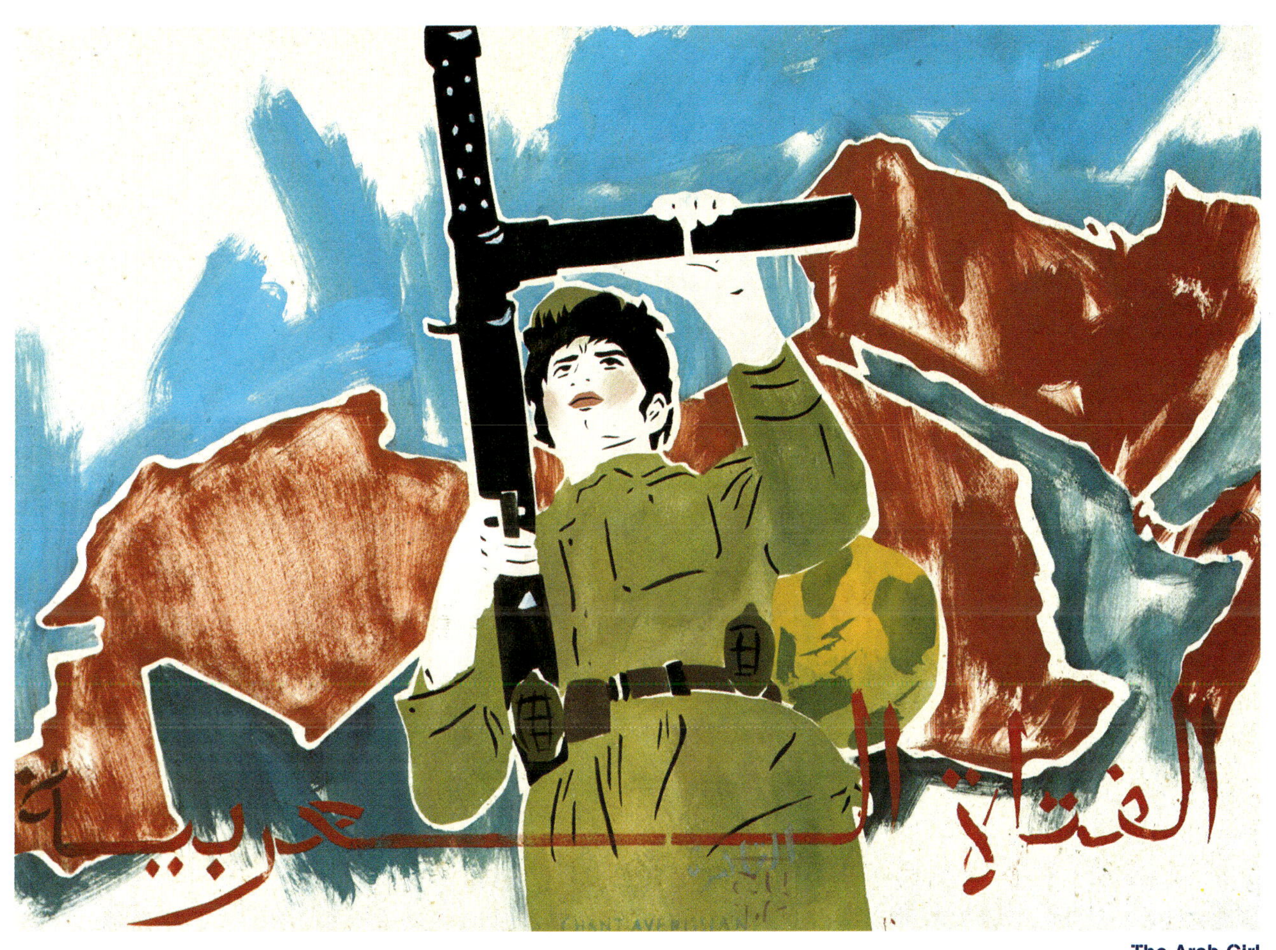

The Arab Girl

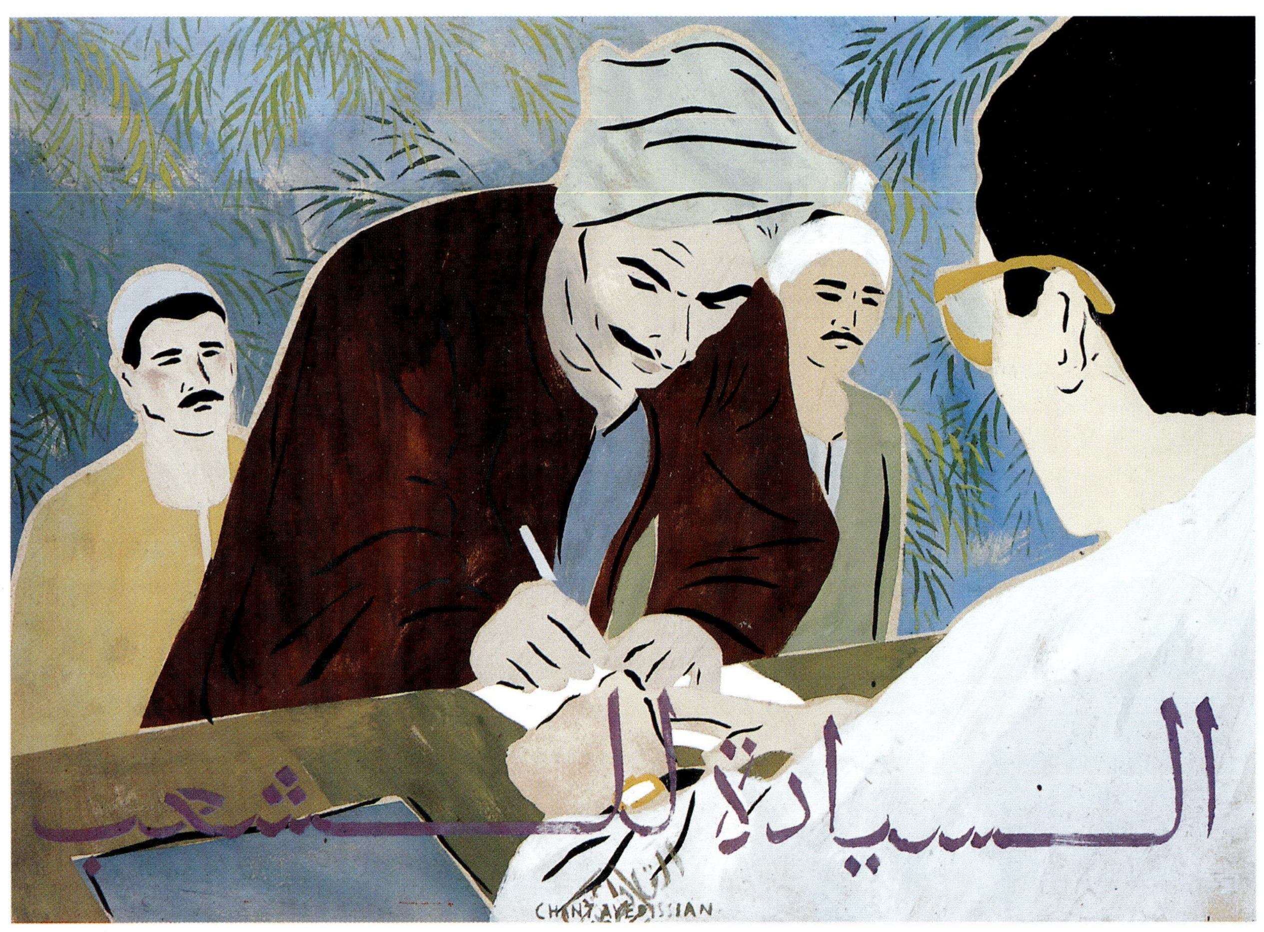

Power to the People

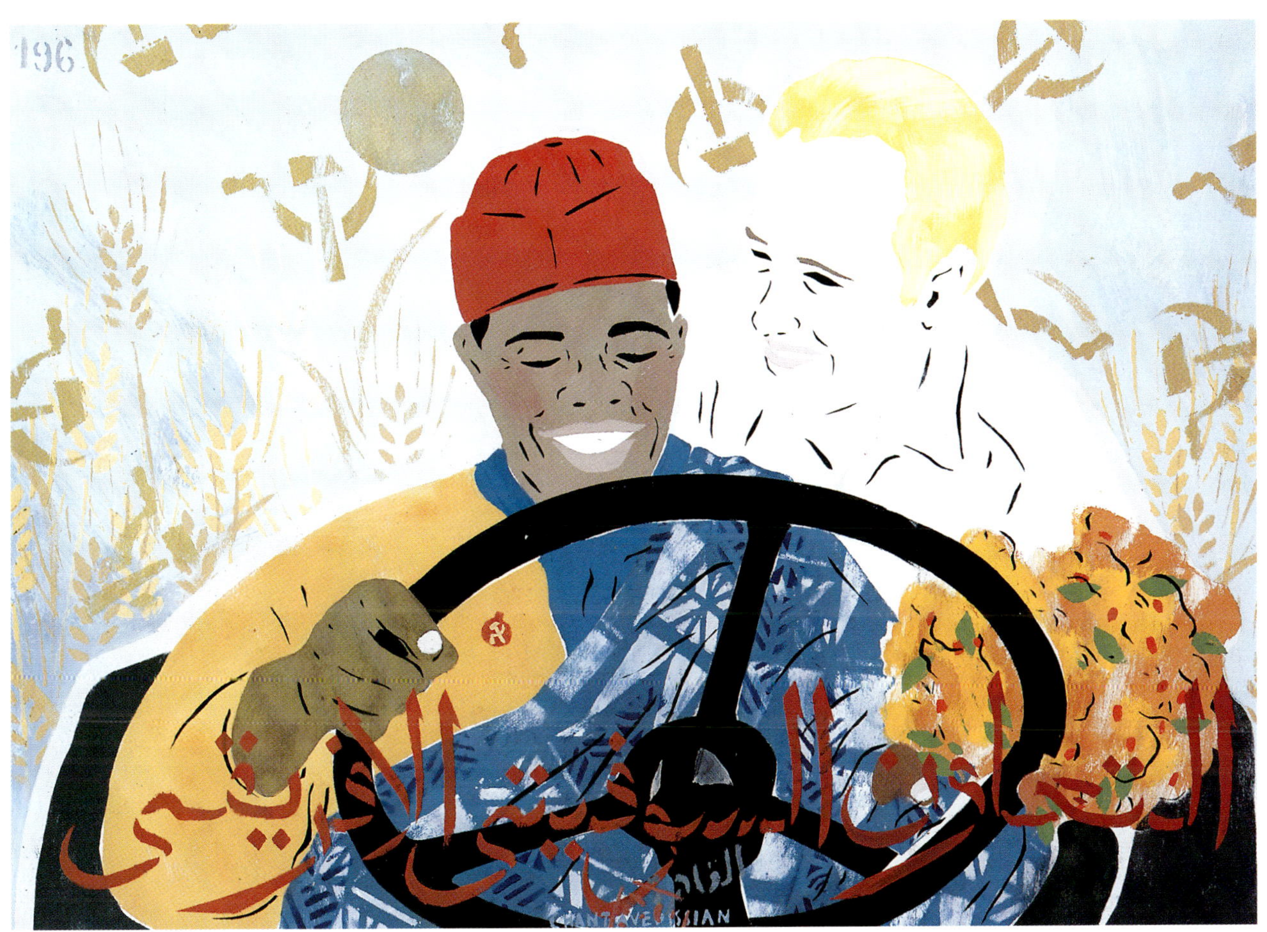

Soviet-African Cooperation

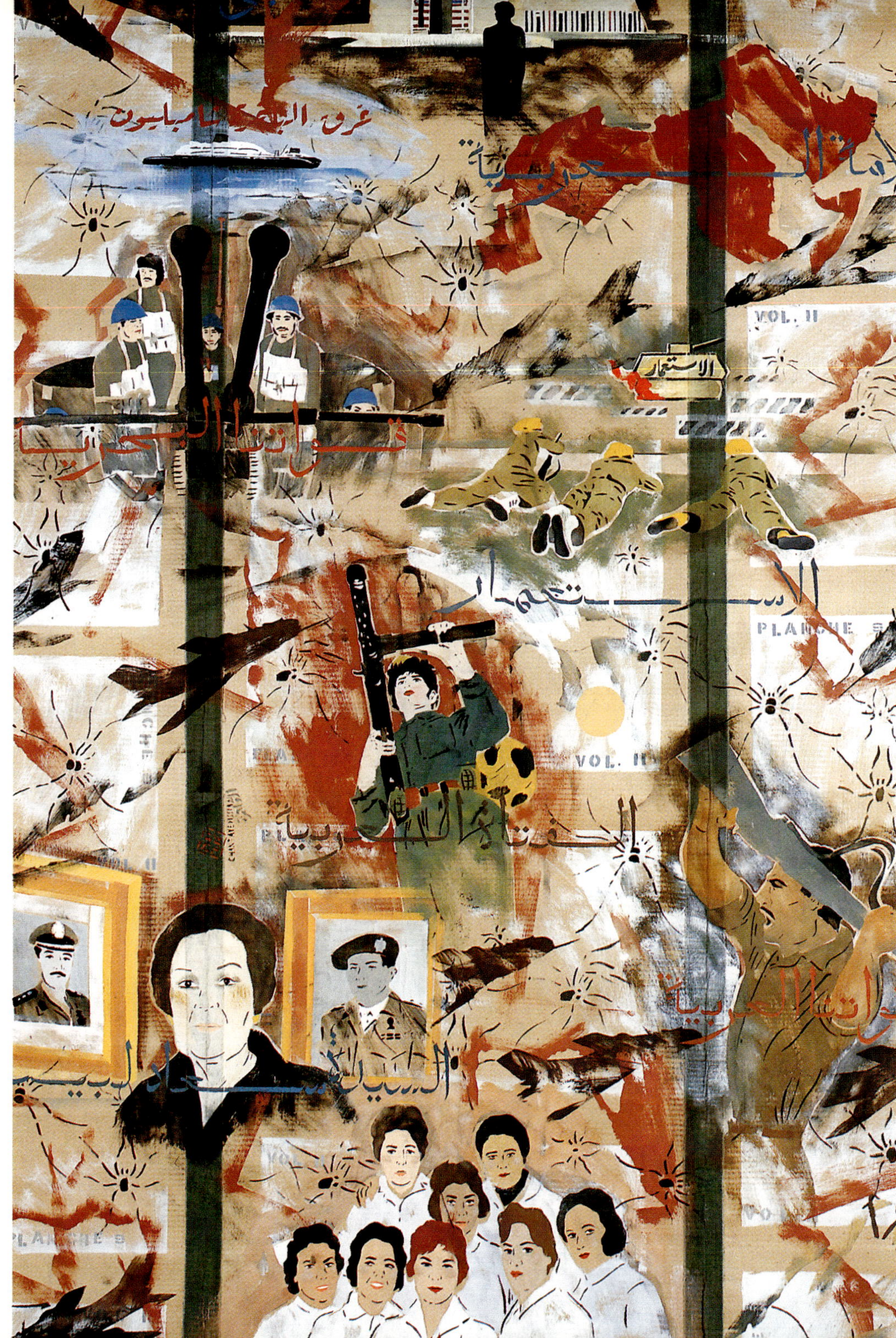

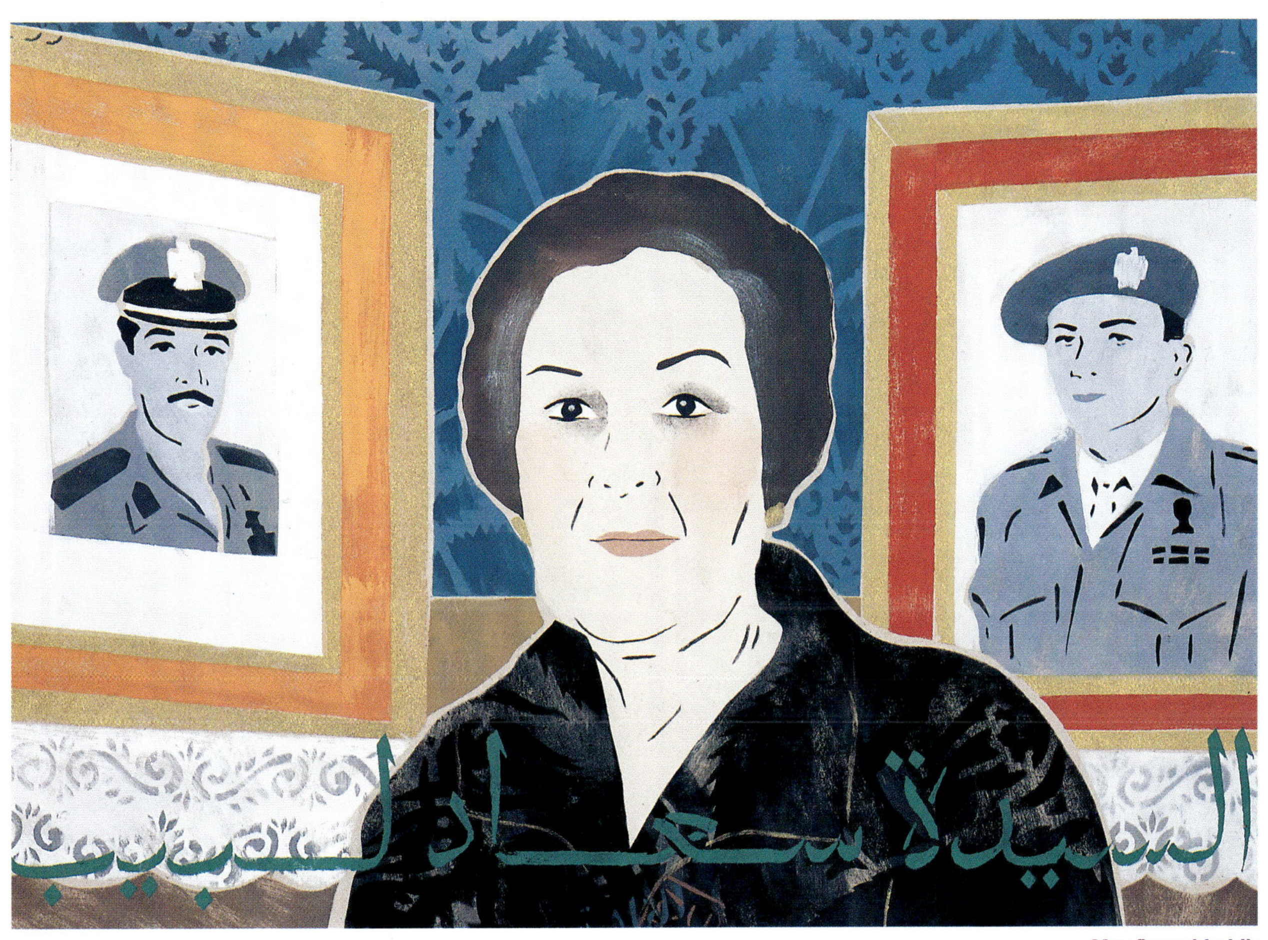

Mrs Souad Labib

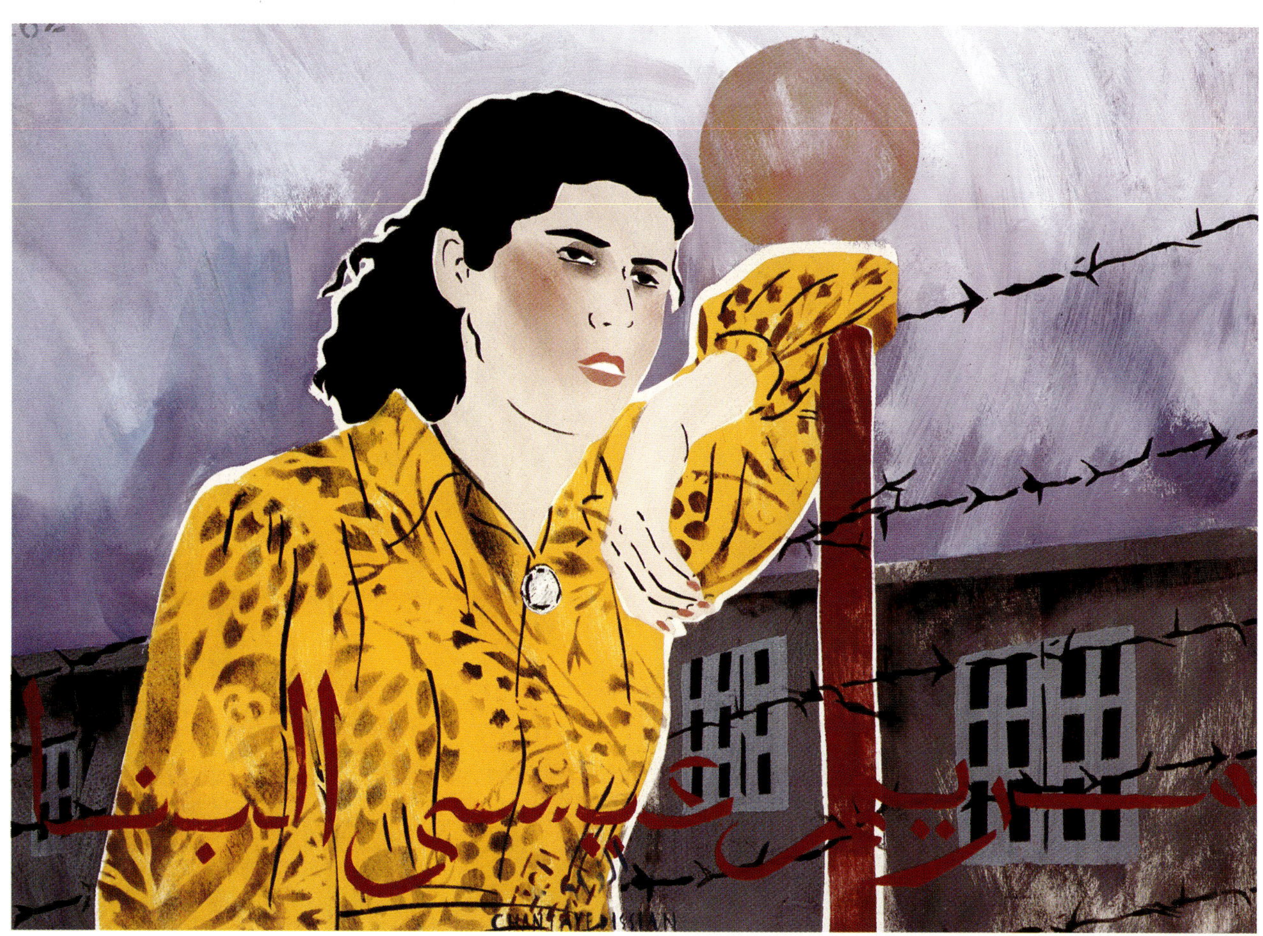

Mariam Issa al-Banna

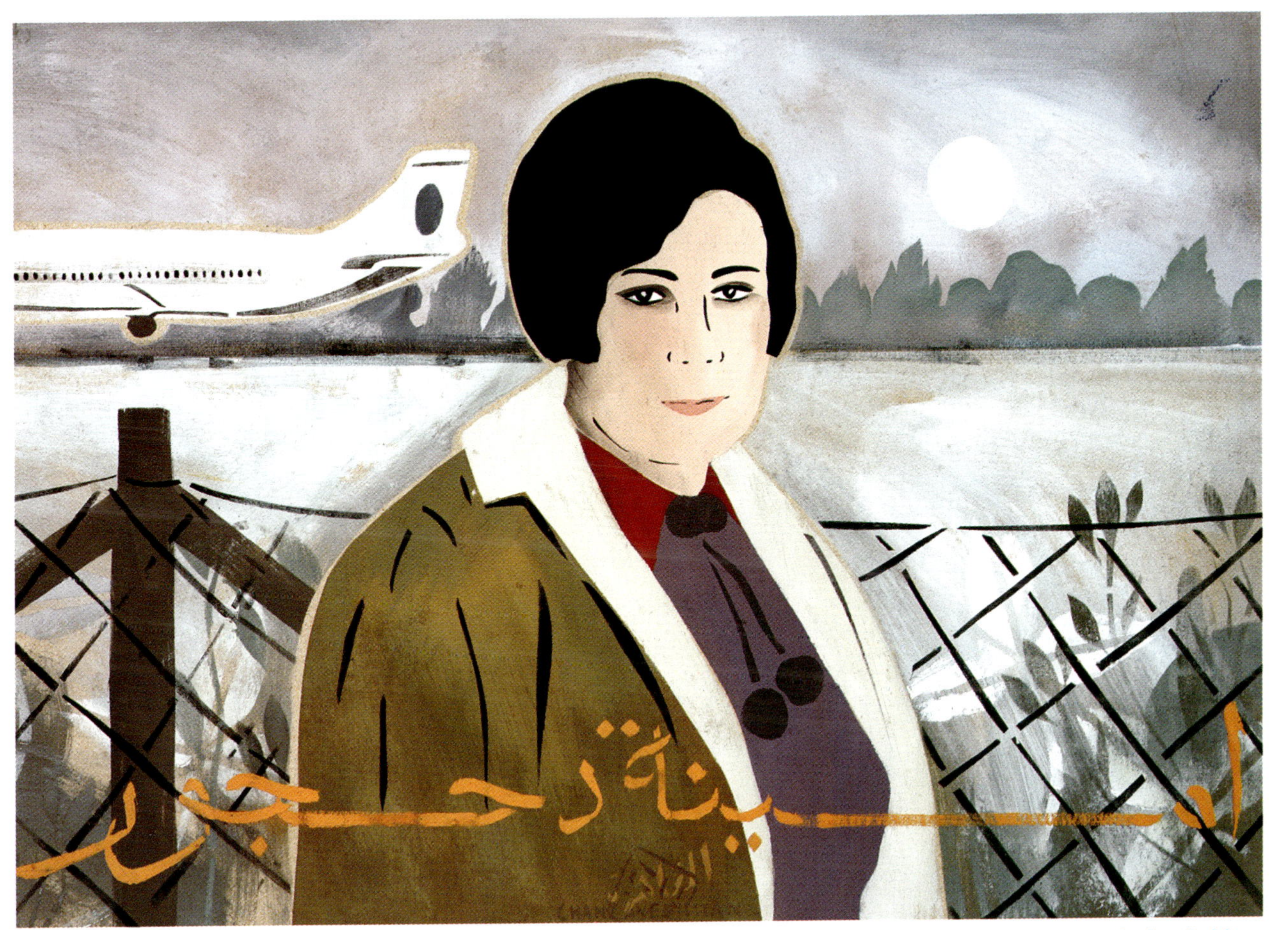

Amina Dahjour

Society

Society

In seeking to forge a modern, indigenous, post-colonial identity, Nasser's regime became dependent on Soviet military and economic support and adopted similar propaganda, mobilising the media to keep up the momentum of socialist values.

Following decades of activism, mostly by upper- and middle-class feminist groups such as the Bint al-Nil Association founded by Doria Shafik, Egyptian women were given the right to vote in 1956. This symbolised their new participation in all aspects of life, no longer just as guardians of the family. Nationalist songs and films with socio-political overtones reflected these changes and the new Arab woman, neither a colonised North African nor an 'orientalised' subject, was widely celebrated in the press.

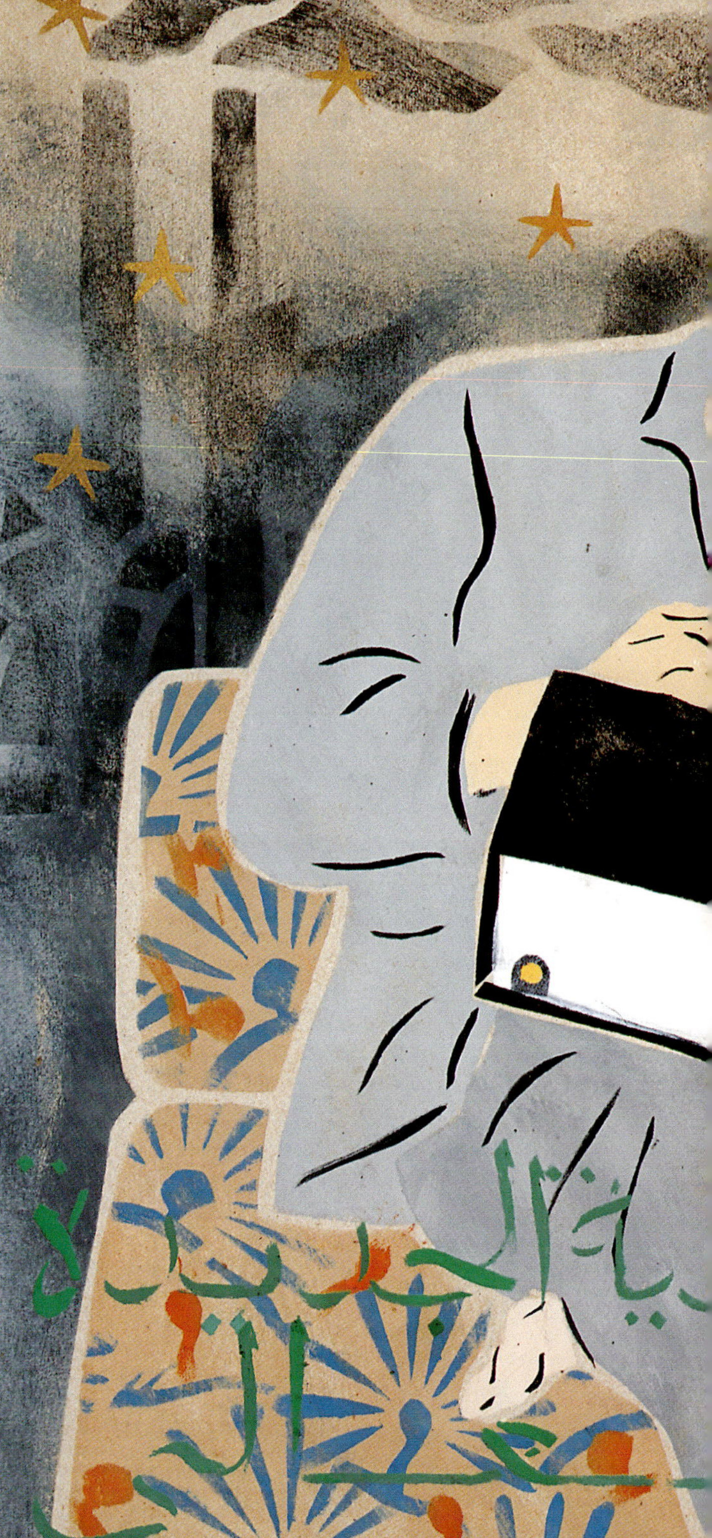

The New Social Life at the High Dam, Aswan

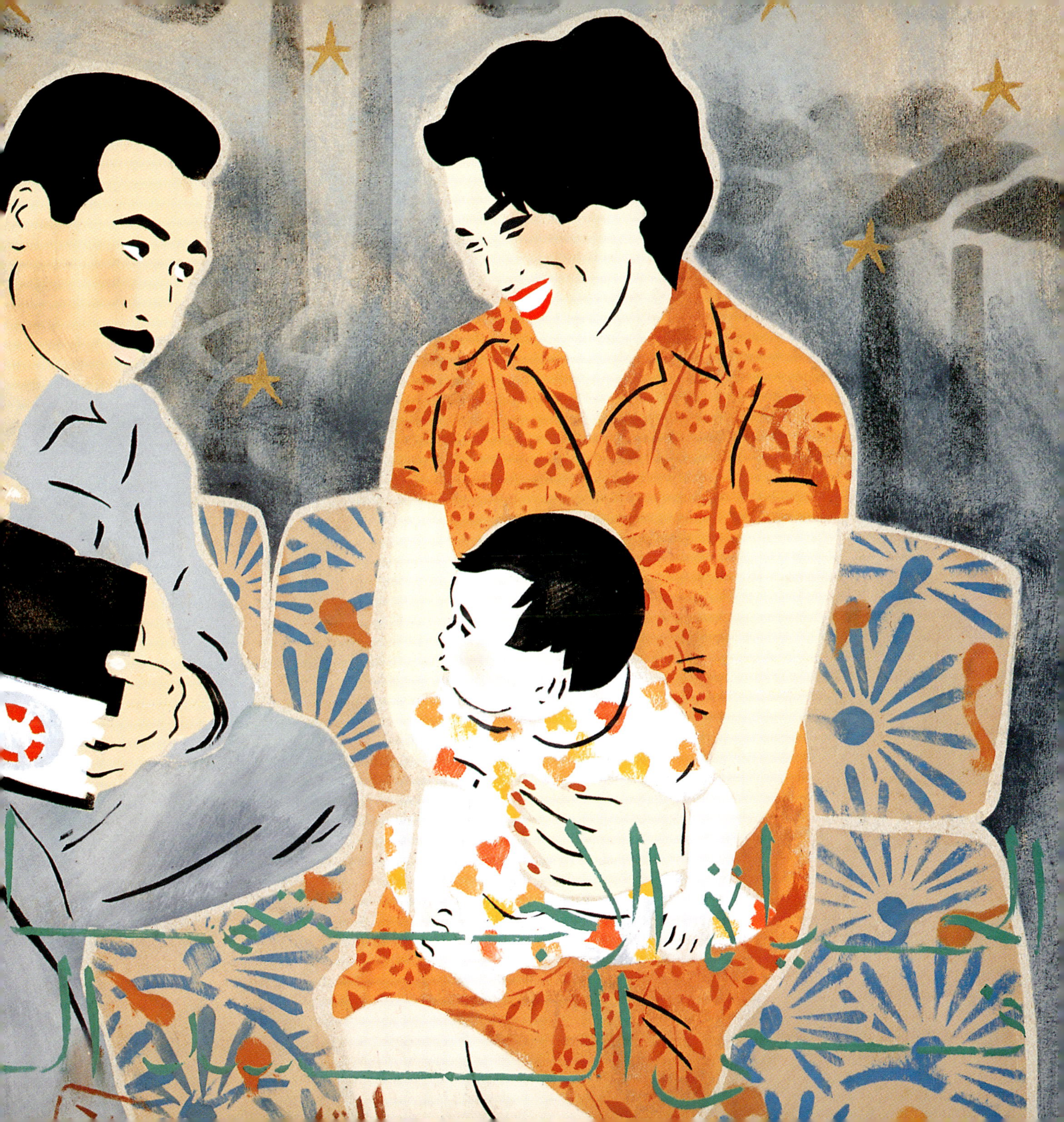

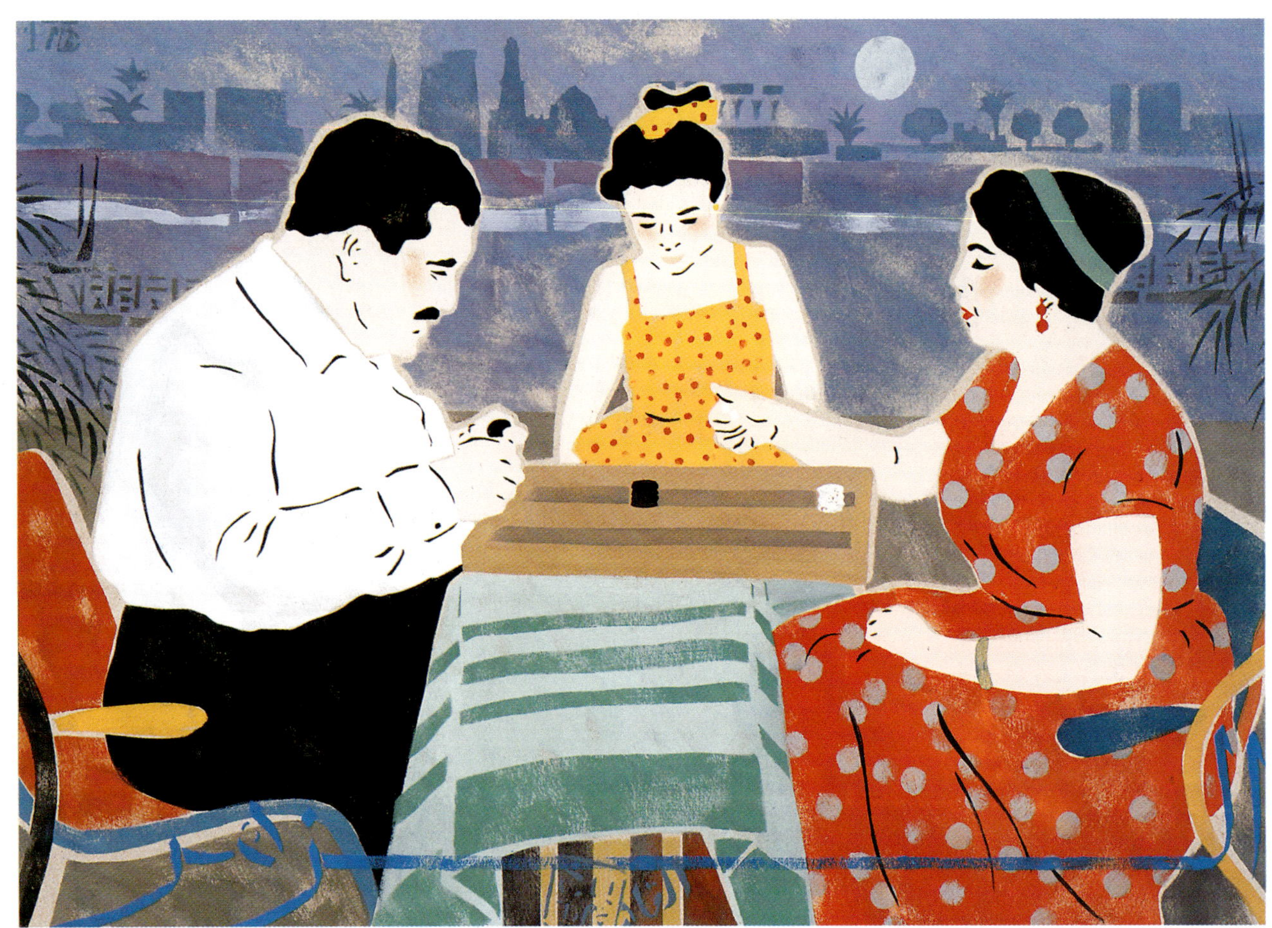

Family at a Kom Ombo Social Club

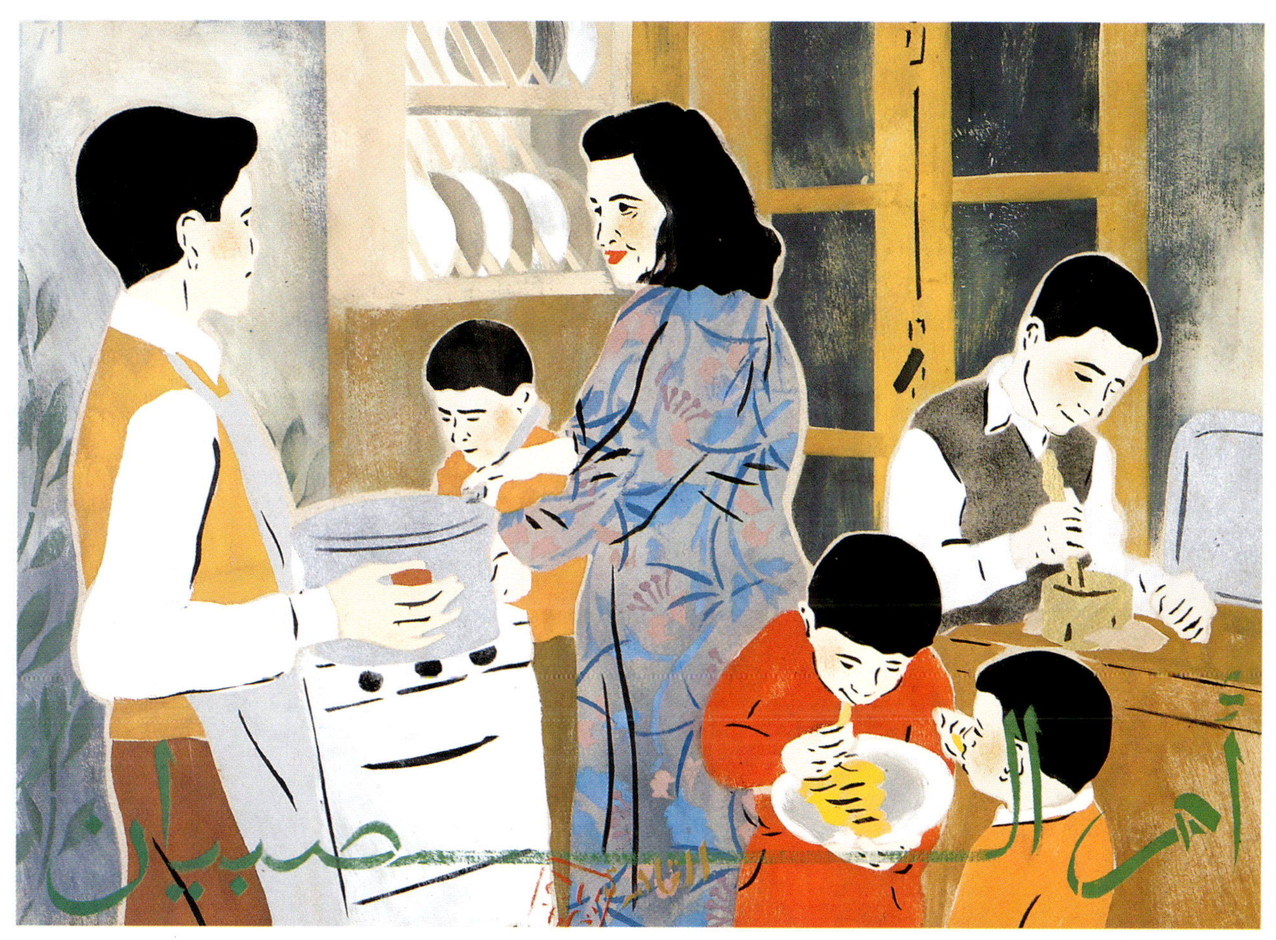

Mother of Boys

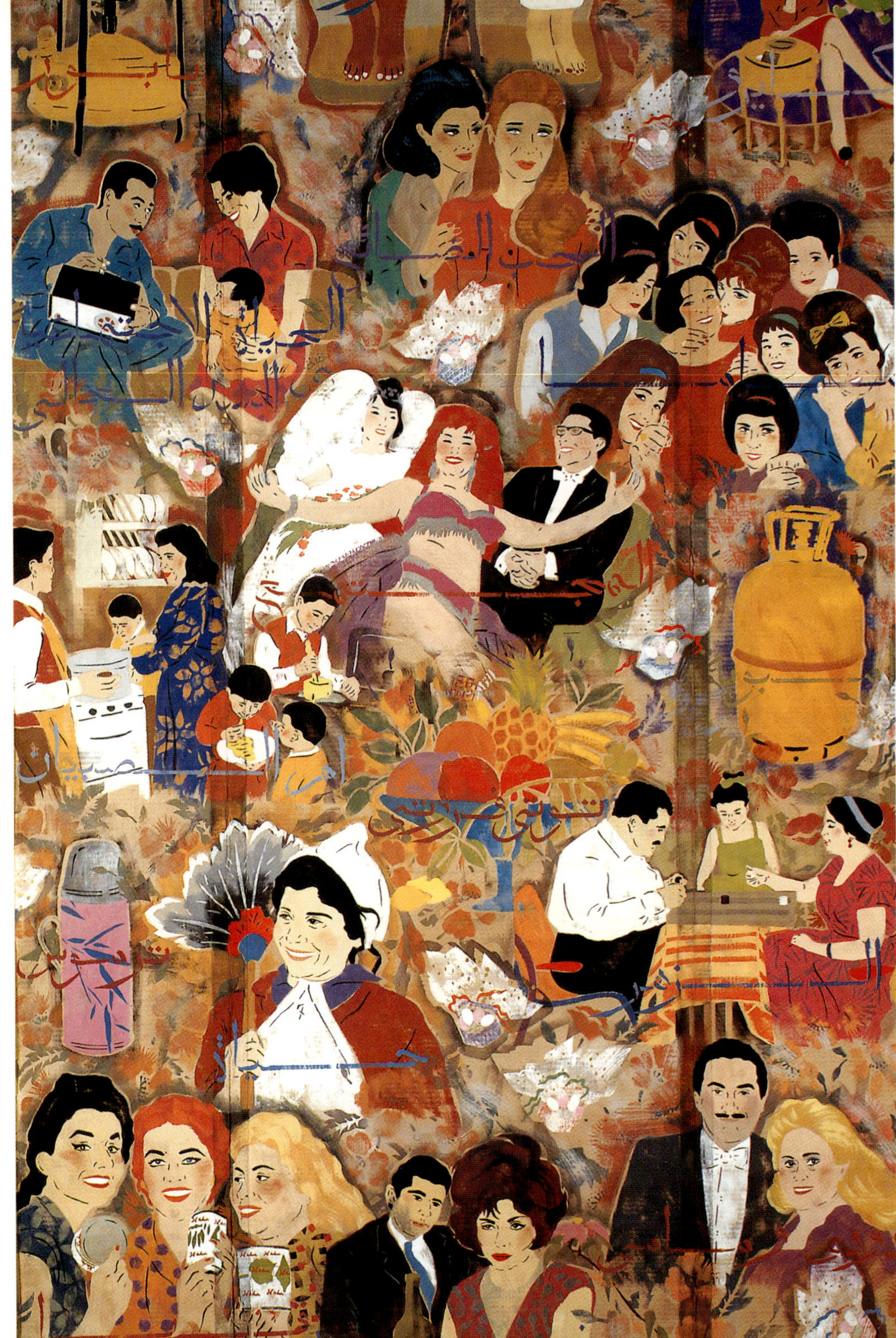

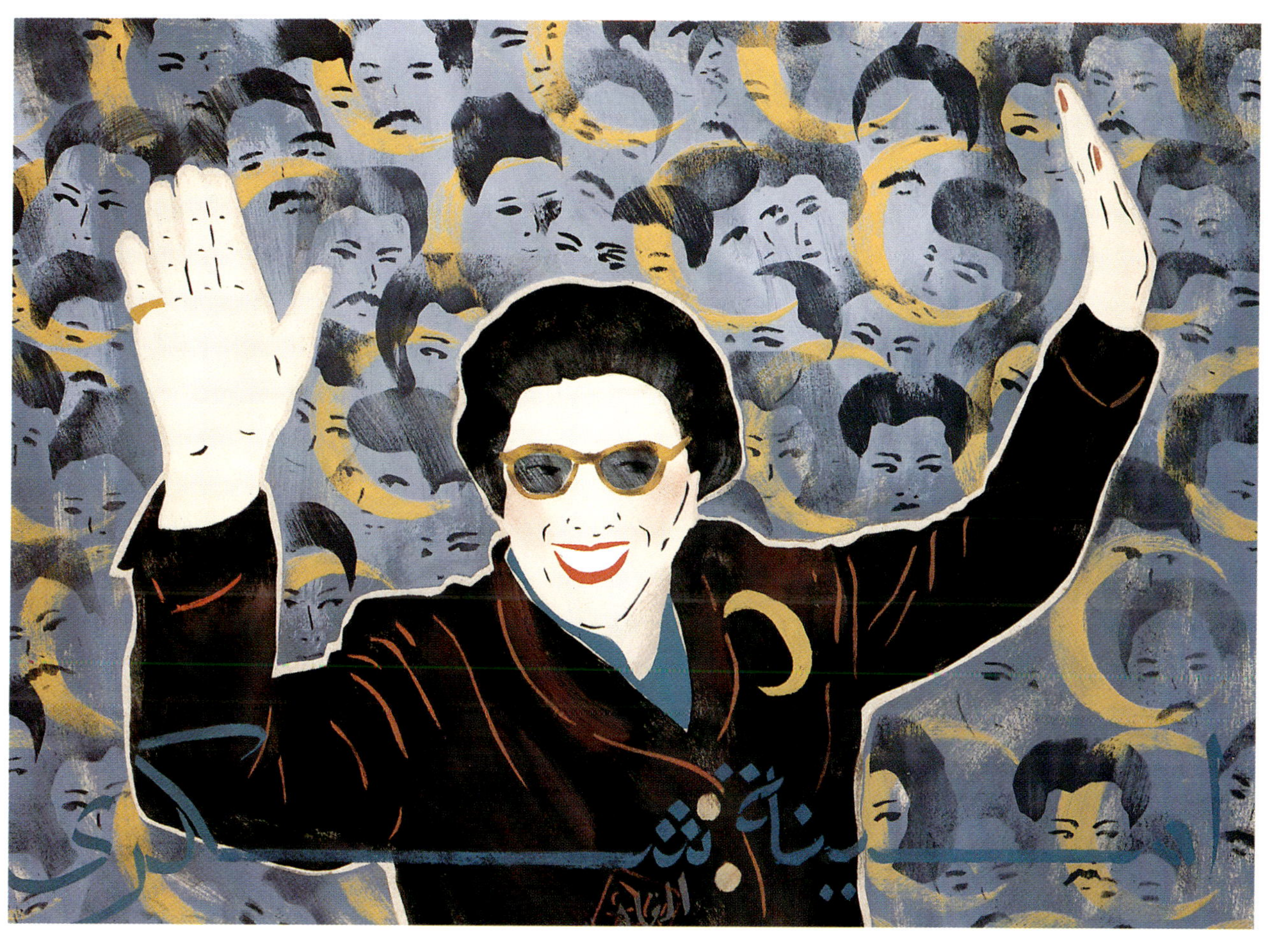

Amina Shokry

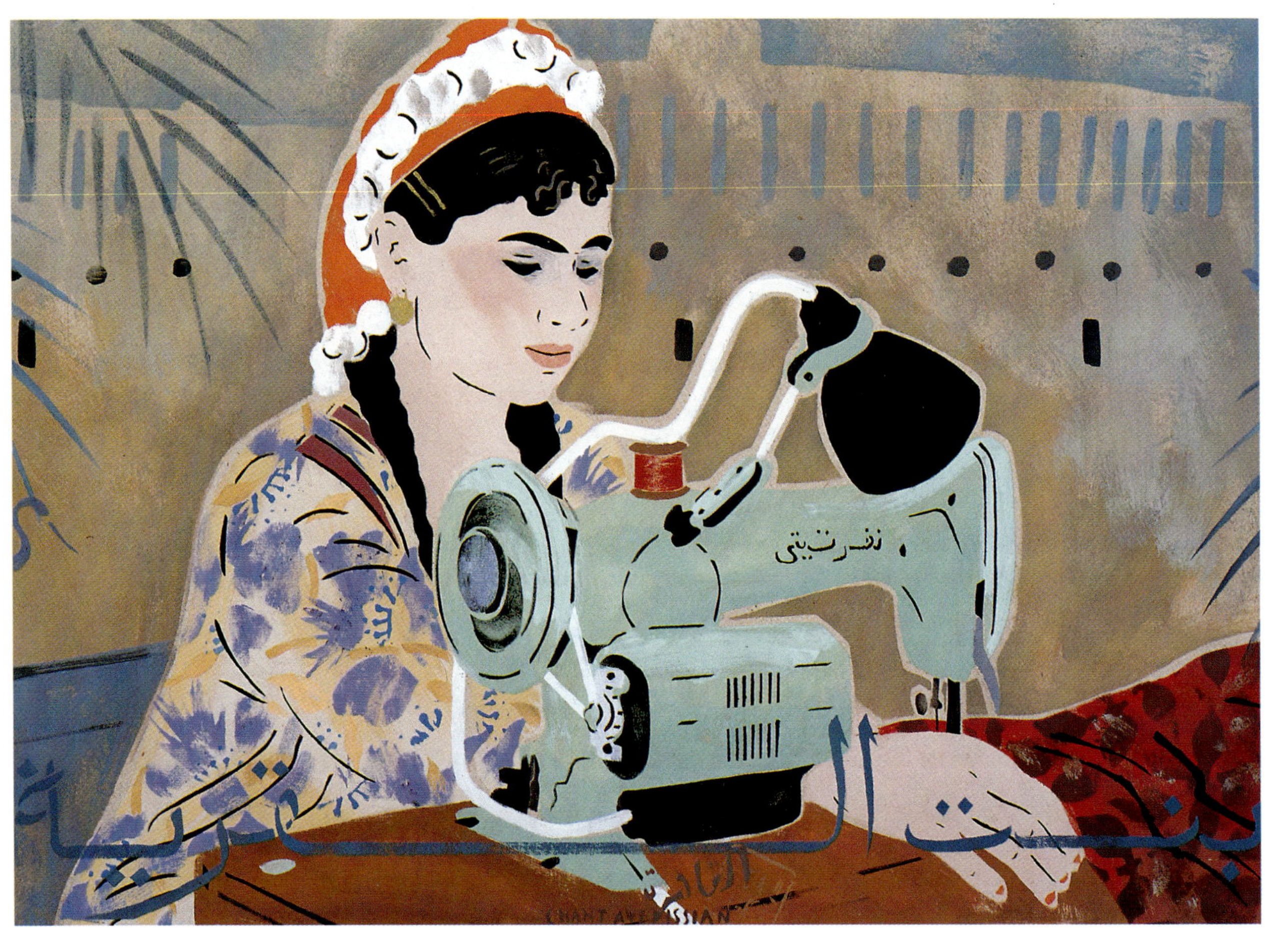

The Village Girl

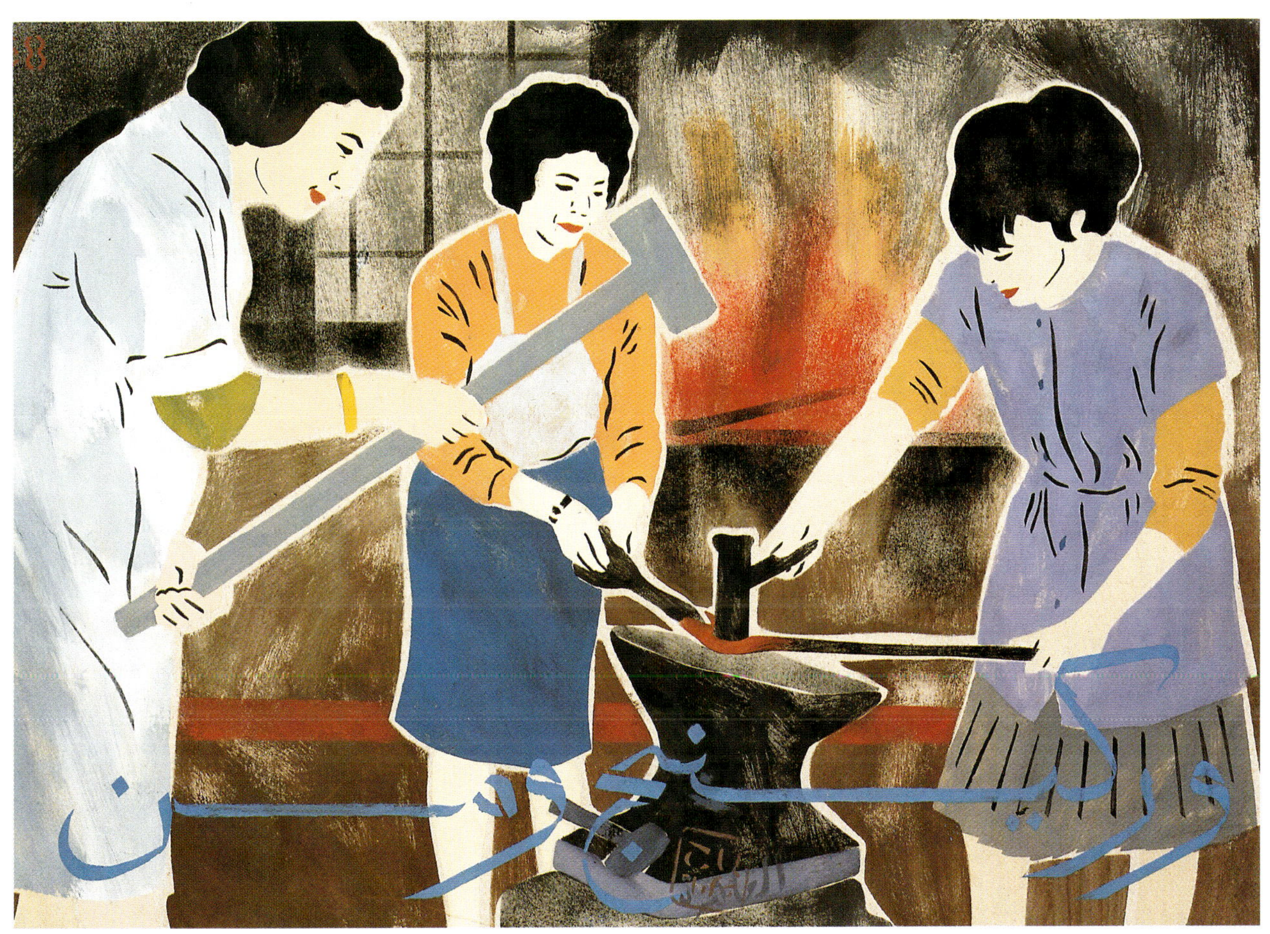

Working Women

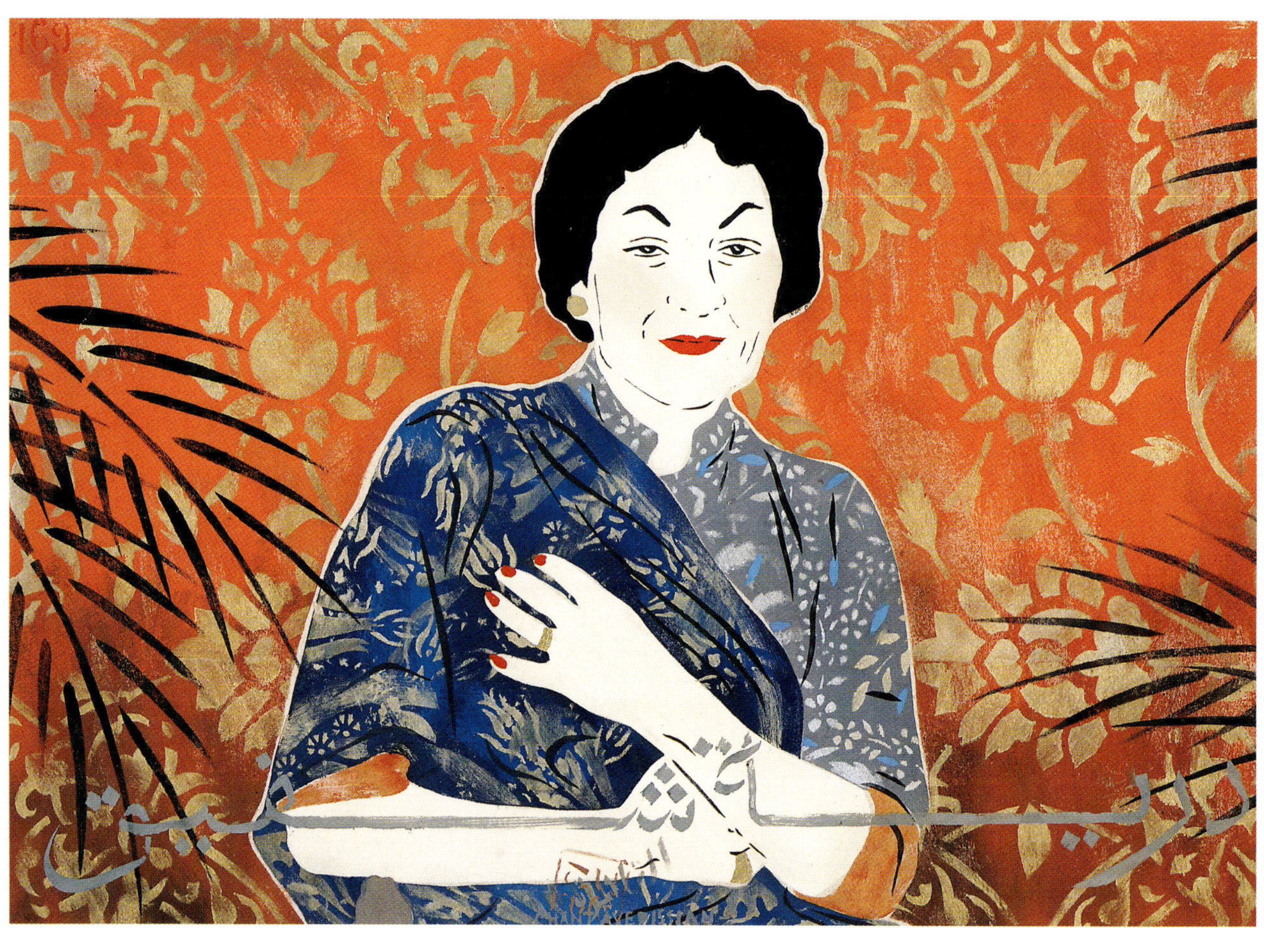

Doria Shafik

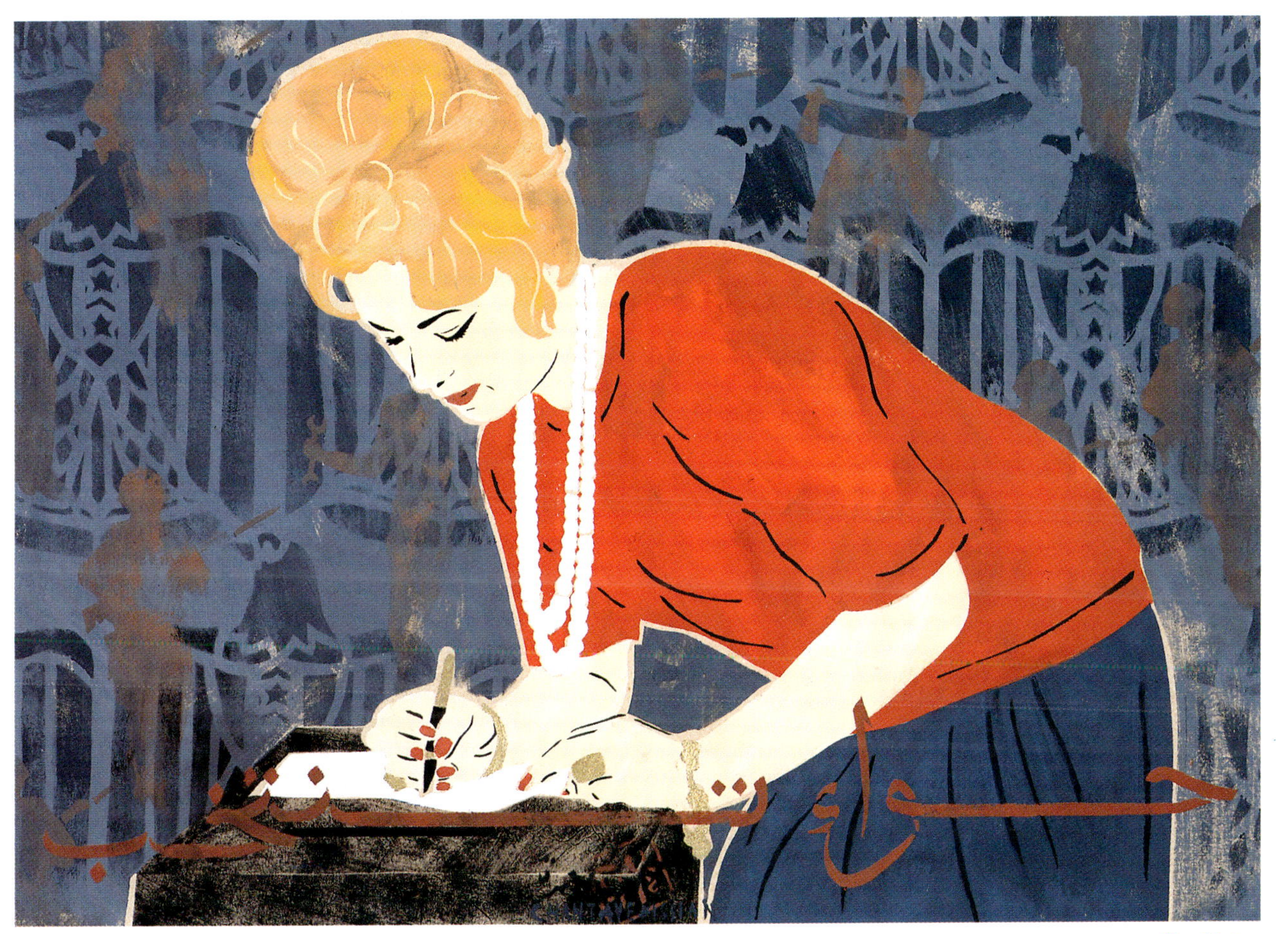

Eve Votes

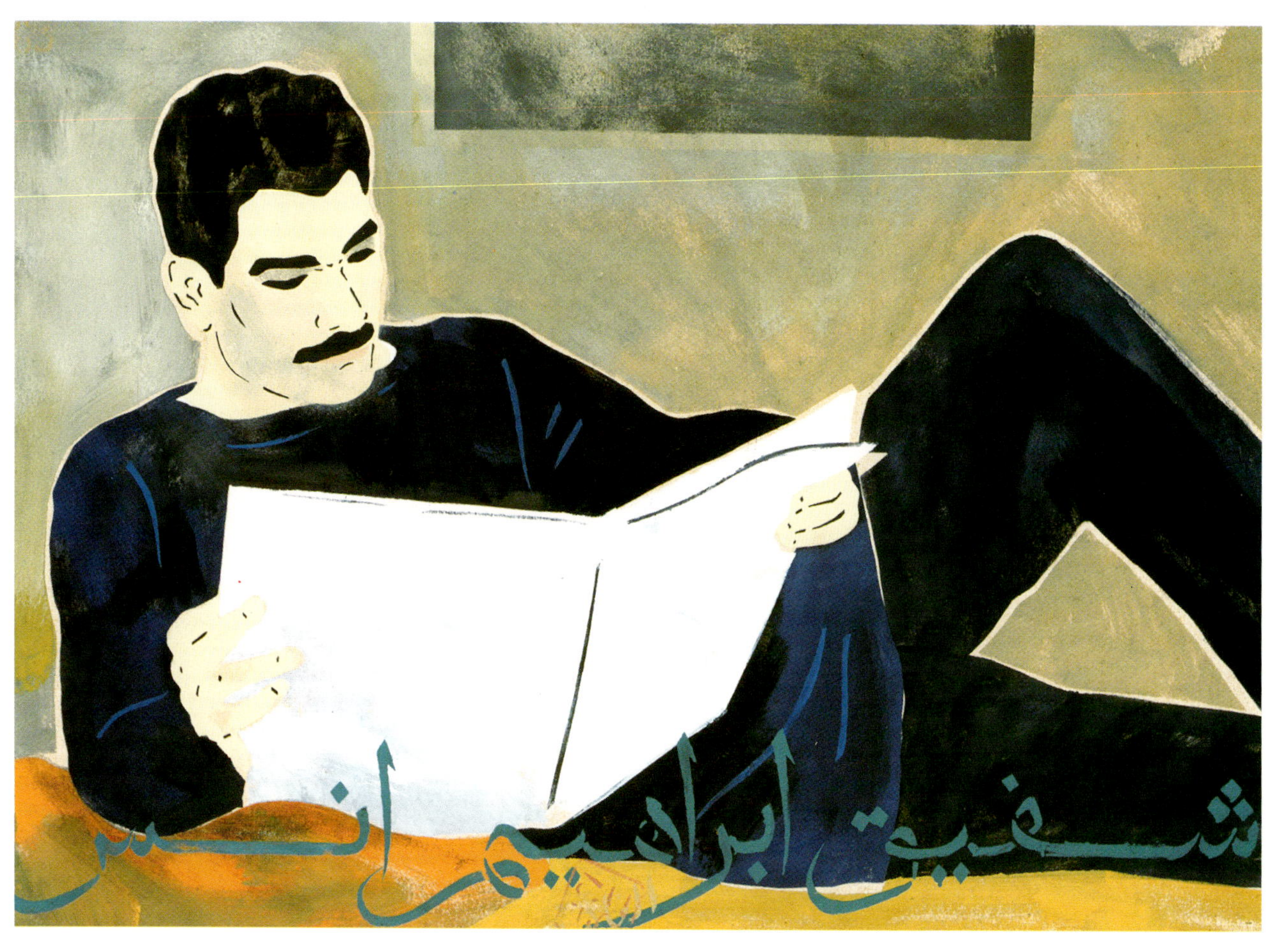

Shafik Ibrahim Onse

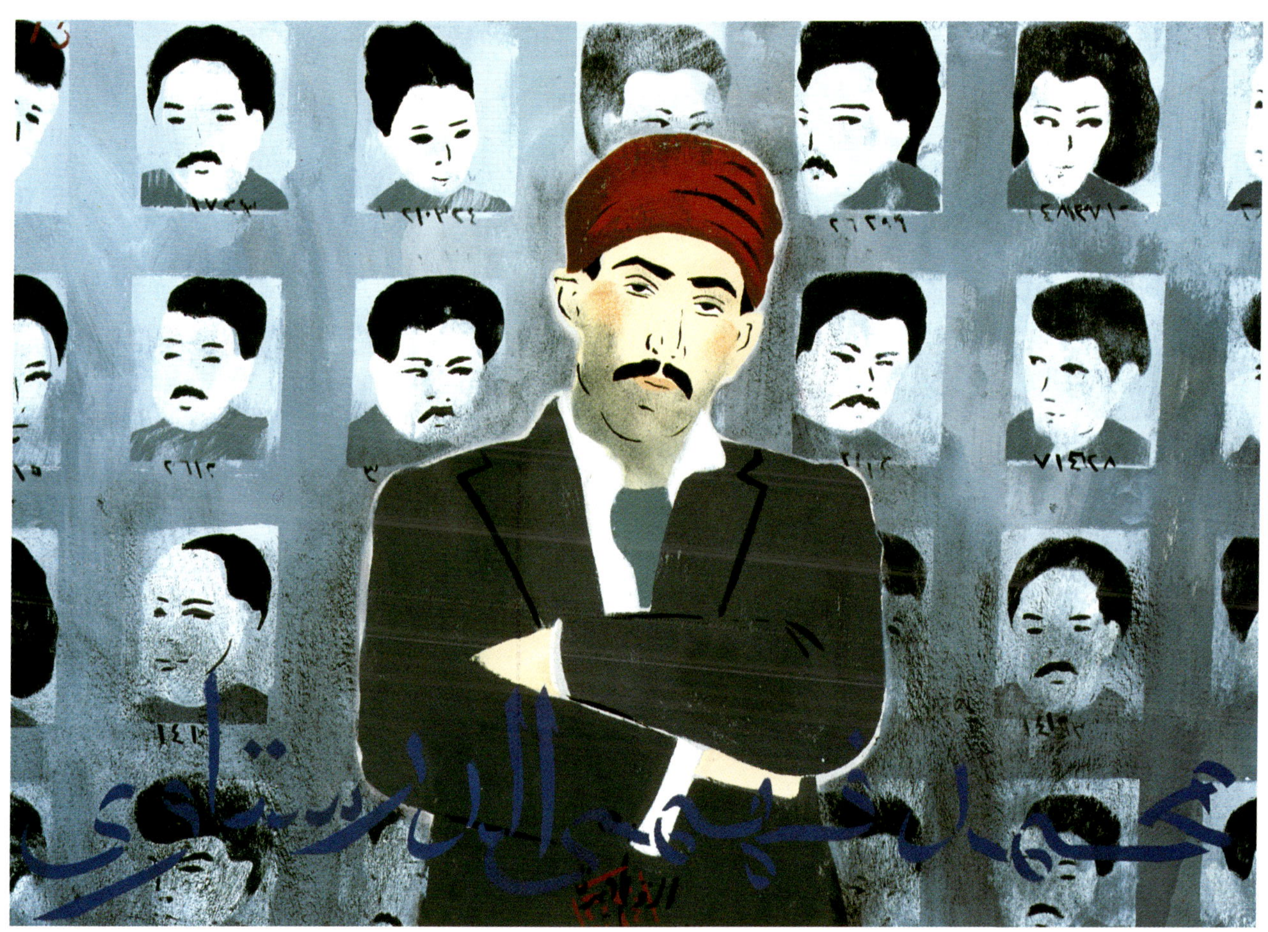

Mohammed Fahmy al-Darestawy

Rural
& Urban

Rural & Urban

Avedissian's discovery of his country was greatly due to the journeys in which he undertook, from Upper to Lower Egypt, to document the buildings of the architect Hassan Fathy, commissioned for a monograph by the Aga Khan Foundation. Fathy's influence on 'architecture of the poor' and 'architecture without architects' was to leave a great impact on many artists and architects worldwide. The cityscapes and landscapes Avedissian photographed represent long-standing traditions in ancient and modern local architecture and craftsmanship. He pays homage to Fathy's unit, the hand-made mud brick (*touba*), as the basis for all vernacular construction. Other works refer to Egypt's pharaonic heritage gradually falling into ruin, as illustrated in *The Mummy*, a stencil inspired by the late Shadi Abdel Salam's classic film that denounced the plundering of cultural sites. Views of the old Cataract Hotel or glimpses of Cairo's old city further symbolise the motif of permanence and transience.

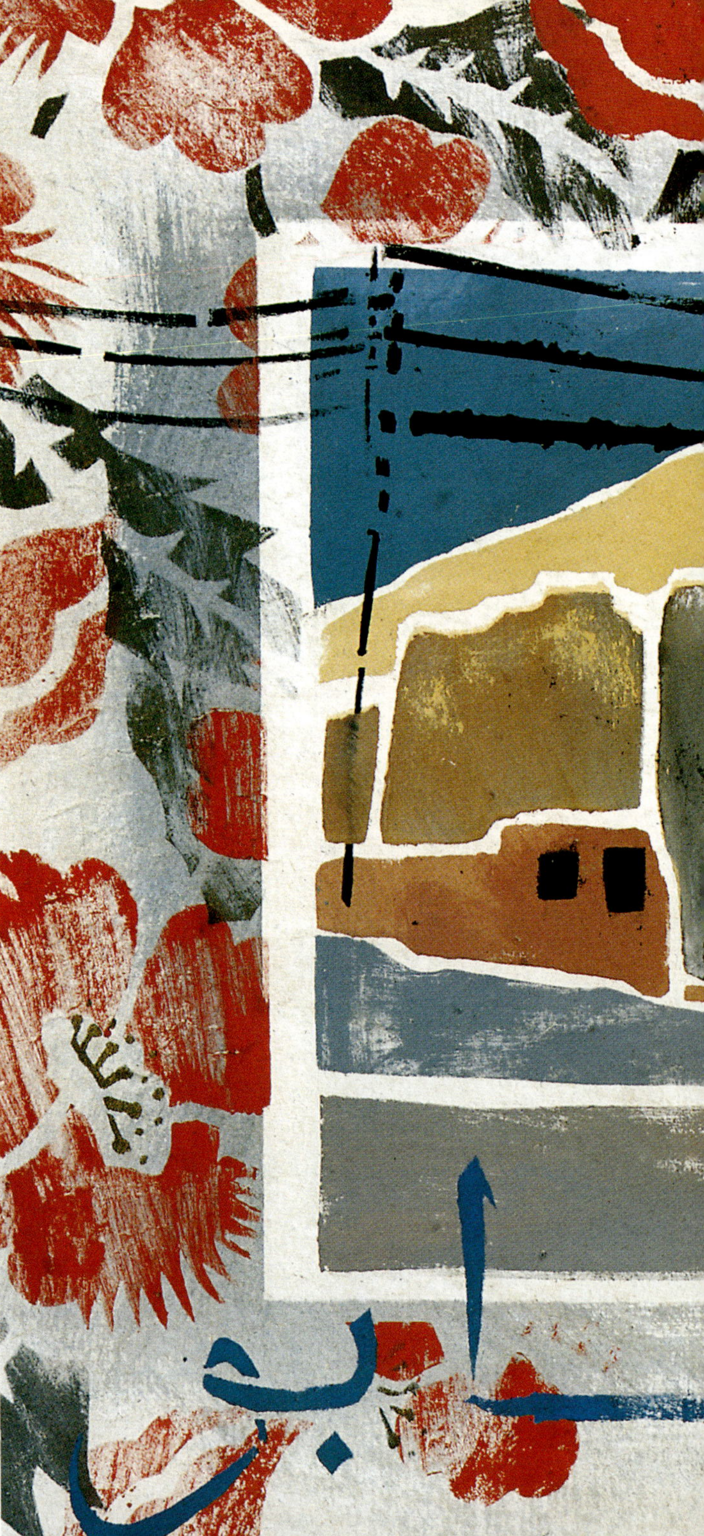

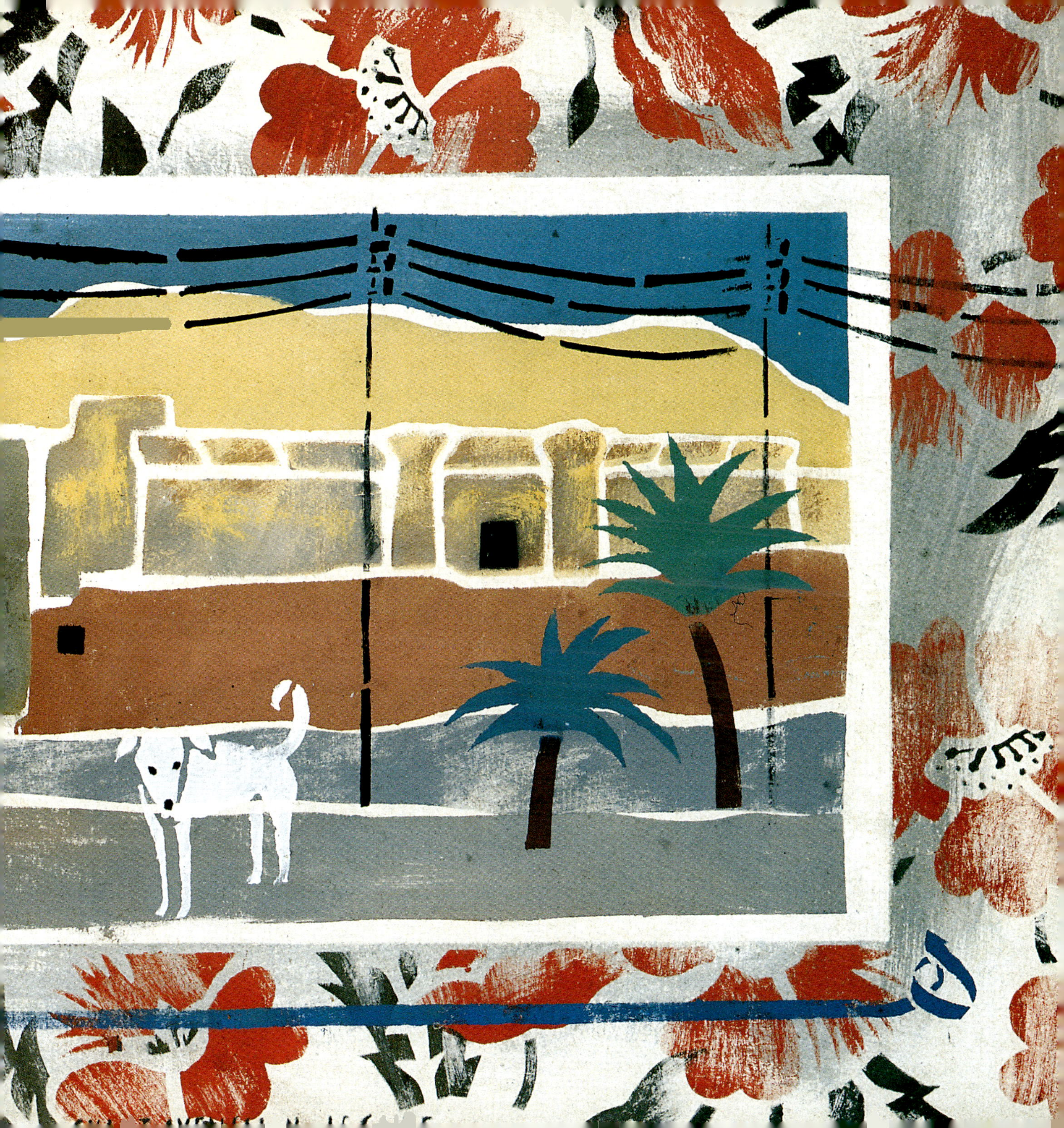

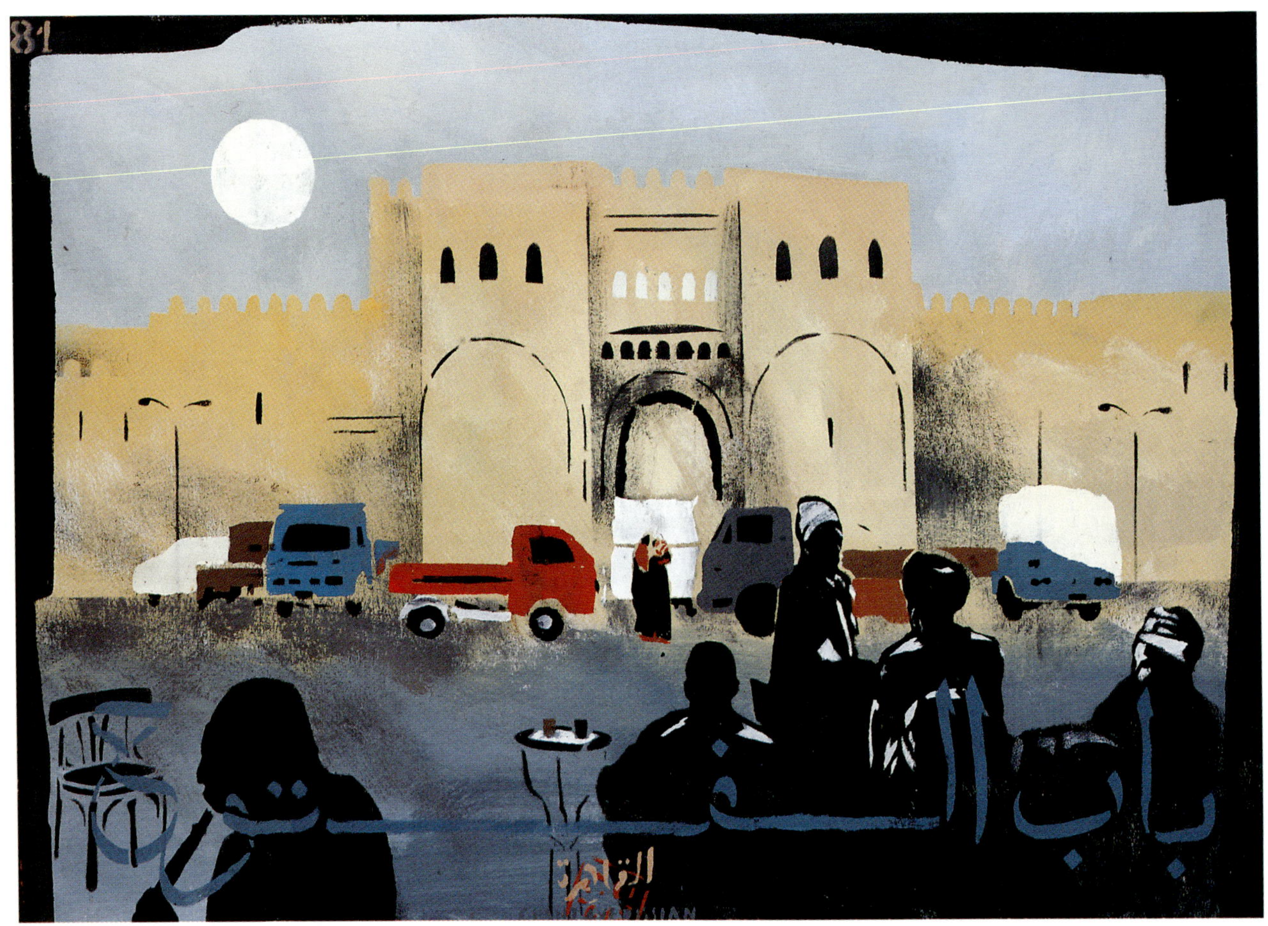

Bab al-Fetouh

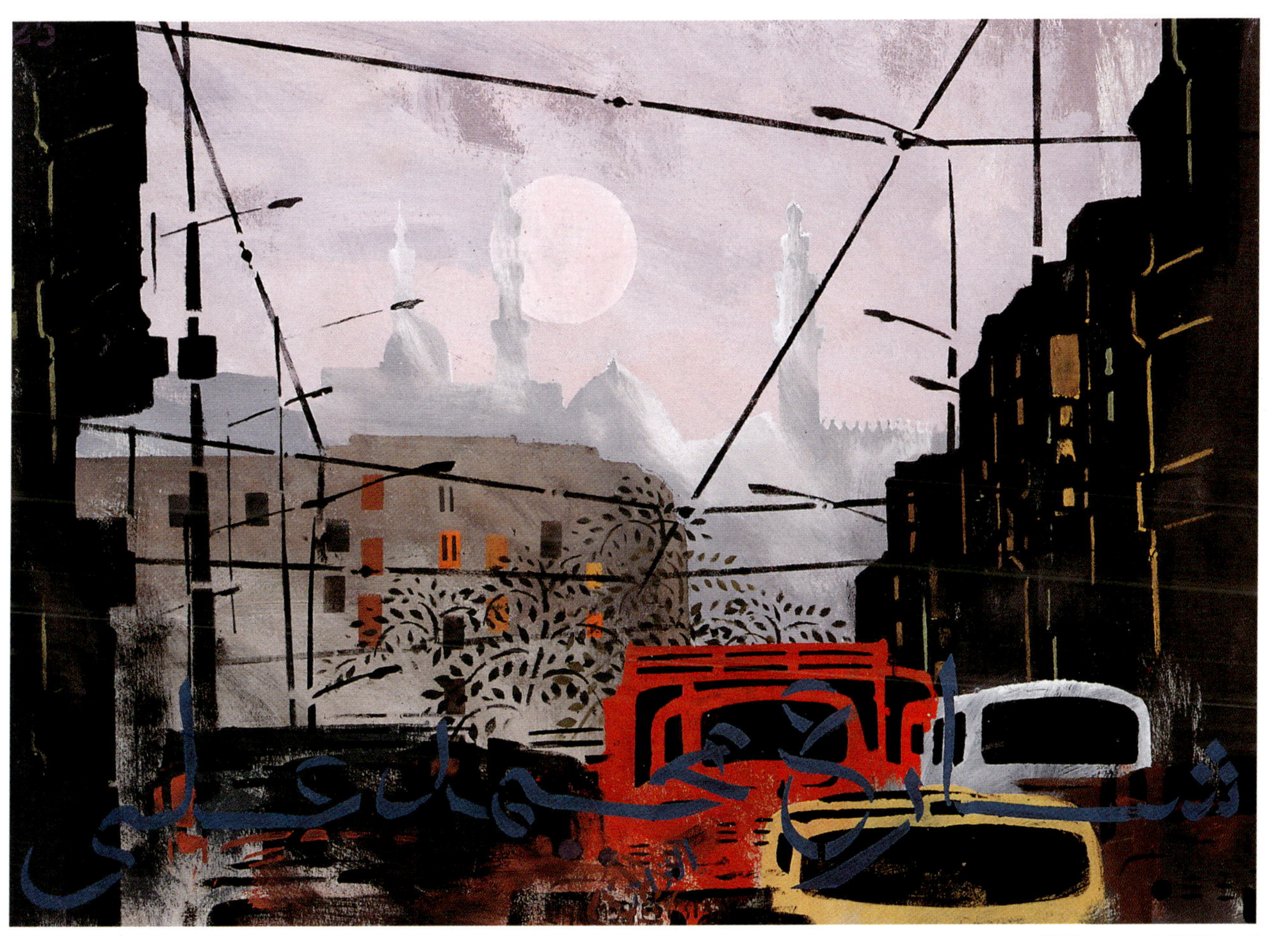

Mohammed Ali Street

Greetings from Misr

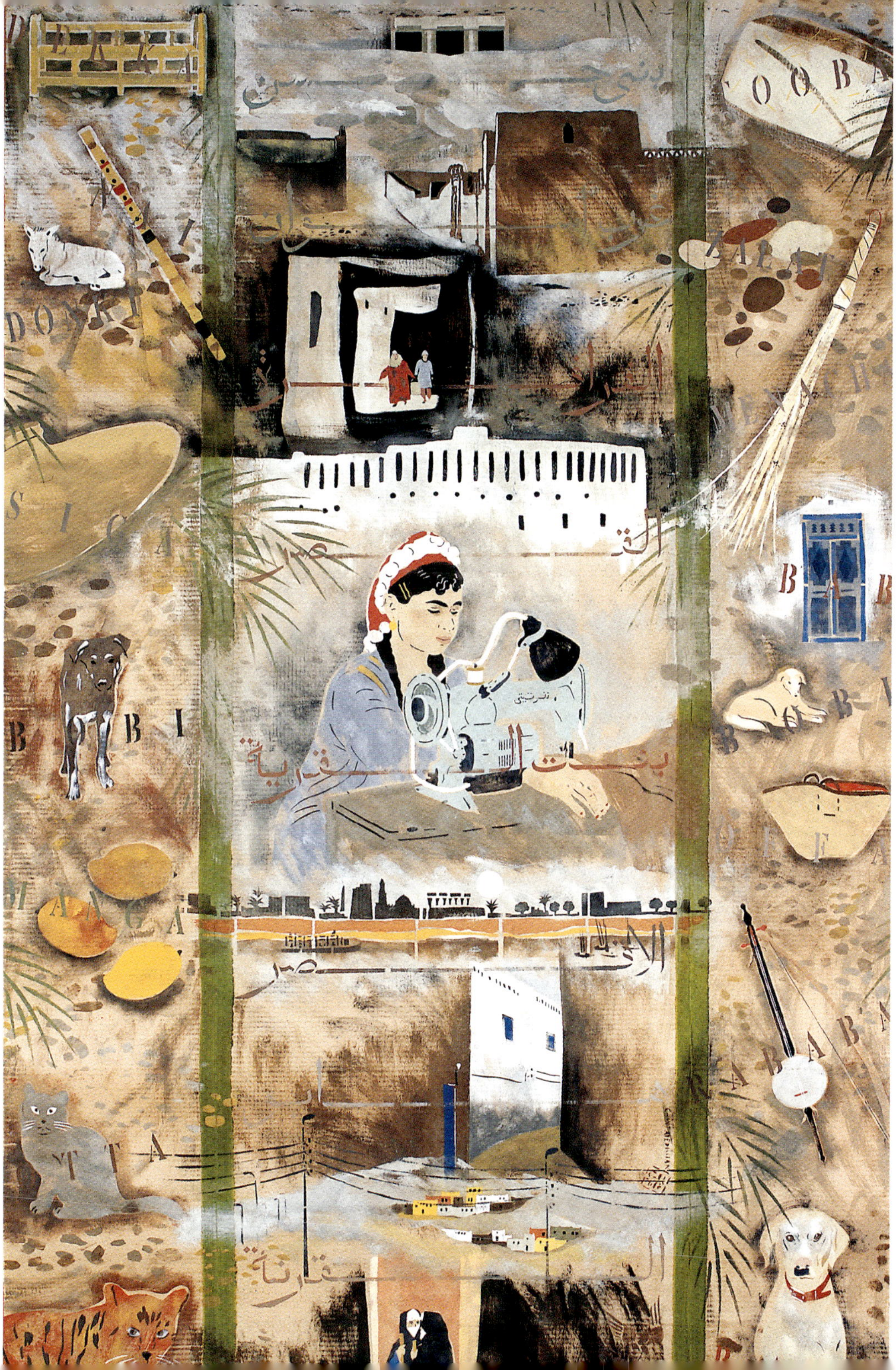

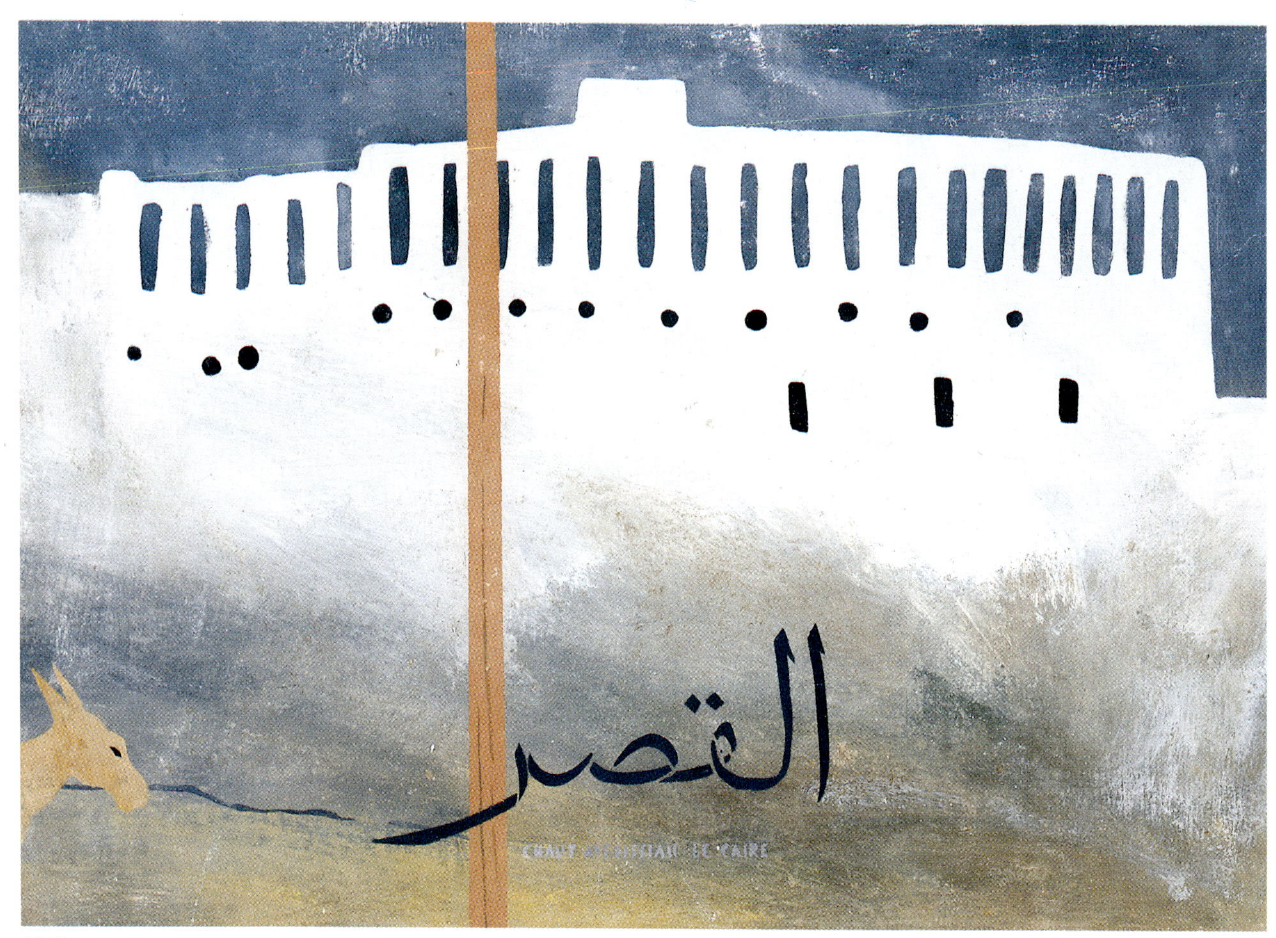

Al-Kasr

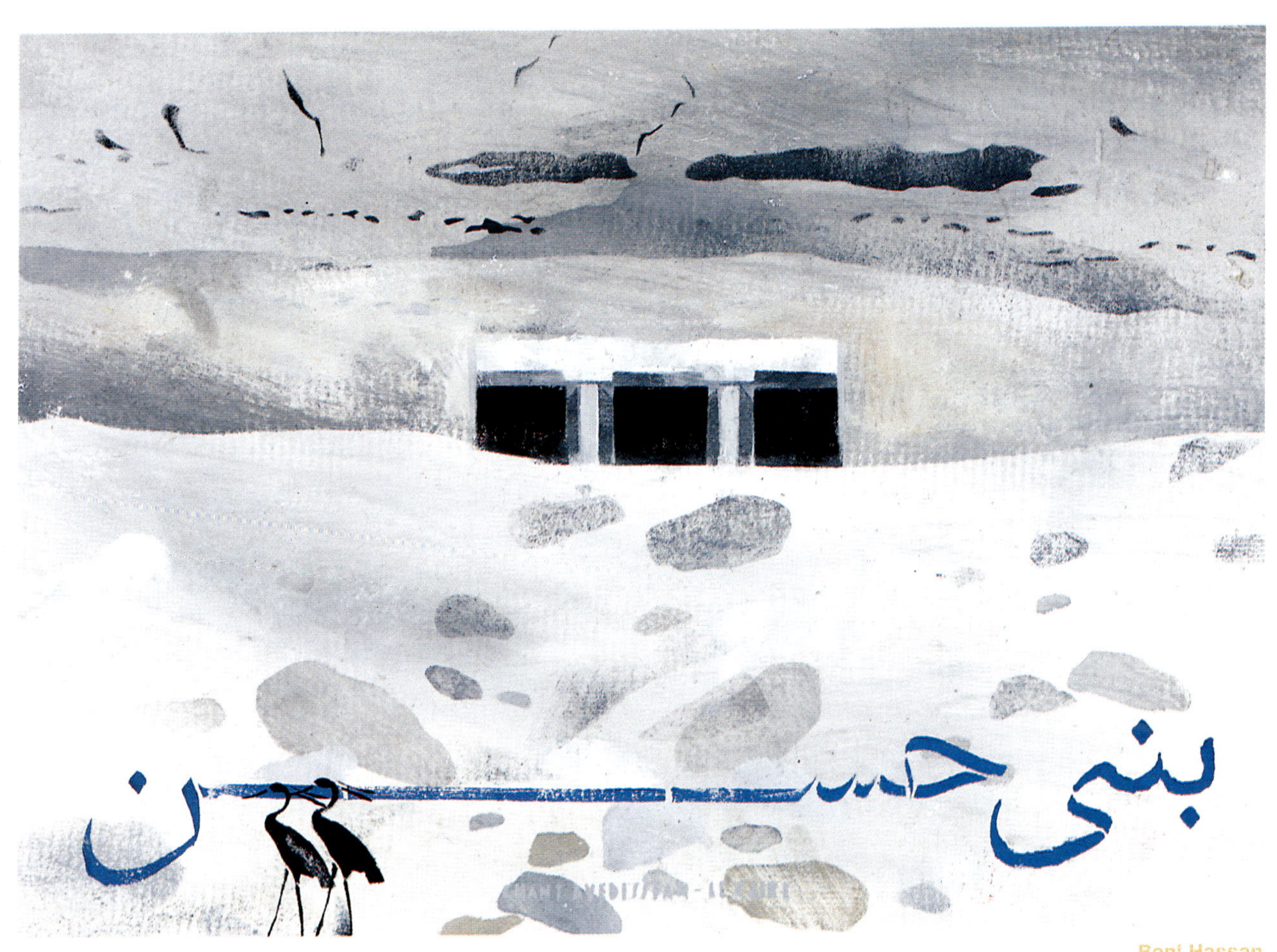

Beni Hassan

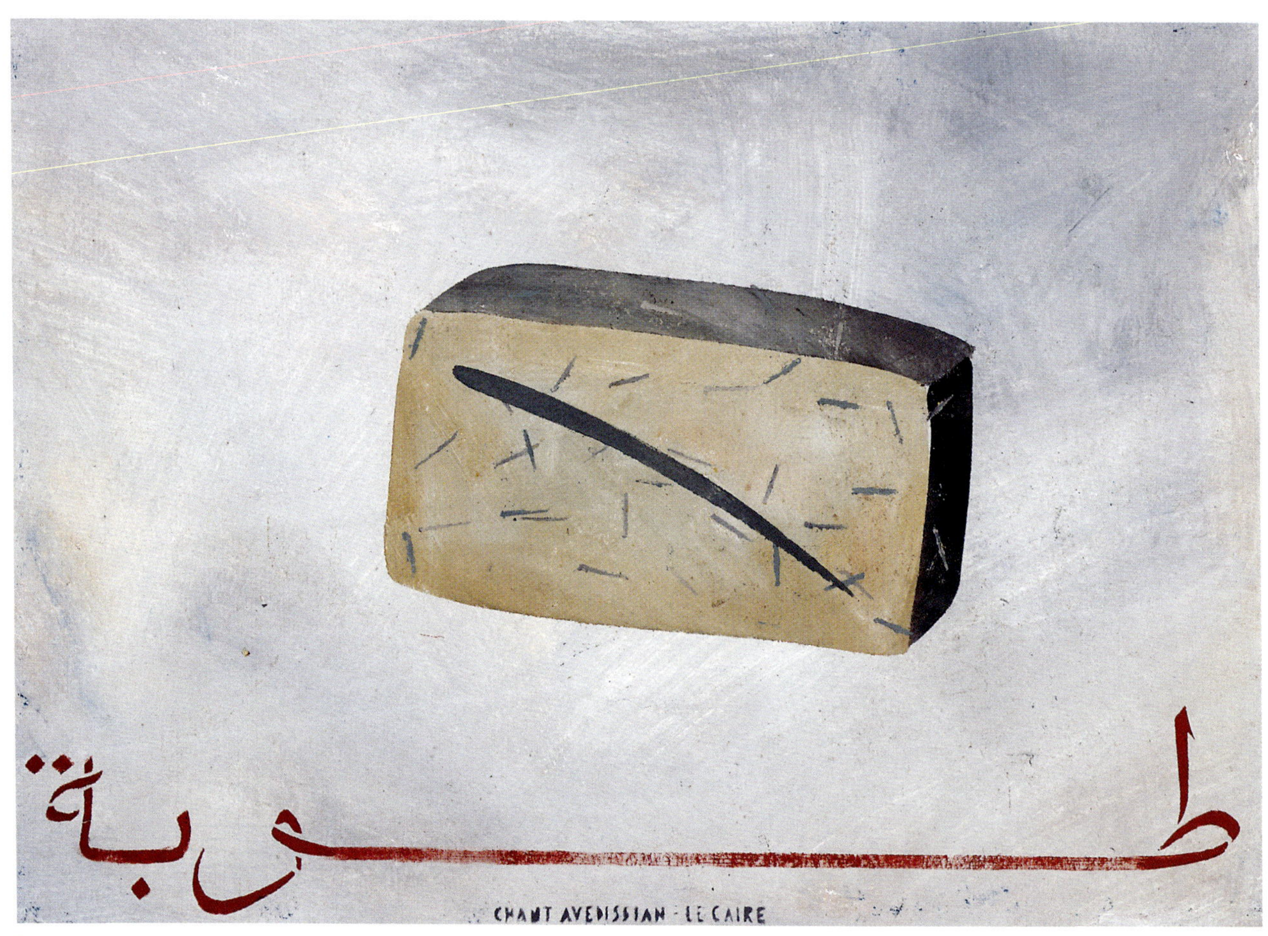

Touba

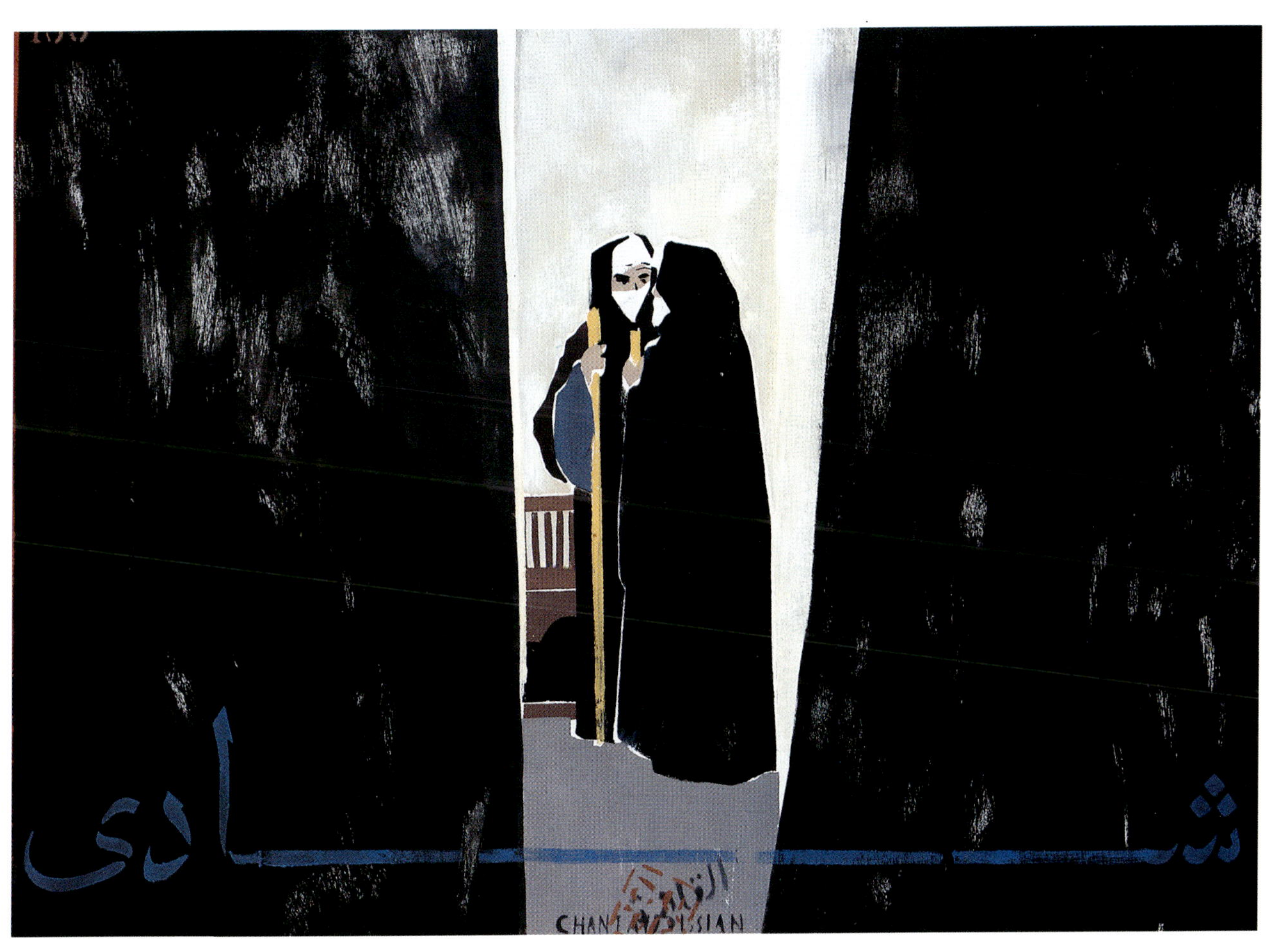

The Mummy

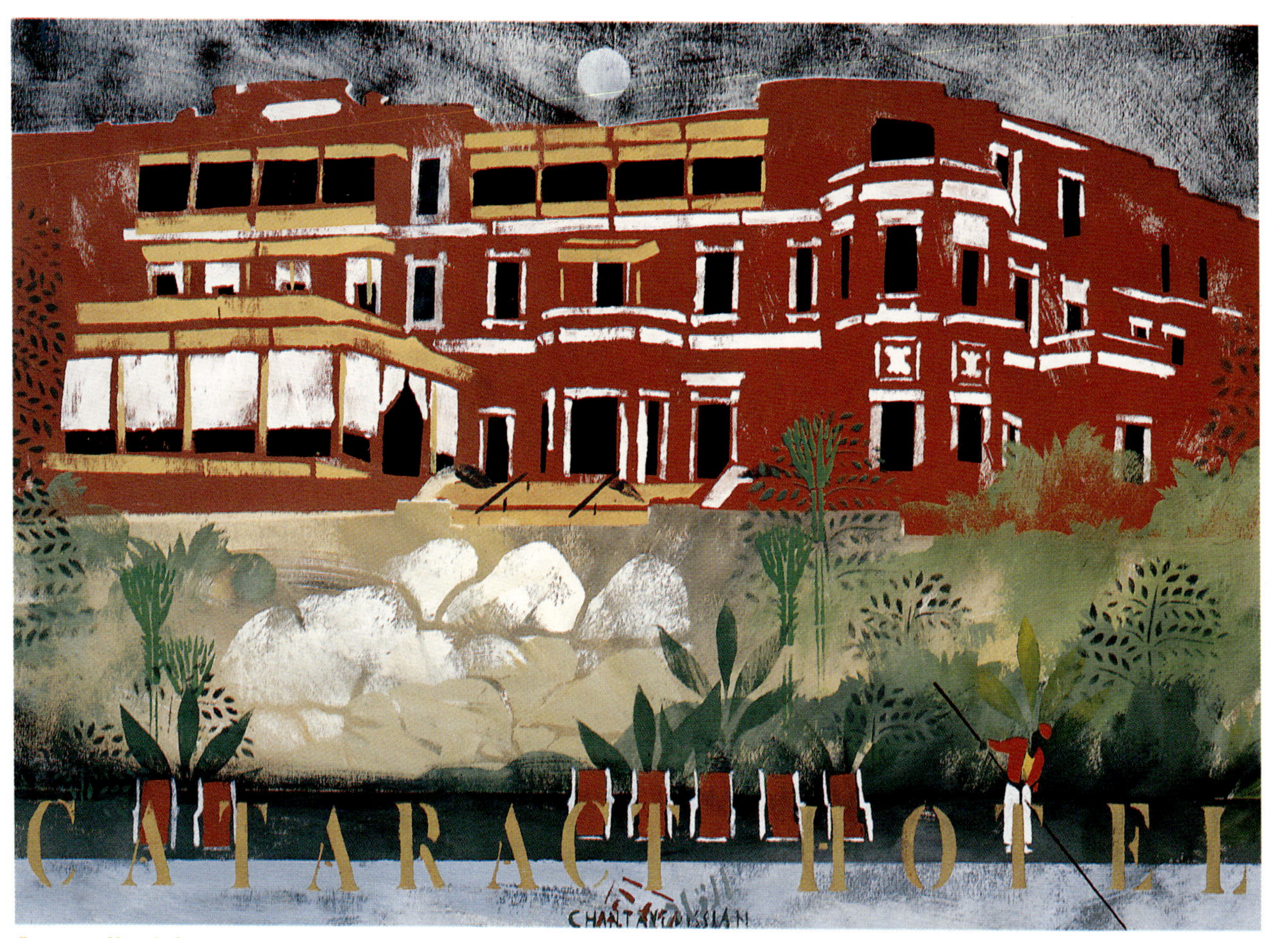

Cataract Hotel, Aswan

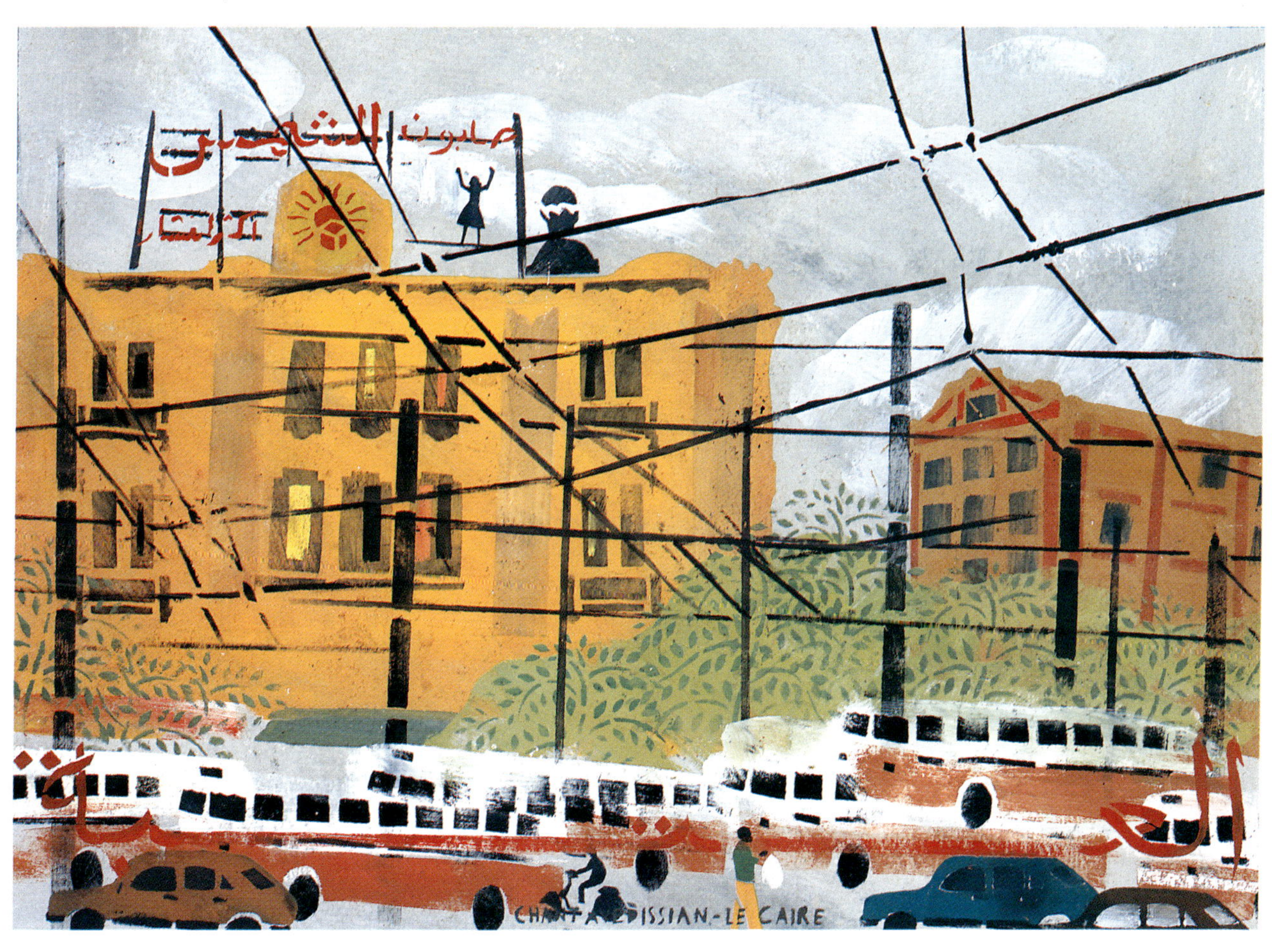

Ataba Square

Athletes

Athletes

These images from the 1950s and 1960s are from posters and magazines of the Egyptian-Soviet era, which promoted the cult of the body. In the nationalist propaganda machine, sport symbolised Egypt's development in the modern world. Sport was associated with the notion of beauty and perfection, competition and progress in a modern way. 'Palaces of Culture' and 'Sport Clubs' were promoted from the north to the south of Egypt. These were places where youths from humble backgrounds could have free access to sports that were previously the exclusive preserve of the rich. Encouraging national and international competition was a way to overcome the class and gender divides. The motto of the socialist era was 'a good mind in a good body'.

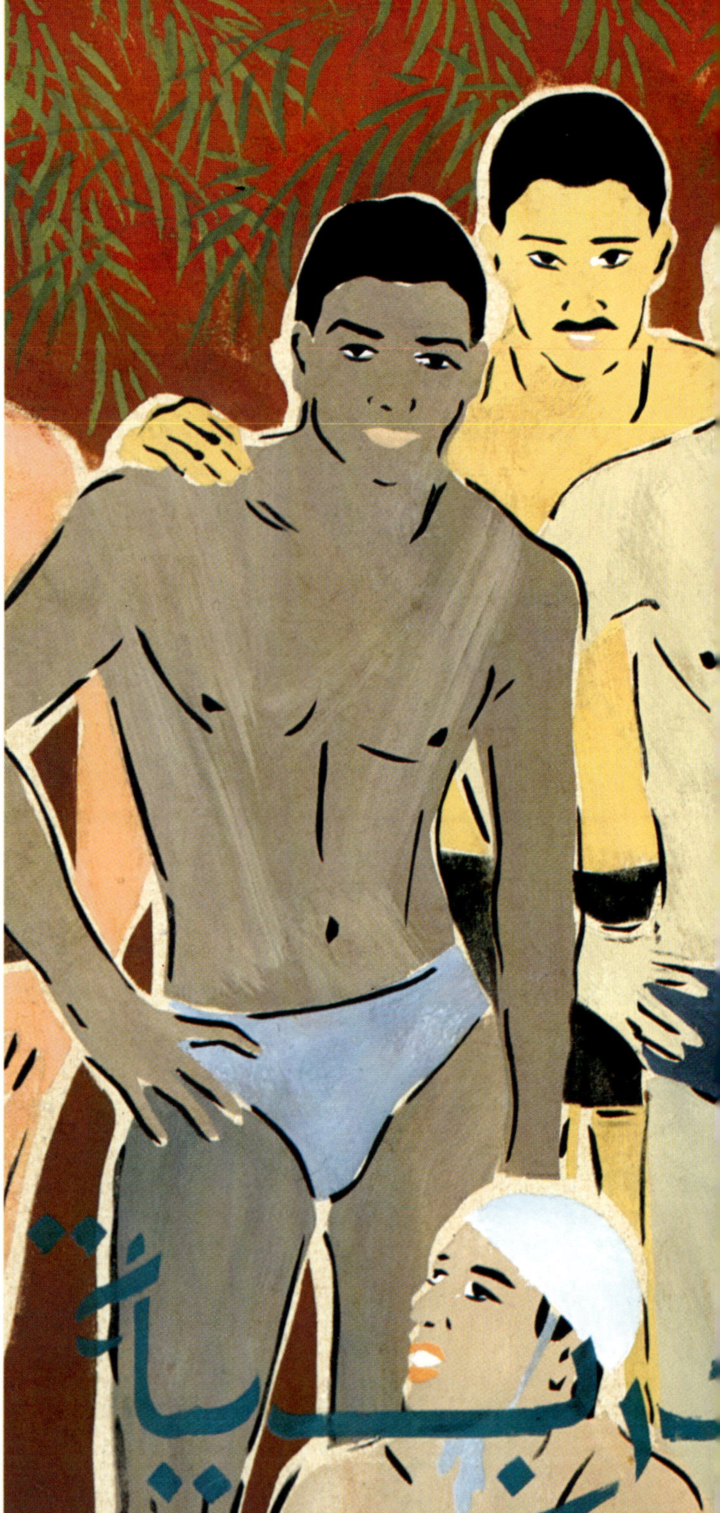

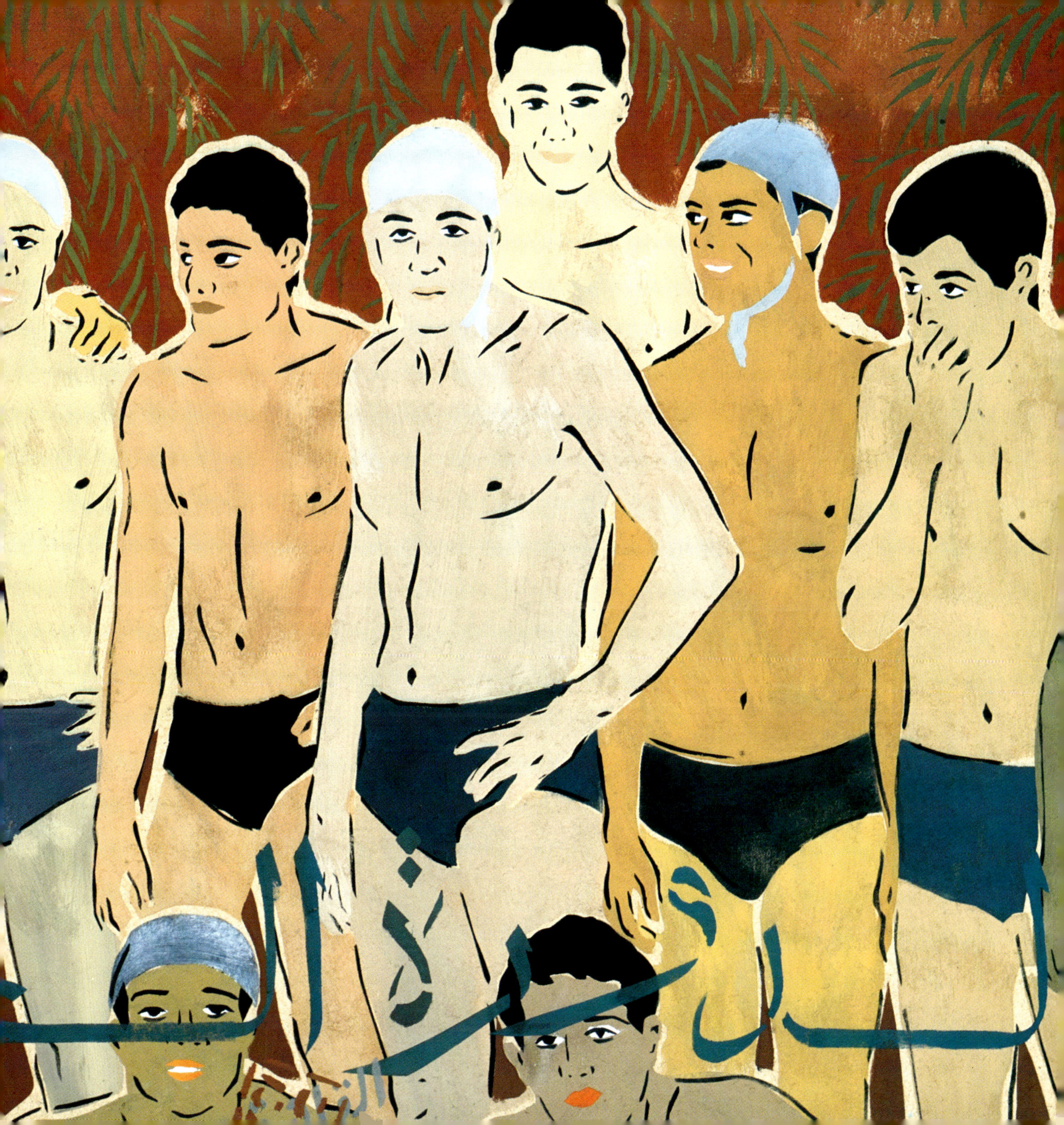

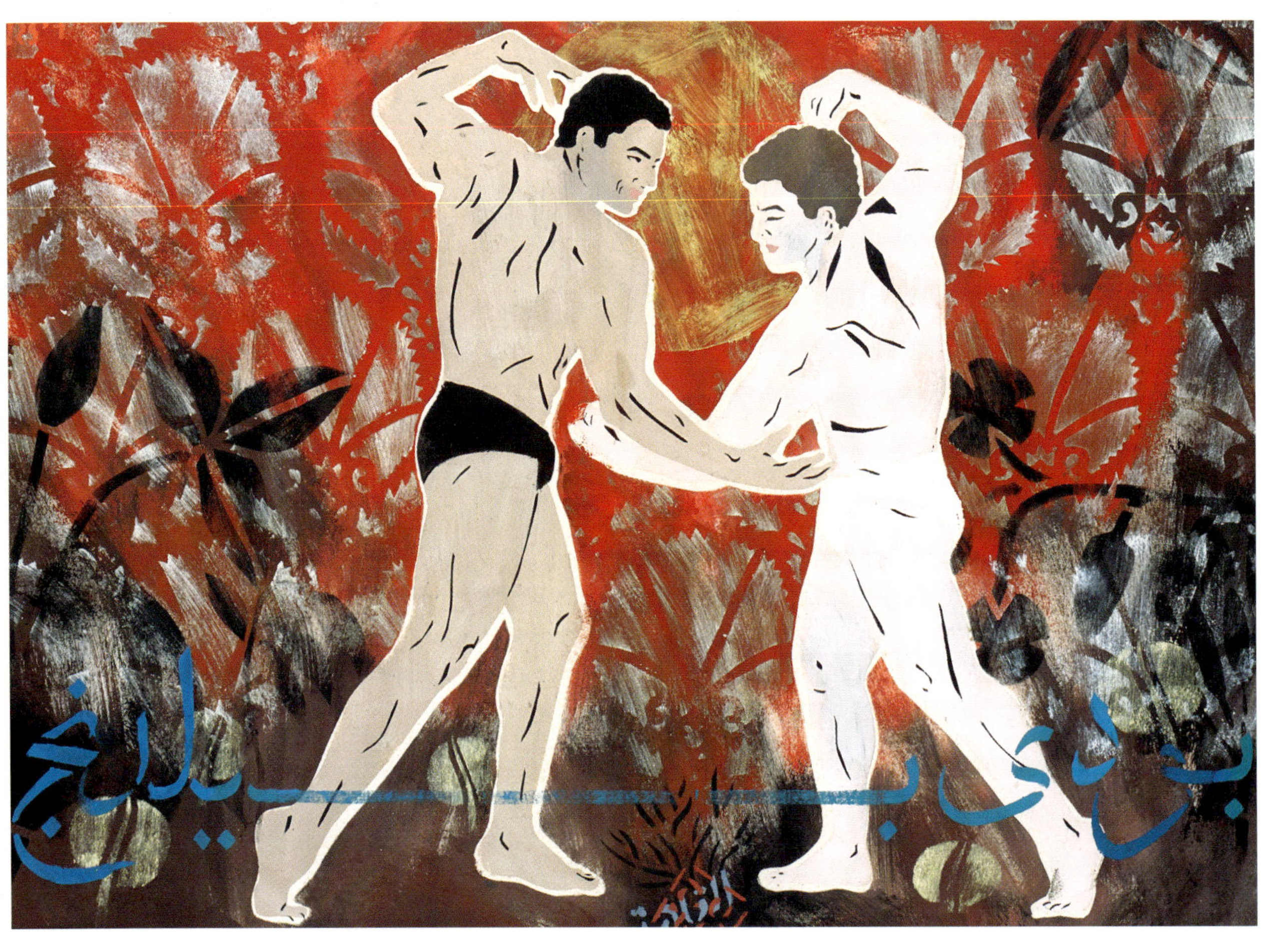

Body Building

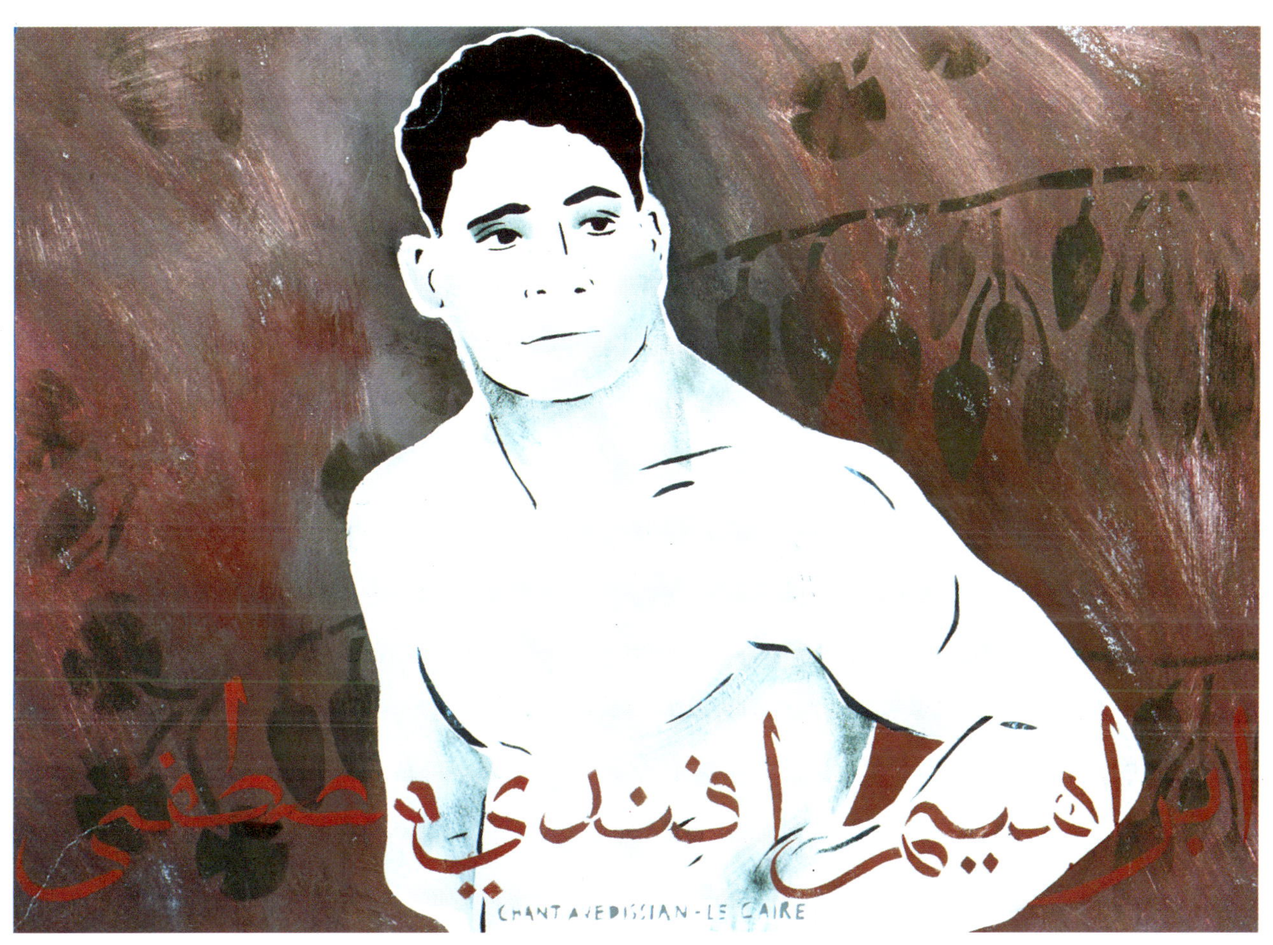

Ibrahim Afandi Mustapha

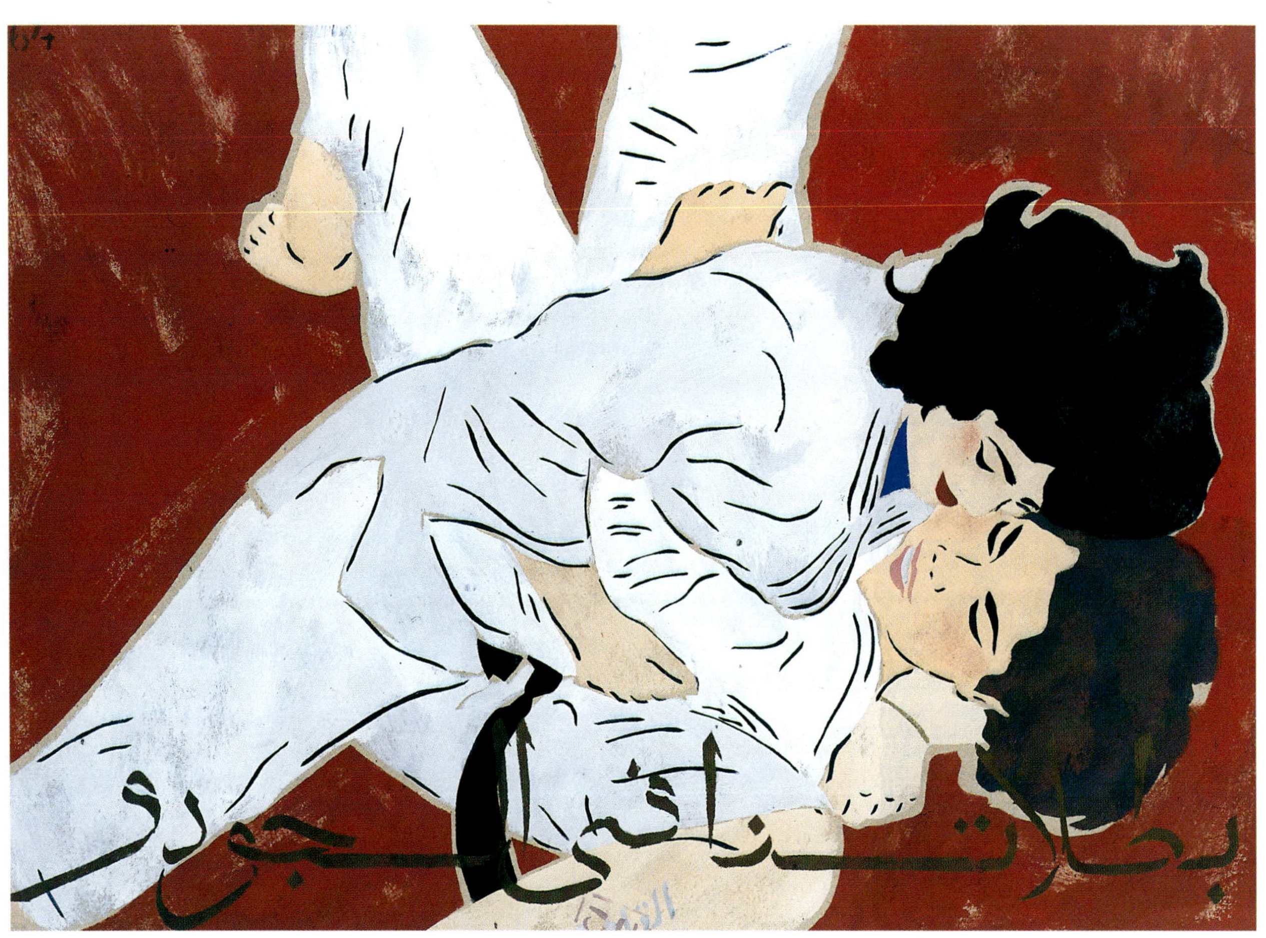

Our Judo Heroines

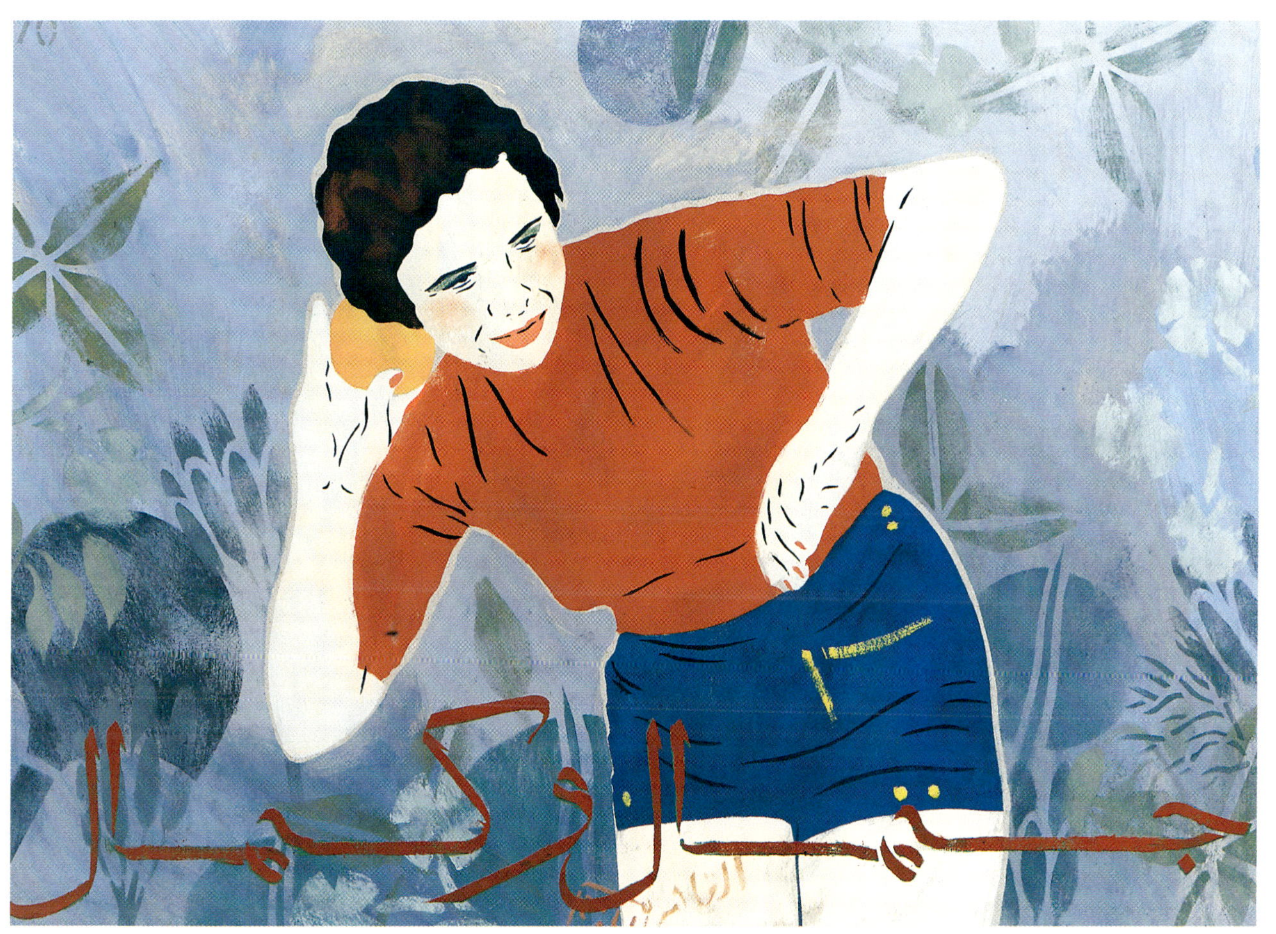

Beauty and Perfection

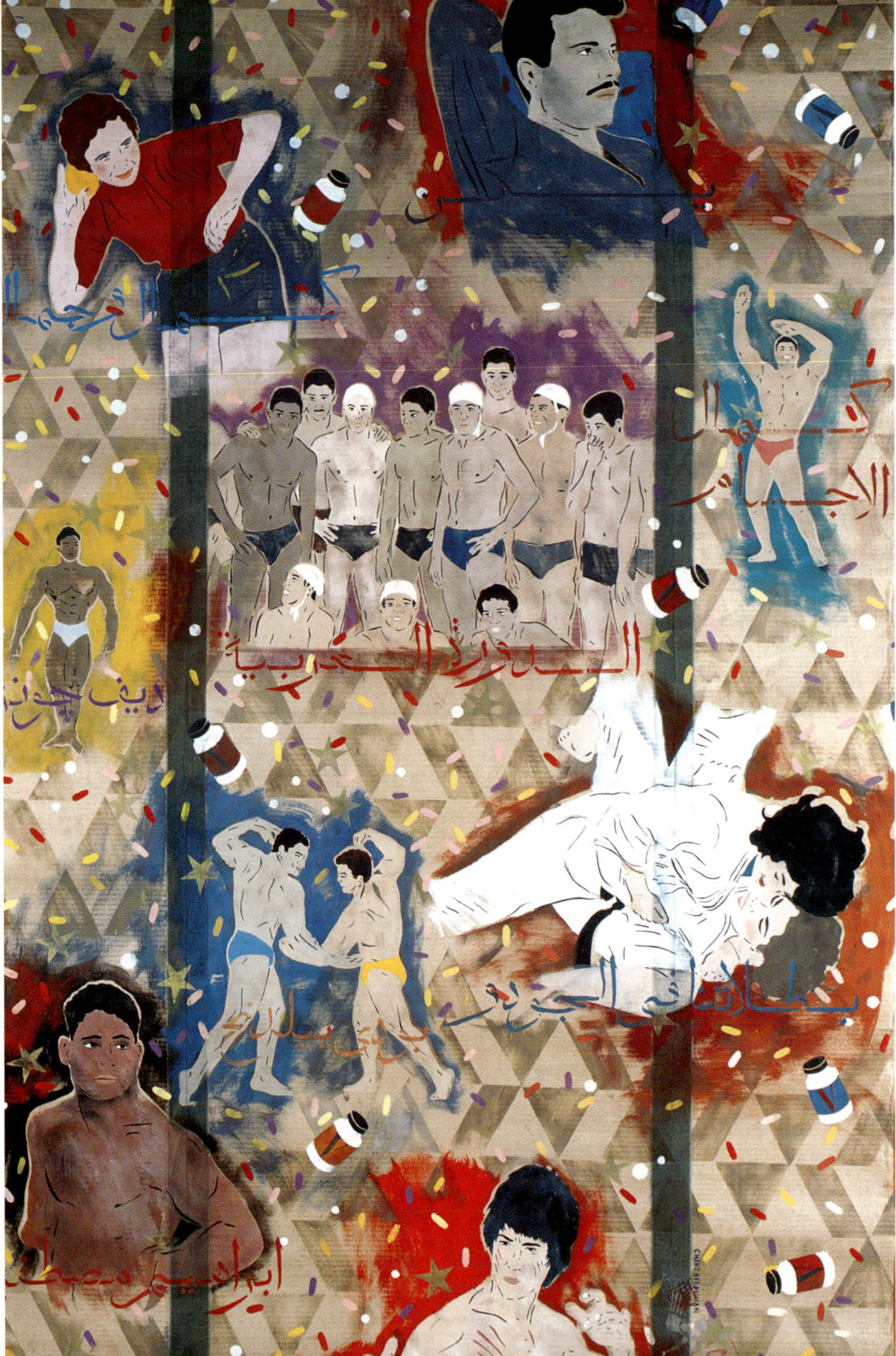
الاجسام
كمال
السباحة العربية
بطولة الجودو
ابراهيم مصطفى

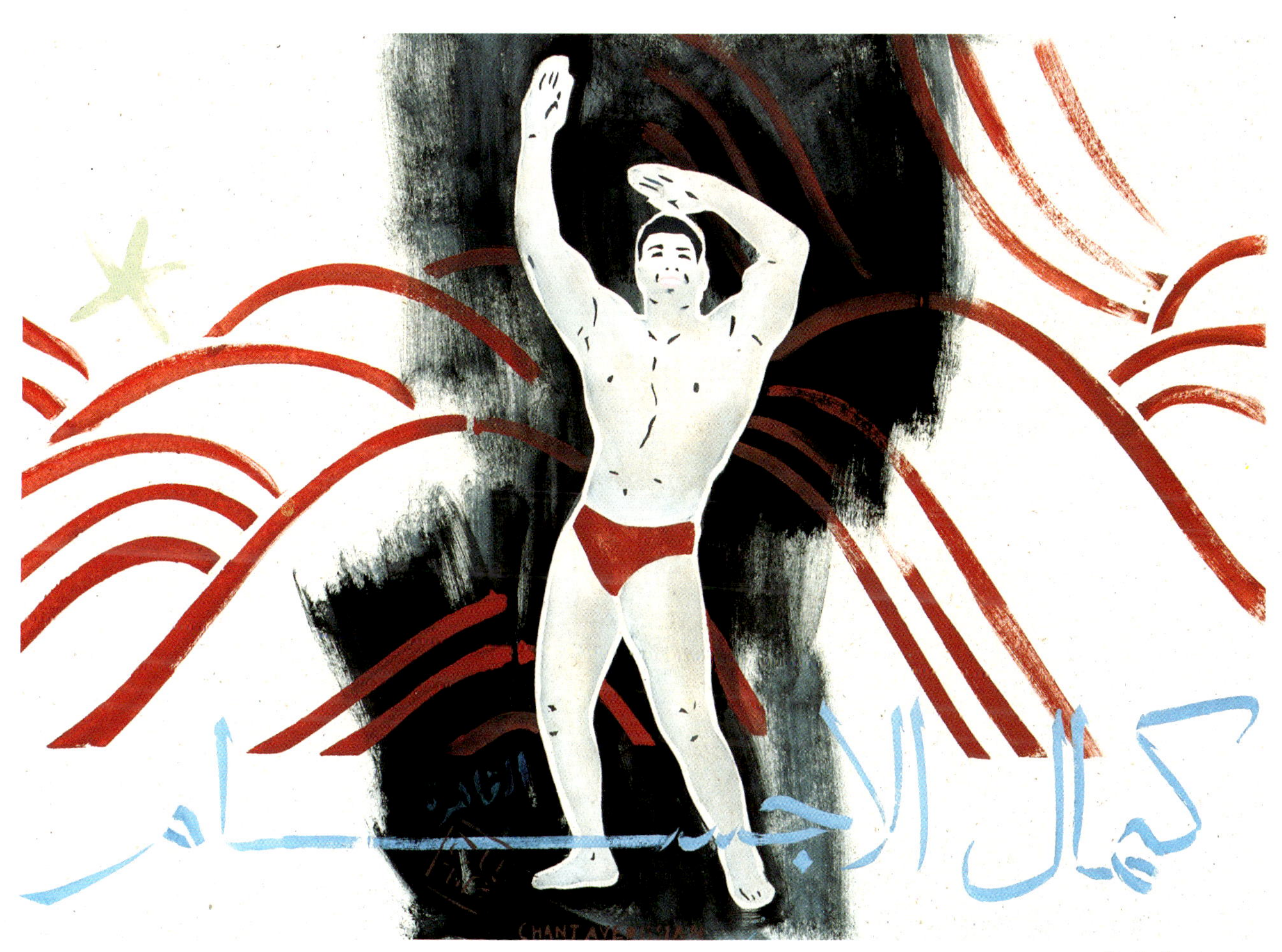

Body Perfection

Tutti Frutti

Tutti Frutti

As well as hand-painted film posters, the walls of Cairo are plastered with advertising panels promoting the latest Western imports – something inconceivable in Nasser's time. Here, Avedissian records memories of his own world, from favorite pet parrots to everyday objects such as fly whisks; the cooking equipment *ambooba* and *baboor*; the thermos from which he drinks his green tea; Bimbo, the only brand of biscuit available under Nasser; and Ika, a popular chewing gum.

Egypt, the great tourist destination, has millions of visitors every year who mix languages in order to communicate. This mix of foreign words is reflected in the playful illustrated alphabets, 'English ABCs' and 'Arabic ABCs', with T for Tourist, C for Camera and X for Madame X.

Here is a world full of life, charm, nostalgia and fun; of words and images colonised and decolonised; a world of small frustrations and great pleasures.

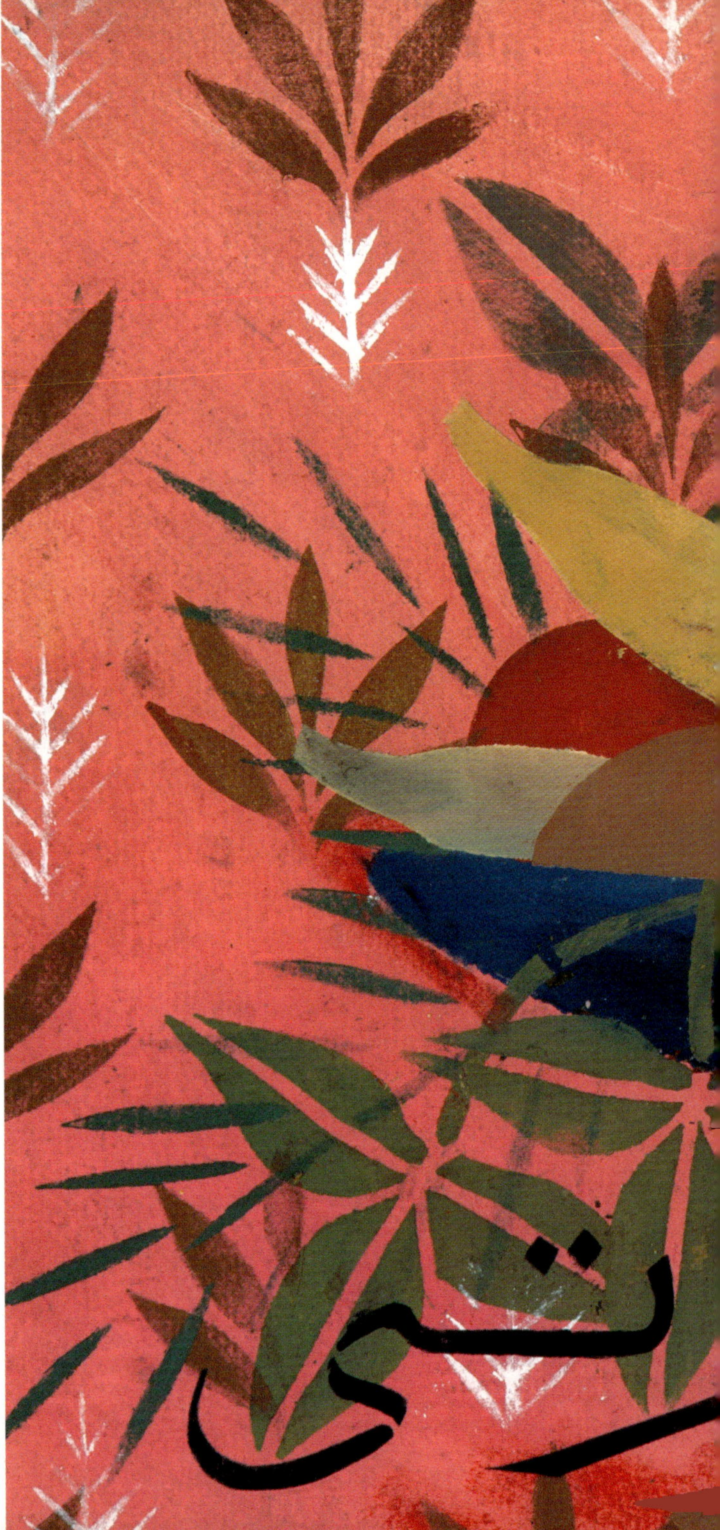

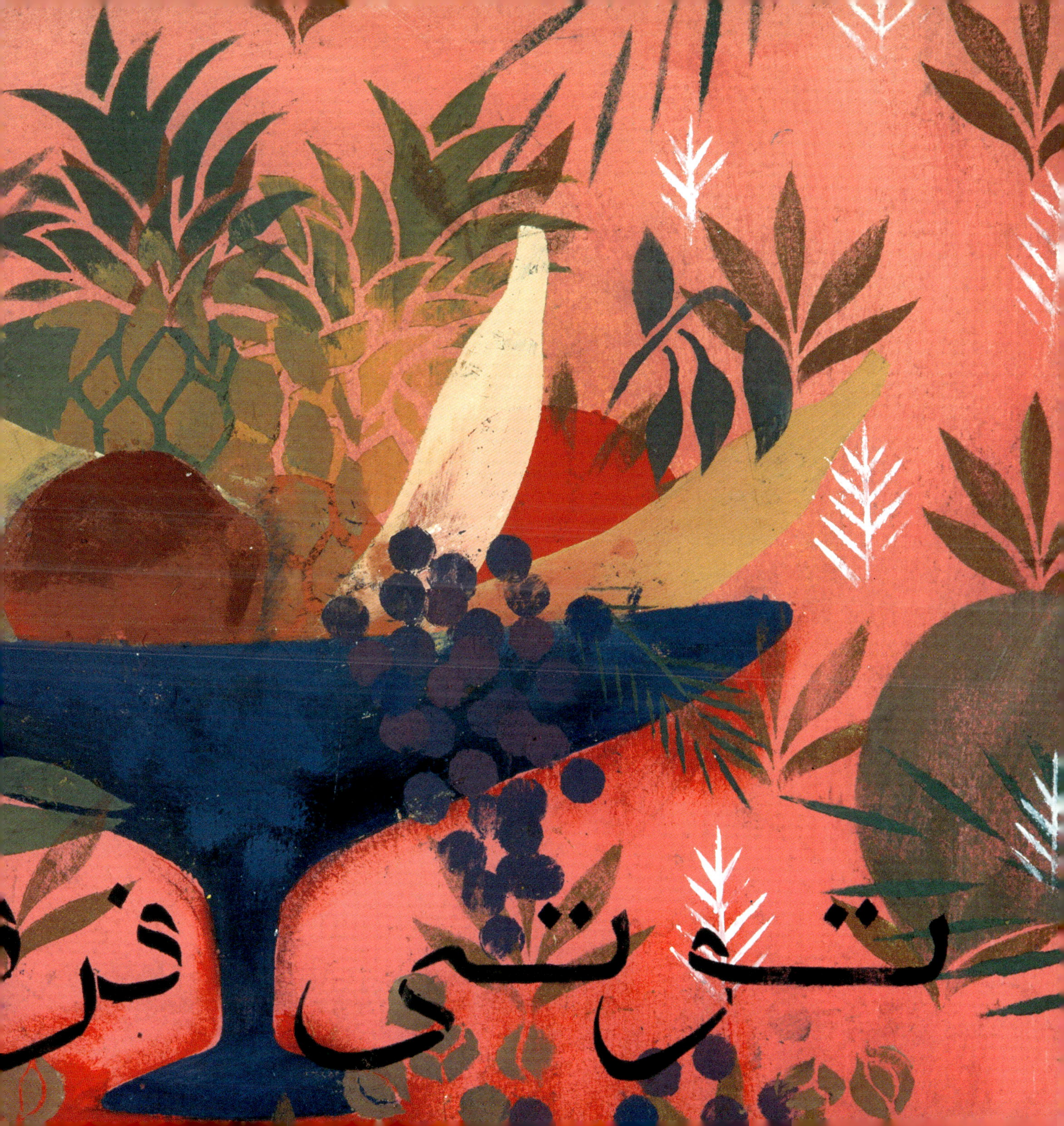

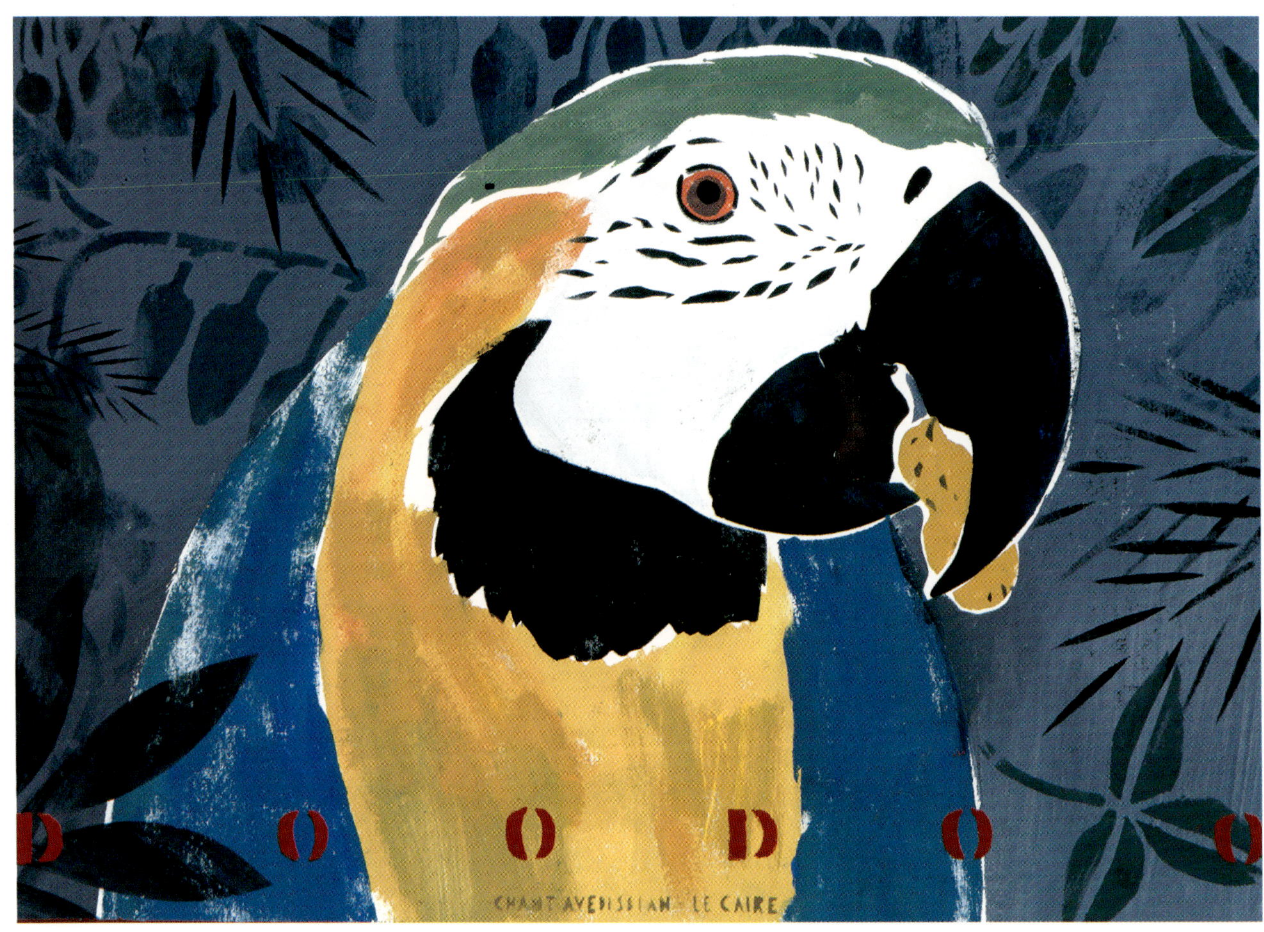

Doodoo

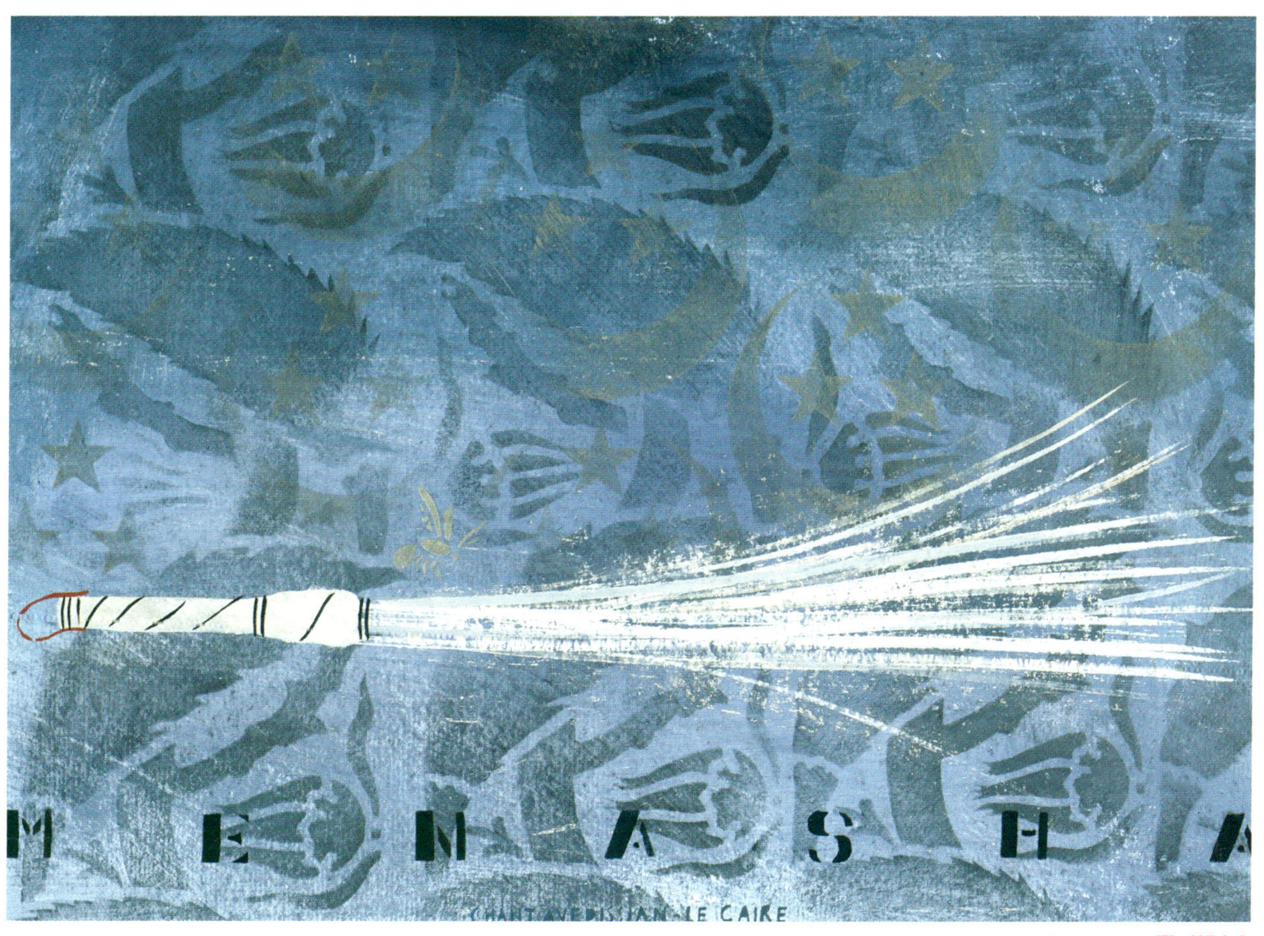

Fly Whisk

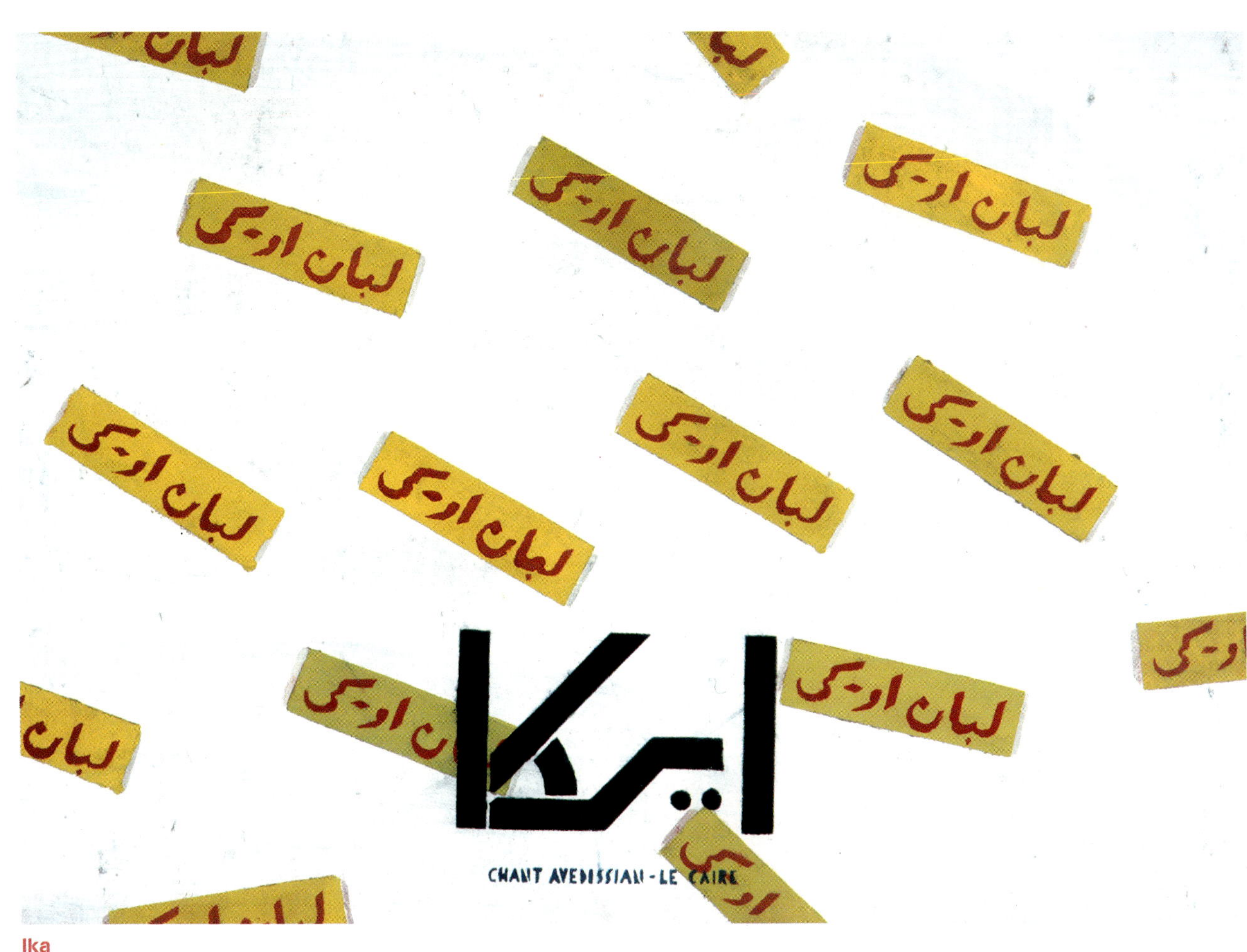

Ika

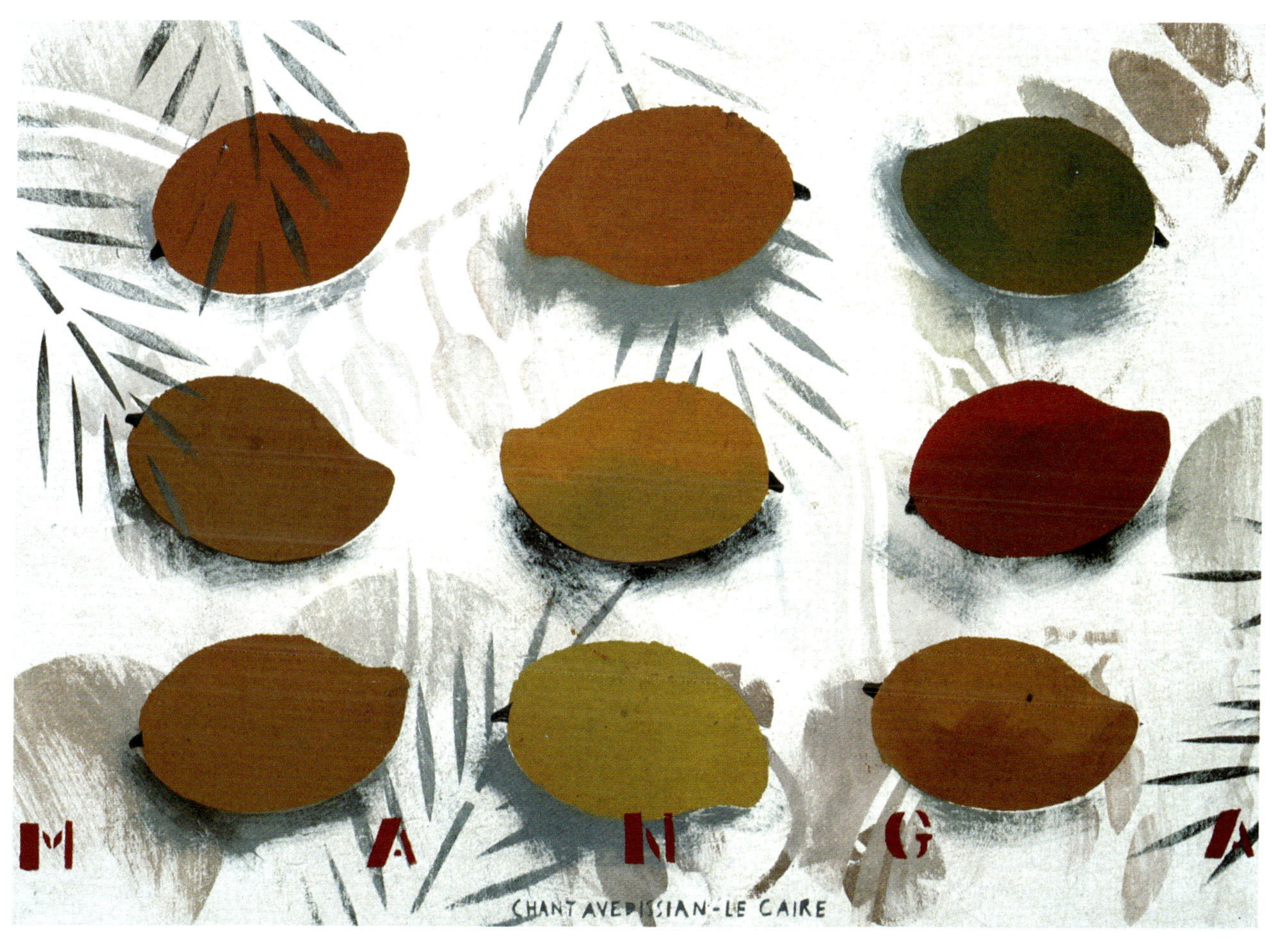

Mango

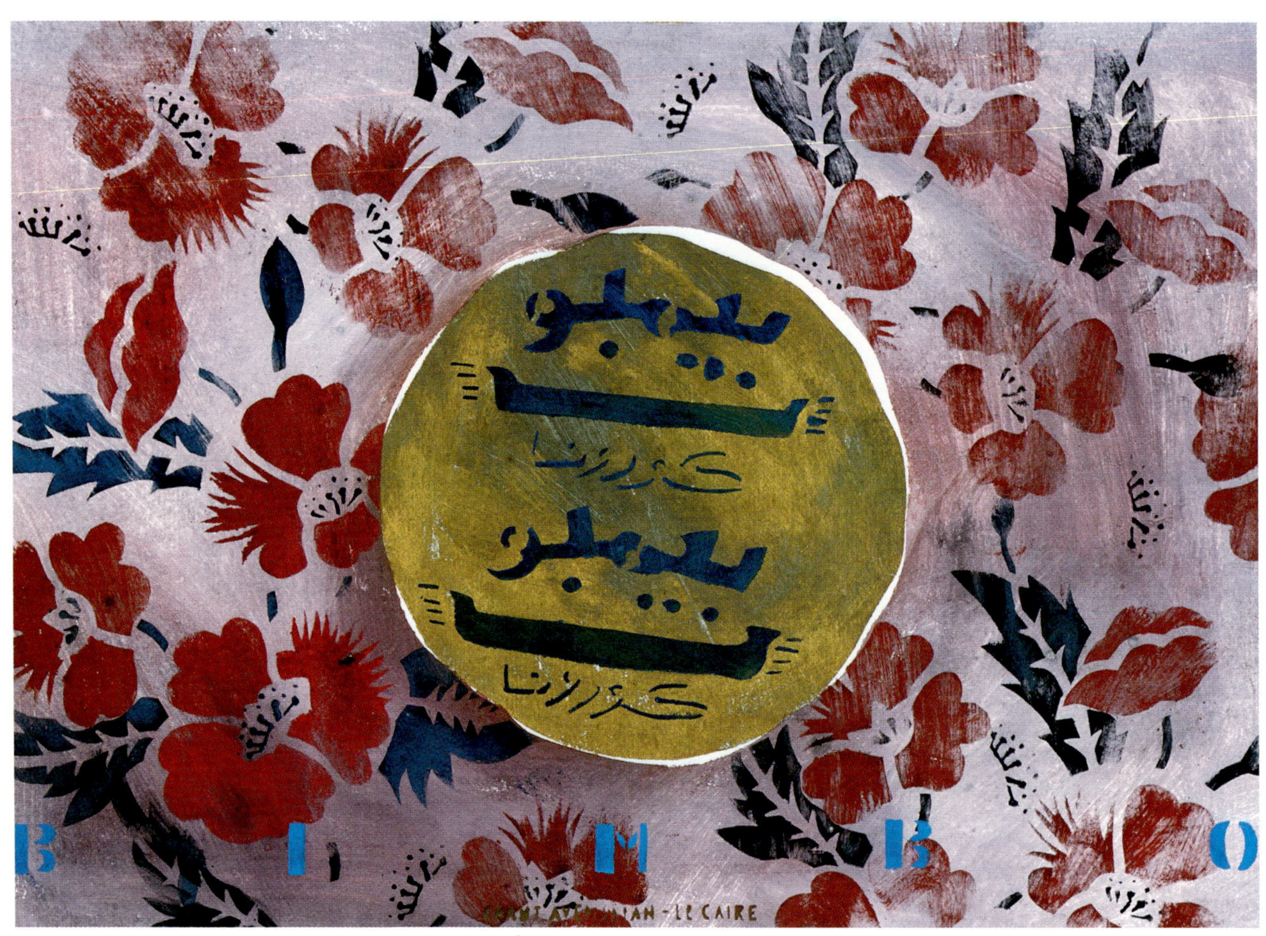

Bimbo

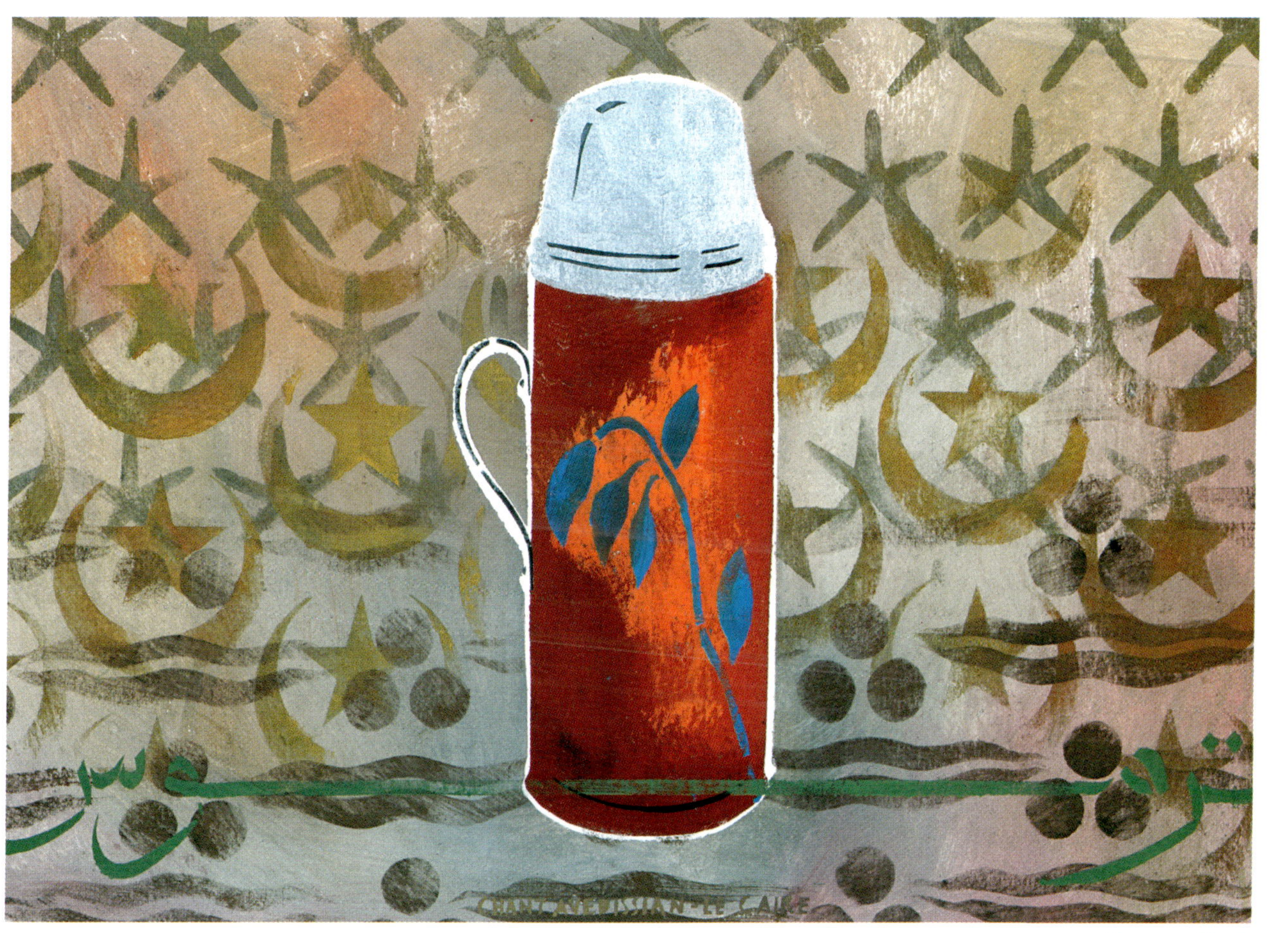

Thermos Flask

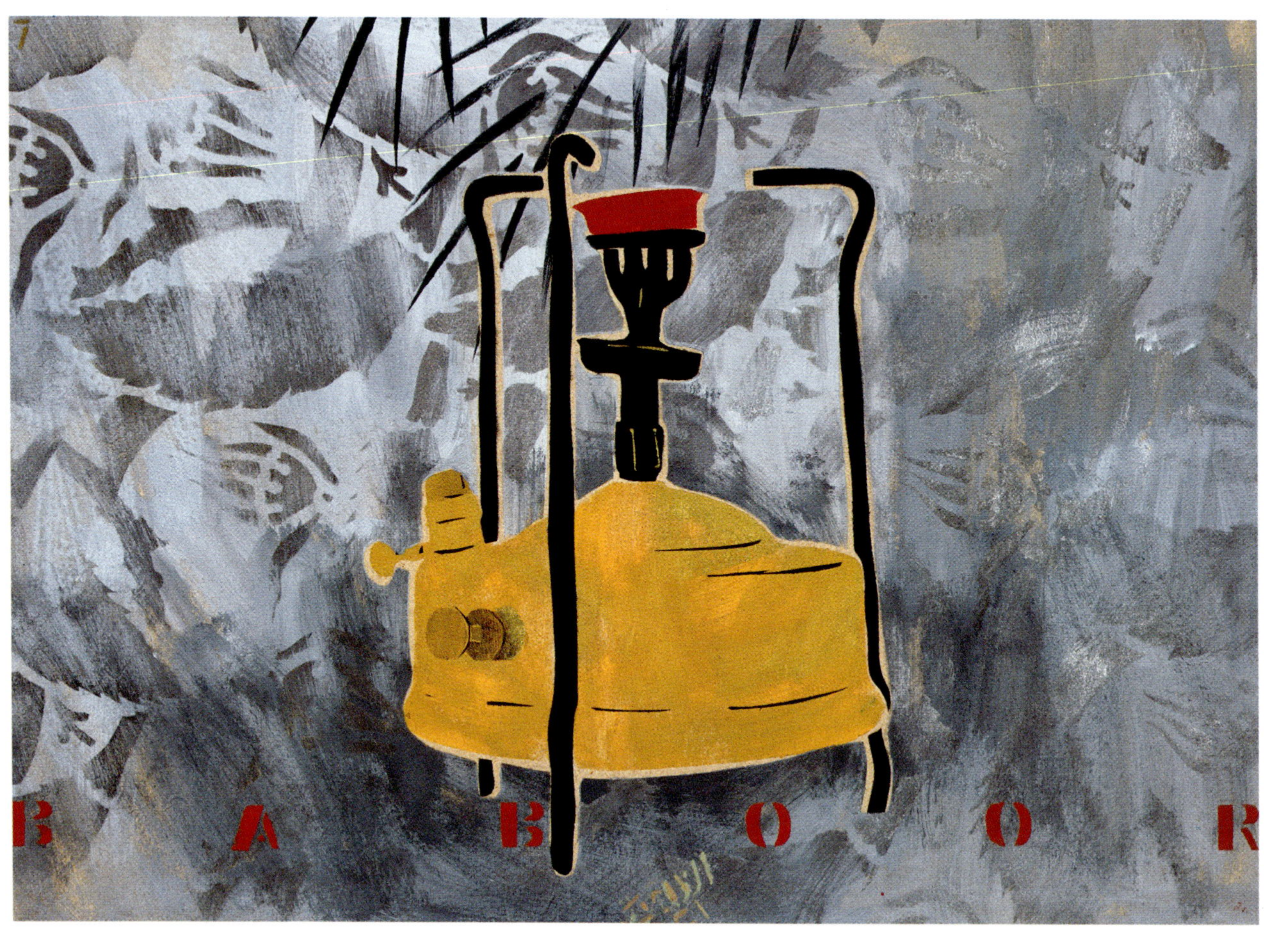

Baboor

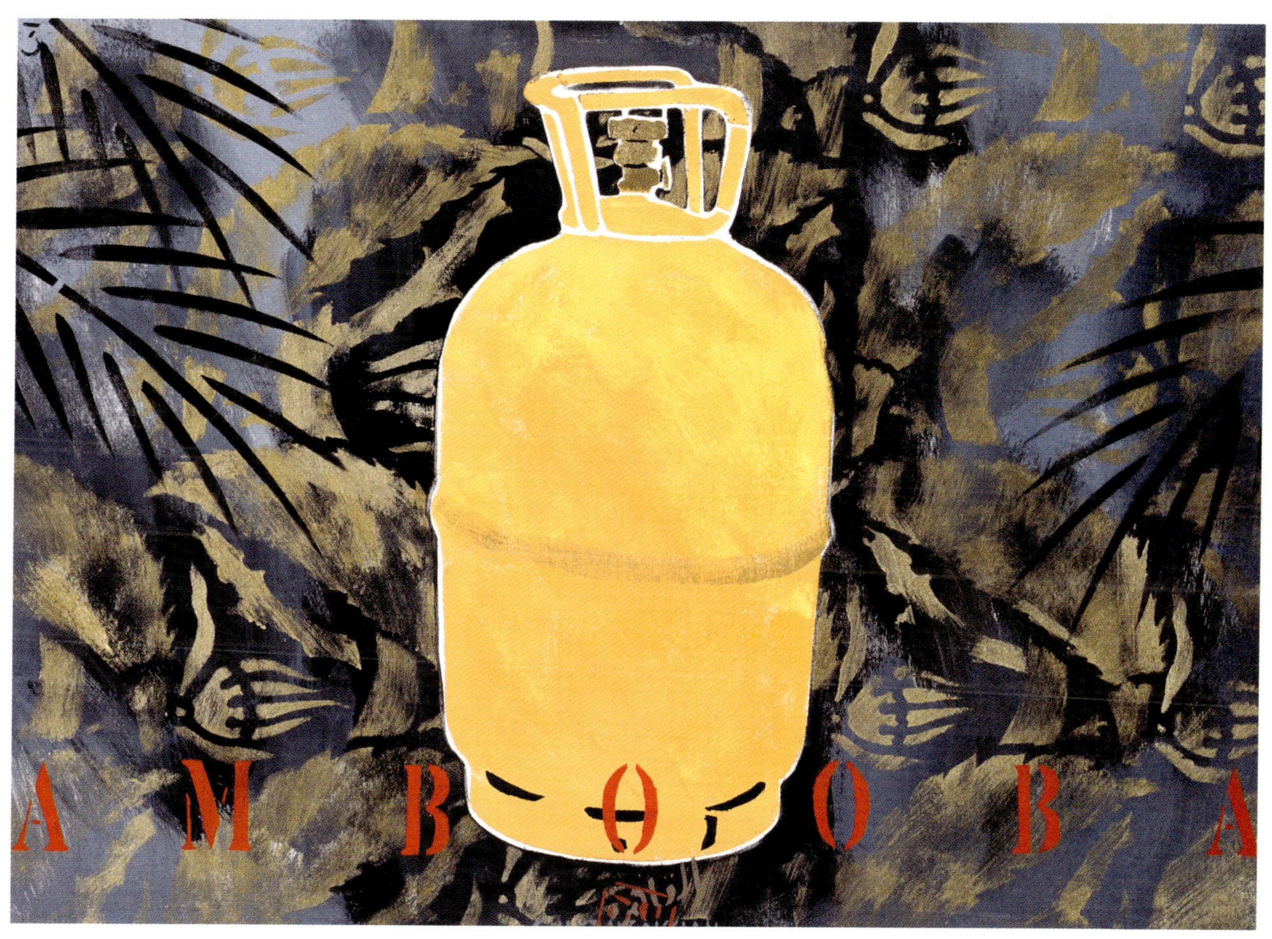

Ambooba

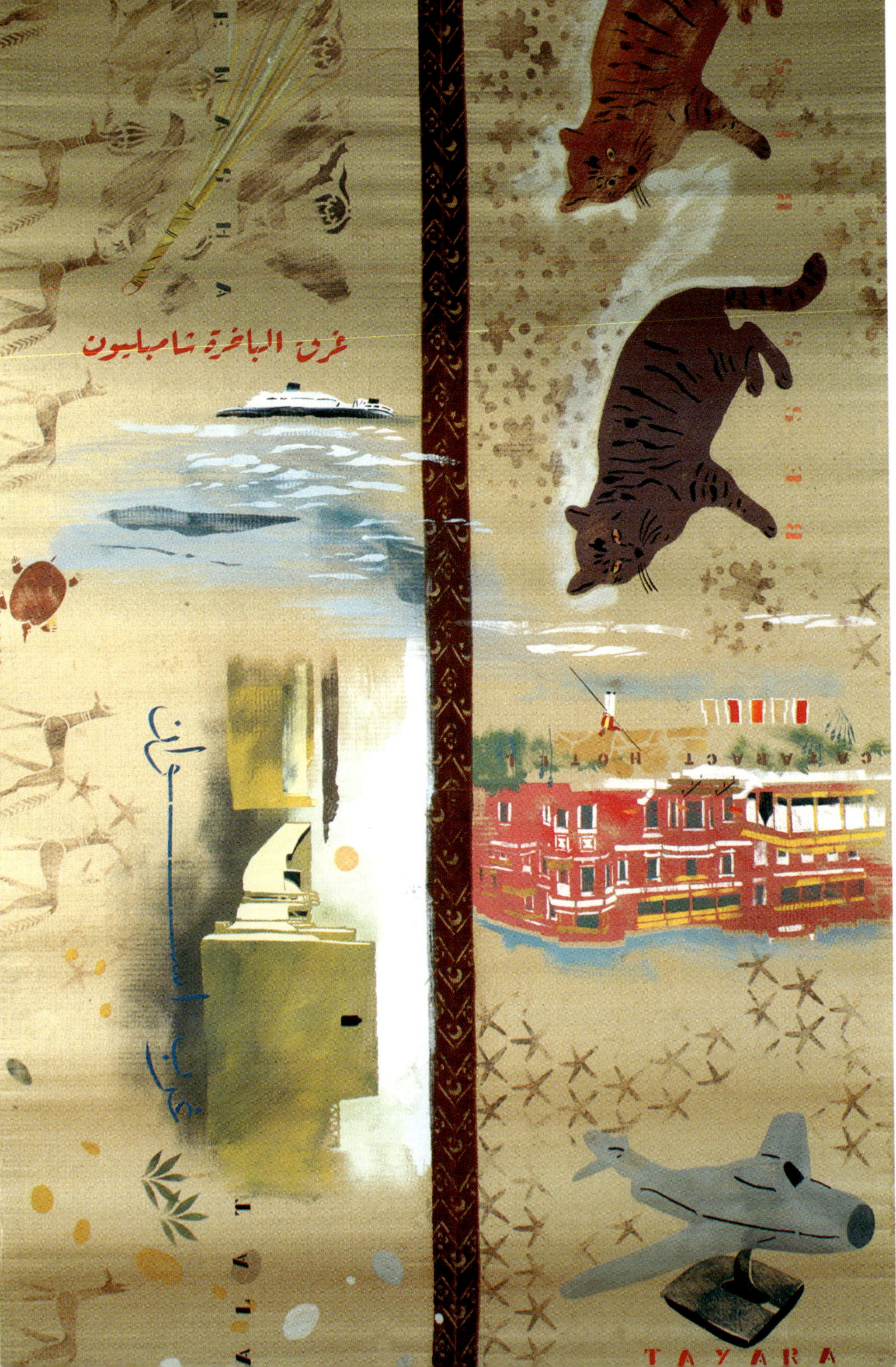
غرق الباخرة شامبليون
Aswan
CATARACT HOTEL
TAYARA

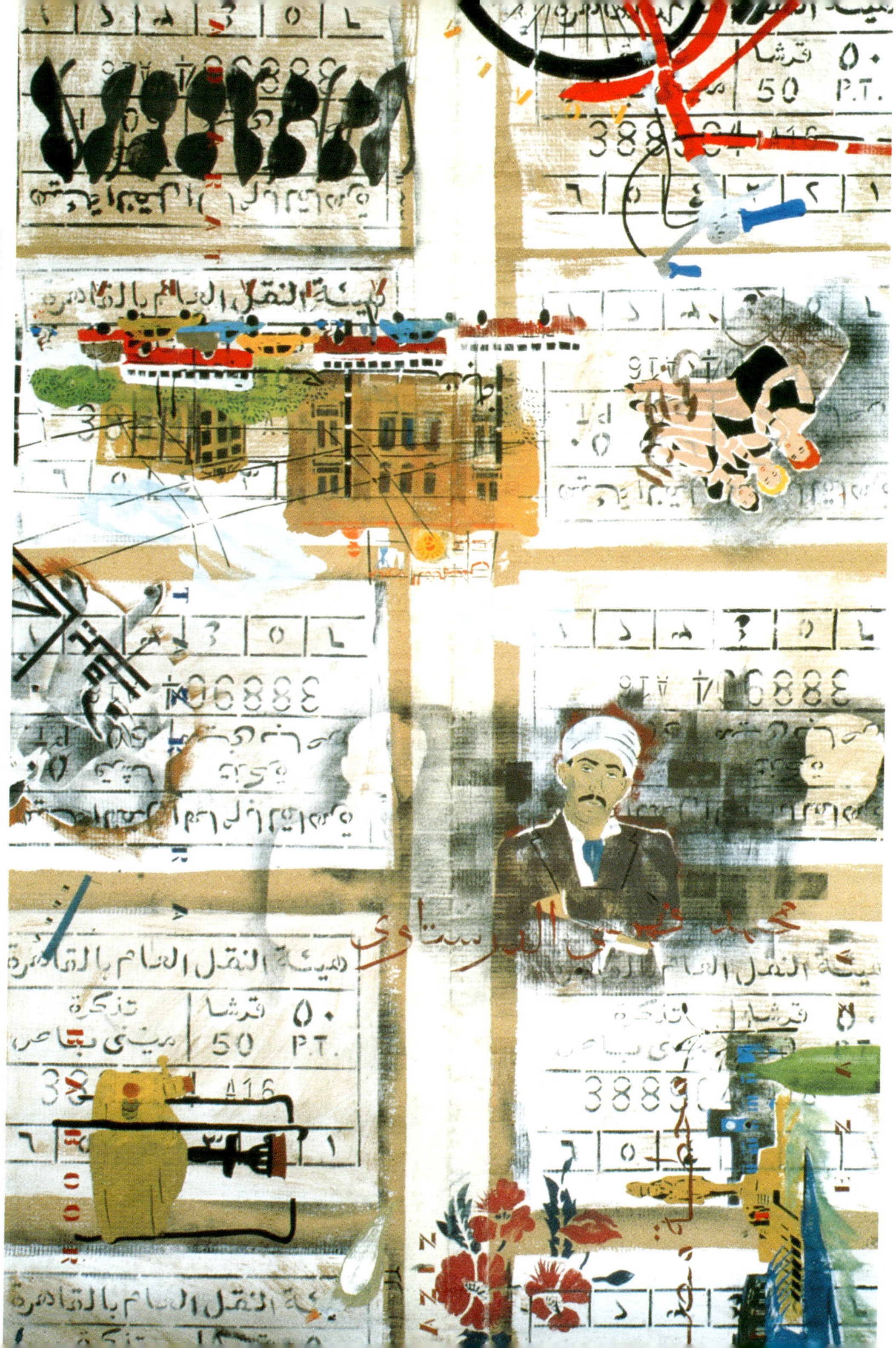
هيئة النقل العام بالقاهرة
تذكرة
قرشا
٥٠
50 P.T.
A16

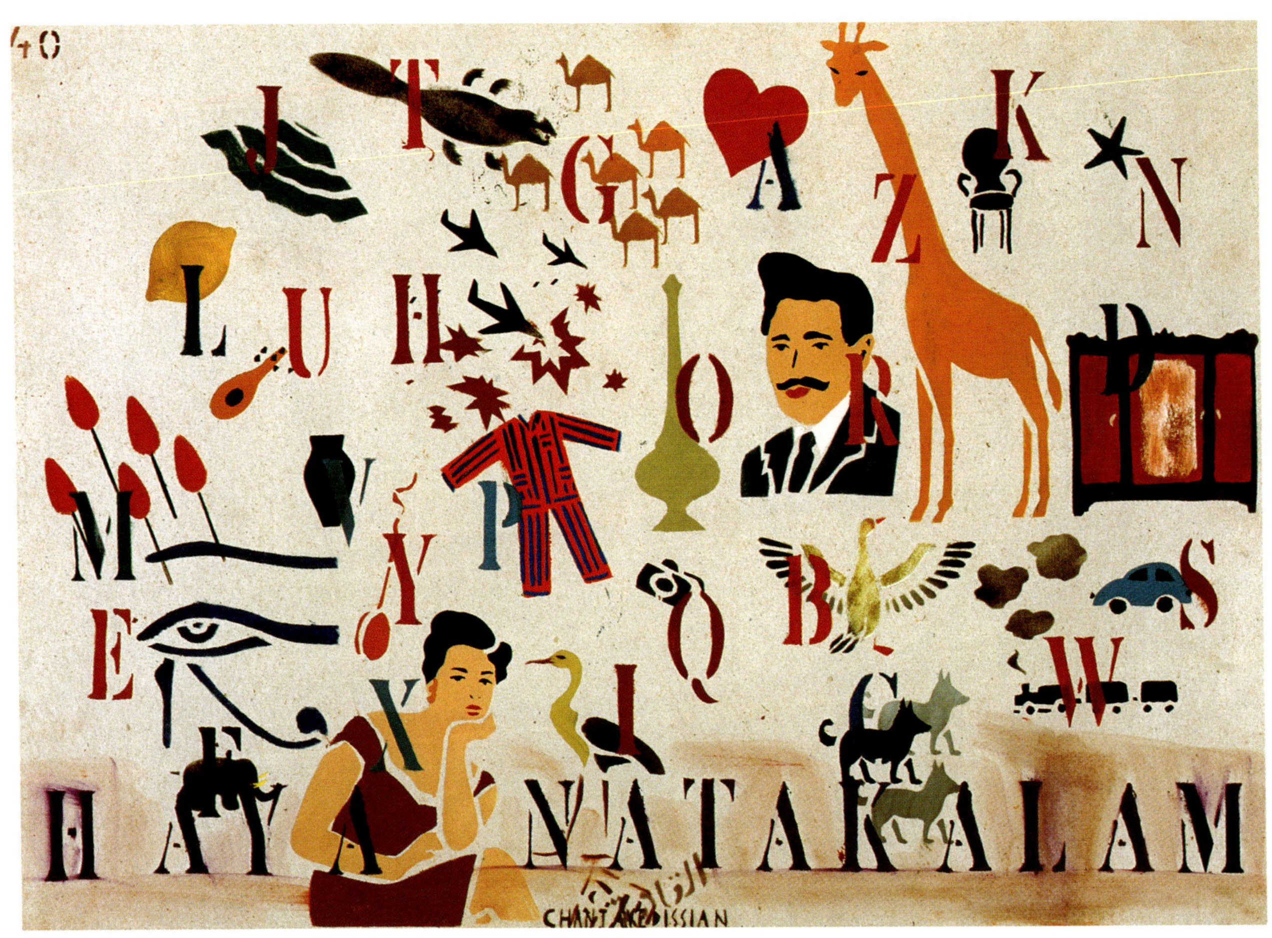

English ABCs

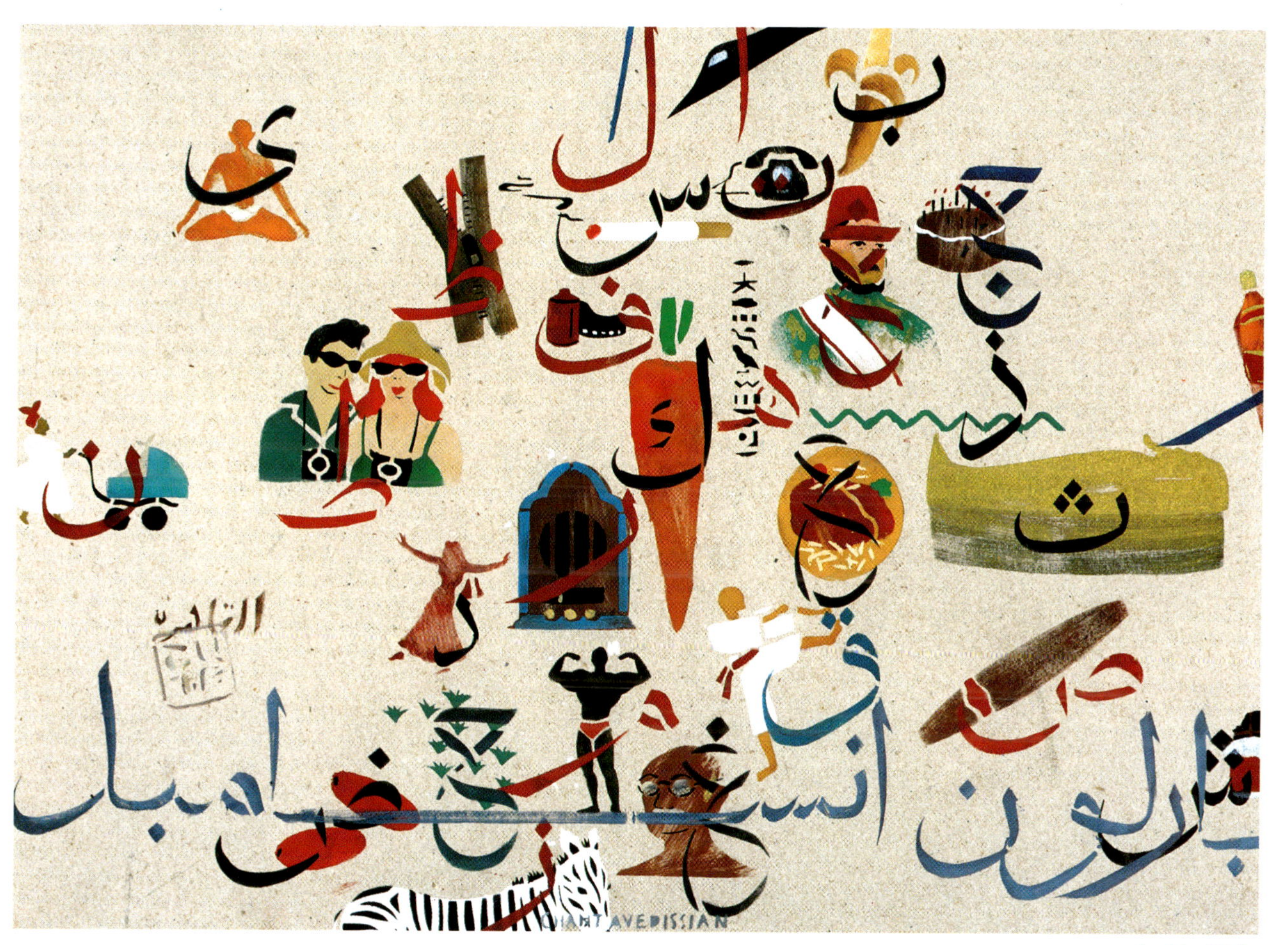

Arabic ABCs

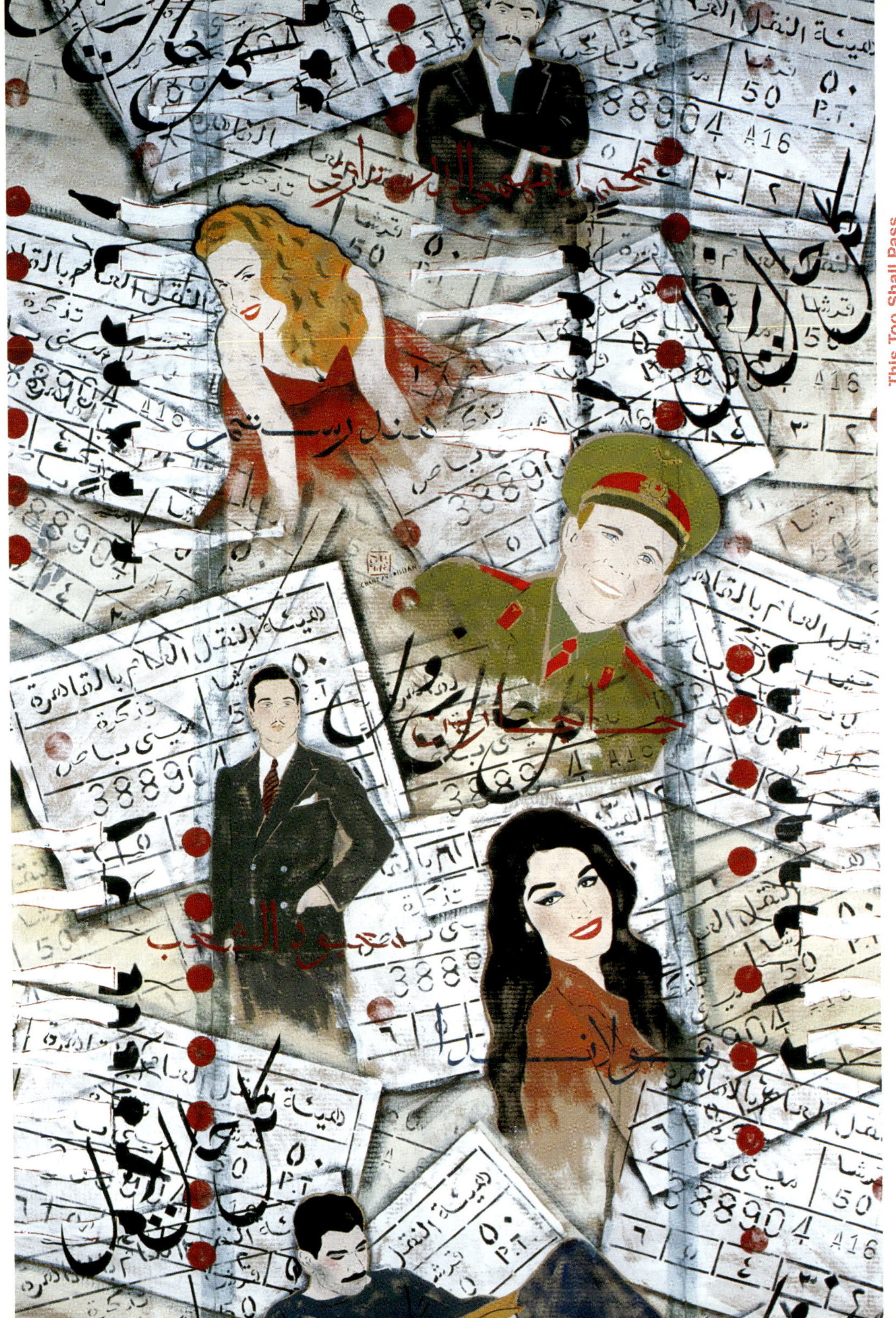

This Too Shall Pass

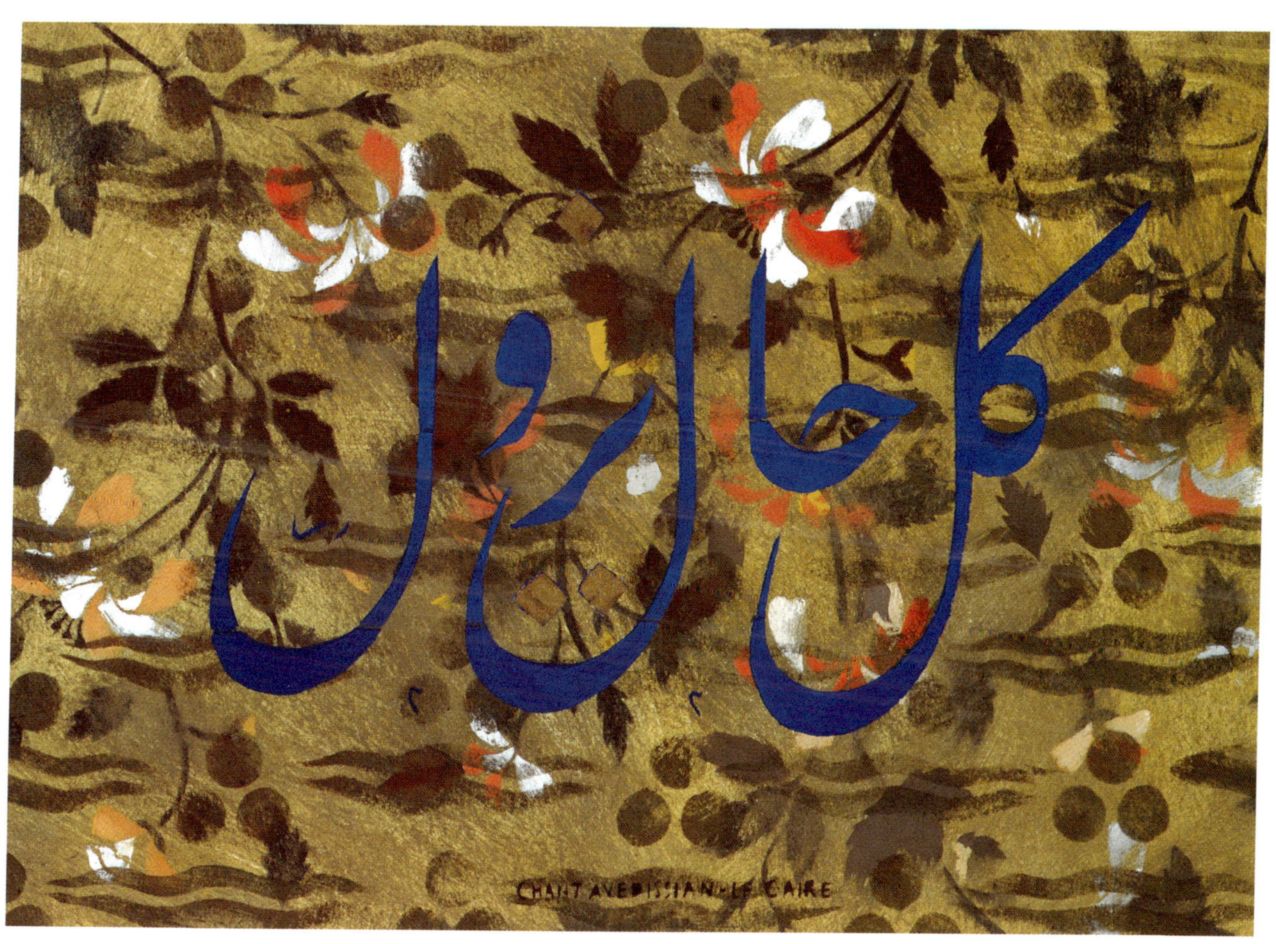

Nothing is Forever

Biography

Chant Avedissian

Chant Avedissian was born in Cairo in 1951. He studied fine arts in Montreal (1970–3) and print-making at the Ecole Nationale Supérieure des Arts Décoratifs, Paris (1974–6). He returned to Cairo in 1980 and worked with Hassan Fathy from 1981–9. He currently lives and works in Cairo and Yerevan.

Selected solo exhibitions

Paris (Institut du Monde Arabe, 1990), Cairo (British Council, 1992), Beirut (Galerie 50X70, 1993), London (SOAS, 1992 & Leighton House Museum, 1995), South Korea (Kwangju Biennale, 1995), Amsterdam (Tropenmuseum, 1996), and Washington DC (NMAA, Smithsonian Institution, 2002).

Selected group shows

Antwerp (In 'Morpheus Armen', Cultureel Centrum Berchem, 1998), Copenhagen (Ekbatana?, Nikolaj Contemporary Art Centre, 2000), and Germany (Love Affairs, IFA in Frankfurt, Bonn and Berlin, 2003–4).

Public collections

The British Museum, London; the Museum of Mankind, London; British Airways, London; National Museums of Scotland; Tropenmuseum, Amsterdam; National Museum of African Arts, Smithsonian Institution, Washington DC; The World Bank, Washington DC; Aga Khan Foundation, Switzerland; The National Gallery of Jordan, Amman; The British Council, Cairo.

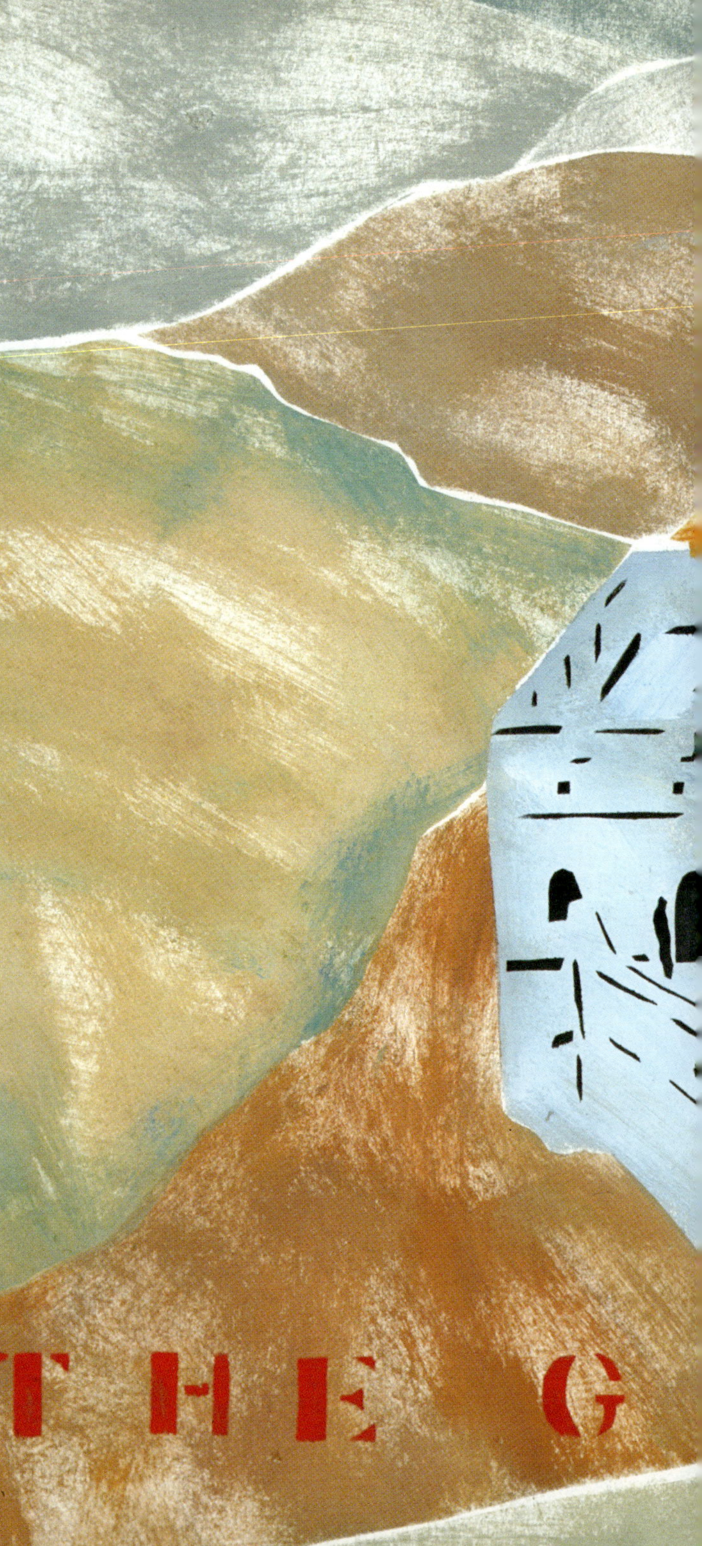

Self-Portrait

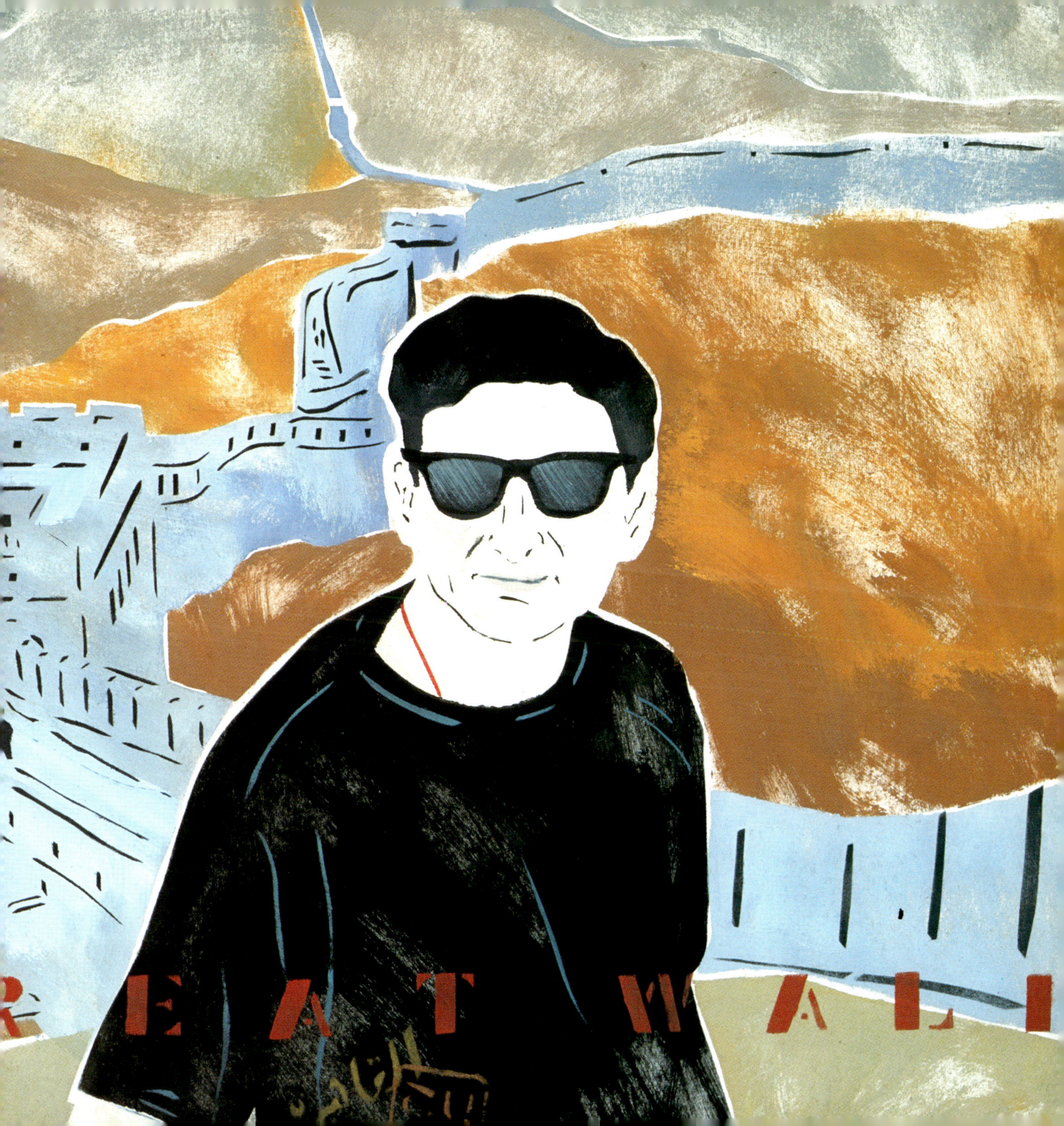
REAT WALL

Details of Artworks

All small horizontal stencils measure 50 x 70 cm, pigments and gum arabic on recycled cardboard.

All large vertical stencils measure 150 x 250 cm, pigments and gum arabic on corrugated cardboard.

All works date between 1991–2004.

Special thanks

This publication would not have been possible without the support of

Saeb Eigner

Anwar Gargash

Rose Issa

TANK Magazine